Tree Cultures

Tree Cultures

The Place of Trees and Trees in their Place

Owain Jones and Paul Cloke

BERG

Oxford • New York

First published in 2002 by
Berg
Editorial offices:
150 Cowley Road, Oxford, OX4 1JJ, UK
838 Broadway, Third Floor, New York, NY 10003–4812, USA

Berg is the imprint of Oxford International Publishers Ltd.

Library of Congress Cataloging-in-Publication Data

Jones, Owain.
The place of trees and trees in their place / Owain Jones and Paul Cloke.
p. cm.
Includes bibliographical references and index.
ISBN 1-85973-498-7 (cloth) -- ISBN 1-85973-404-9 (Paper)
1. Trees--Symbolic aspects. 2. Trees--Psychological aspects. 3. Landscape. 4. Human ecology--Philosophy. 5. Forest conservation. I. Cloke, Paul J. II. Title.
GT5150 .J66 2002
302.2′223--dc21

2002000206

British Library Cataloguing-in-Publication Data
A catalogue record for this book is available from the British Library.

ISBN 1 85973 498 7 (Cloth)
1 85973 404 9 (Paper)

Typeset by JS Typesetting, Wellingborough, Northants
Printed in the United Kingdom by Antony Rowe Ltd, Chippenham, Wiltshire

Dedications

Paul as always thanks Viv, Liz and Will for their precious love and support.

Owain's dedication is to Sue, Sam and Luke and his parents with love.

Contents

Acknowledgements

The authors gratefully acknowledge the financial support of the ESRC for their research on 'Arbori-culture: the significance of trees to places' (R000237083).

We also gratefully acknowledge the help of Mr T. Titchen; Mr L. Owen; Mr P. Brain, other members of the Friends of Arnos Vale Cemetery; officers of Bristol City Council; the owner and staff of West Bradley Orchard; officers of Somerset County Council; Mr T. Webber, Mr K. Taylor, Mr A. Rankine; Broadleaf Forestry Contractors; residents of Camerton who agreed to be interviewed; Mr S. Preddy and the Cam Valley Wildlife Group, Dr C. Chilcott; Mr J. Cornwell; residents of Victoria Square who agreed to be interviewed; and Mrs J. Machin.

Thanks to Theresa Andrews and Elaine Osborne for their cheerful and tireless work on the manuscript.

Thanks is also due to an anonymous reader for helpful comments and Kathryn Earle for her patience.

Chapter 6 is a revised version of Cloke, P. and Jones. O. (2001) 'Dwelling, place, and landscape: an orchard in Somerset', *Environment and Planning A,* 2001, 33, 649–66. We are very grateful for permission from Pion, London to reproduce it in altered form here.

Chapter 8 is a revised version of Cloke, P. and Jones, O. (2000) 'From Wasteland to Woodland to "Little Switzerland": Environmental Management in Place, Culture and Time', Chapter 10 in X. Font and J. Tribe (eds) *Forest Tourism and Recreation*, Oxford: CABI Publishing. We are very grateful for permission from CABI, Oxford, to reproduce it in altered form here, and for the reproduction of figures 8.1, 8.2, 8.3 and 8.5.

List of Figures

–1–

Introduction

> Trees are large and conspicuous objects in the landscape, and they endure over long periods of time. We cannot ignore them even if we should wish to do so, and happily they are lovely at every season.
>
> (Edlin, 1970: 165)

> Our culture is rich with trees, wood and green-men – from pollards and timber barns to painting and poetry, from the Green Knight and Robin Hood to Constable and Elgar. We urgently need to find new ways of living with trees as cultural, spiritual and emotional companions – as well as for ecological reasons.
>
> (Sinden, 1990: 9)

> Every tree counts.
>
> (Common Ground slogan)

This book is set within the context of recent attempts within the social sciences to construct closely theorized and firmly grounded analyses of the interconnections between nature–society relations and place relations. Our contention is that nature–society relations are continually unfolding in the contexts of specific places, in which meanings will arise from particular interactions between different assemblages of social, cultural and natural elements.

The last twenty years of the twentieth century witnessed a very significant increase in the importance of understanding nature–society relations as an integral part of the political, economic, social and cultural constitution and reconstitution of changing places. Not only has the prominence of environmental issues placed nature firmly in the glare of the media and of the political and academic discourses on conservation, but also there has been an increasing theoretical sophistication by which nature has been accepted as something more than an 'empty canvass' onto which society and culture are constructed. It is now recognized that non-human life-forms and materials can be thought of as having 'agency', and that the biological and physical dynamics of life-forms and processes need to be recognized both in their own terms and in terms of the relational agencies which are established among themselves with humanity. Structures of nature-social articulation will be spatially as well as historically specific. As a living complex of life-forms and processes, natural relations will always be embedded in, and thereby interact with and condition, human social relations to varying extents and in different ways in specific times and spaces.

In order to explore these themes, this book chooses *trees* as its focus. This trajectory can be understood partly in terms of the status of trees as a major global icon of terrestrial nature conservation and nature destruction (Schroeder, 1995). The fate of trees is often emblematic of the wider environment; Gates (2000: 1), for example, writes, 'if we can't protect threatened tree species, it does not bode well for the rest of the biosphere'. In Britain, trees have on the one hand been the focus or touchstone of the most prominent and bitter conservation battles in recent years, yet on the other they form the core of other initiatives such as the Community Forests or the National Forest which are held up as emblematic of progressive environmental policies. As well as these more 'immediate' discourses of nature and the environment concerning trees, they are also embedded in other cultural contexts which assemble complex layers of meaning. For example, Schama (1995) has produced a historical account of how the meanings of forests differ dramatically in the differing national cultures of Germany, France, England, America and Poland. In the context of Britain, Schama (2000) tells us that the greenwood was seen as a refuge from state tyranny, and also the provider of England's 'Heart of Oak' (see also Tsouvalis, 2000). Such images of England as pastoral and 'green at heart' had hedgerow trees, patchworks of deciduous woodland and the great forests as central icons. This iconography, for example, is confirmed in many of the famous war posters, travel posters, and covers of the Batsford's guide books which proliferated in such a distinctive style in the middle decades of the twentieth century, yet Britain is the least wooded country in Europe (Evans, 1992; Shoard, 1980) and contemporary discourses from media and pressure groups tell us that trees continue to fall under the spread of development and modern agricultural processes. In urban contexts, trees are vital in hopes of 'greening' the cities to make them more habitable. Consequently, there is now a plethora of organizations which are solely or partially dedicated to some or other aspects of tree conservation and/or management in Britain.

Our fascination with trees has also to be acknowledged in personal terms. When planning the research on which this book is based, we realized that we both were variously inspired by trees as an attribute of nature. We were drawn to their aesthetic beauty and their shadowy meaningfulness. We had both previously compiled personal photographic essays on different aspects of trees, and the patterns, colours and emotions they project. These fascinations resonated with our desire to accentuate the importance of the non-human in studies of nature–society and place. It also quickly occurred to us that trees *in particular places* could be highly valued. Indeed our research was partly inspired by one of the direct action tree protests which marked Britain in the 1990s. In this instance, in Bristol, a row of street lime trees was to be cleared to make way for the development of a new Tesco supermarket. This threat to the trees prompted a 90-day protest, where a sustained presence was kept at the base of the trees and in the trees themselves. In the end, the protestors were removed and the trees felled, all in front of the cameras of local and national media.

It was clear there was much to learn from this protest, as from other tree protests in Britain and further afield. The first thing which we were interested in was that these lime trees were not of particular 'scientific' or 'aesthetic' interest, and they had therefore slipped through the net of conservation discourses and legislation. Despite this, the trees were significant to local people; their meaning had a *local* dynamic, and they were obviously valued by those who were concerned with their felling. This concern appeared to enrol *both* broad disquiet over the destruction of natural habitats at whatever scale, *and* very specific disquiet over the destruction of particular trees which were regarded as palpable living individuals. From the complex interconnections visible in this one 'tree-place', we wanted to think through all kinds of wider considerations of what we began to call 'arbori-culture' especially relating to myriad social constructions which positioned trees as anything from sources of timber to living spirits. We further realized that arbori-culture was itself placed, and represented as an integral part of nature–society relations in the places concerned. As with the lime trees, such relations are refolded, resisted, and magnified in the complex milieu of any particular place where trees stand or fall.

In this book, then, we want to bring together these two strands of arbori-culture. We want to discuss particular trees and tree places, and we want to deploy theoretical ideas about nature, place, agency and ethics. Do trees represent a particularly vivid and important articulation of ideas about social nature (Cloke et al., 1996a/b)? How does the agency of particular trees fit in with current popular perspectives associated with Actor Network Theory (ANT) about the relational and networked nature of nature–society relations? Do ideas of place and geography tend to be lost in ANT's view of the world as topographically fluid networks, and if so, how do trees fit into such networks when they are so palpably rooted in particular places? Is there any value in pursuing nature–society relations in terms of ideas of *dwelling*, which Ingold (1993, 2000) famously illustrates using a painting by Bruegel in which a lone pear tree takes centre stage both visually and in the narrative? What emphasis should be given to environmental philosophy's pursuit of the intrinsic value of nature and natural beings, taking a relational view of the world as co-constituted by biosphere systems in which humans form a small and somewhat problematic part? 'Should', as Christopher Stone (1972) asks, 'trees have standing'?

We address these strands and questions in the book by considering trees contemporaneously as both social constructions and as real dynamic material entities. In so doing we seek to respond to Philo's (2000) concern about the dematerialized nature of much contemporary cultural geography, which ignores 'stubbornly there-in-the-world kind of matter' (33). There is nothing more stubbornly 'there-in-the-world' than the trees which, we guess, you could now take a look at by moving to a window, or taking a short stroll outside. Yet trees also have an extraordinary range of symbolic places within human imagination. We need to deal with things in more nuanced ways which acknowledge these and other dynamics of being and becoming, and the knowing of being and becoming.

Here, then, we are joining the ranks of expanded 'human geographies' into which nature is being incorporated. This perspective has gained momentum particularly via a reconsideration of animals in social processes and formations. Fitzsimmons and Goodman (1998: 194) suggest that across the social sciences and humanities there has emerged a broad if somewhat disjointed front, the concern of which is to bring 'nature' 'back in' to social theory by contesting its abstraction from 'society'. There is a growing corpus of studies (see for example Anderson, 1995, 1997; Philo, 1995; Philo and Wilbert, 2000; Whatmore, 1997; Whatmore and Thorne, 1998, 2000 and Wolch and Emel, 1995, 1998) which suggest that human geography can play an important role in contesting nature's abstraction from society through the development of *animal geographies*. Gaps remain, however, in the canon of non-human geographies. For example, Whatmore and Thorne (1998: 436) point out that 'geographers have paid remarkably little attention to wildlife in recent times'; and addressing that part of the non-human world not seen as 'wild', Anderson (1997: 464) feels that the human sciences have mostly failed to engage critically with the processes of animal domestication, and that this failure 'continues to constrain the imagining of alternative ethical and practical relations between humans, animals and environments'. Similar concerns have been expressed by Philo (1995) about animal geographies in general:

> The tendency has been to consider animals as marginal 'thing-like' beings devoid of inner lives, apprehensions or sensibilities, with little attempt being made to probe the often take-for-granted assumptions underlying the different uses to which human communities have put animals *in different times and places.* (656–7, our emphasis)

If all this neglect is so for fauna, it is even more so in the case of flora, which remains an even more ghost-like presence in contemporary theoretical approaches. Moving 'beyond' animals to plants, and in our case, to trees, represents a further expansion and development of the 'geographical imagination'. Trees, we suggest, are a pressing and vibrant case because of their powerful presence in all manner of lives and spaces. In studying arbori-culture, we are responding to Burgess's (2000) call for cultural geographers to consider society-environment issues 'worthy of attention' (273).

This is not to say that plants, or even trees, woods and forests, have been entirely absent from recent geographical and related discourses. Woodland has been considered through notions of the iconography of landscape (Daniels, 1988); as a symbolic other to western civilisation (Harrison 1992) and in terms of social nature (Cloke et al., 1996a). Tsouvalis (2000) has discussed the meanings and the materiality of British forests and woodlands, while Watkins (1998a) and McManus (1999) have considered national and international histories of how woodlands and forests have been constructed. In addition, Rival's (1998) edited collection has considered the rich range of symbolisms which attach to trees in national and international contexts. In sympathy with much of this endeavour we are in this book beginning to articulate a particular form of *hybrid geography* (Whatmore, 2000) which has the aim of

> exploring ways of recognising and accommodating the presence of non-humans in the worlds we inhabit [and] is concerned with the spaces of social life, relational configurations spun between the capacities and effects of *organic beings*, technological devices and discursive codes. (247, our emphasis)

In pursuit of this aim in the case of trees, we use the first half of the book to explore four conceptual spaces. These are: **culture** – the meanings which orbit around trees and woods in culture; **agency** – the bewildering range of creative capacities trees bring to 'heterogeneous geographies'; **place** – the places which form as trees relate along with particular spun configurations of ensembles of various actors; and **ethics** – considerations of the duties that individuals and societies may owe trees in the light of seeing them as living actors in geographical and conceptual spaces. Each of these conceptual themes will be briefly introduced. But we are also interested in the interactions, or the interstices between these forms and how meaning and practices form within them.

Culture

Trees are implicated in a huge range of cultural formations. There are common understandings of trees and woods, which may be at large in society at a number of scales (national, regional, local) and locations (e.g. the media, the local, state, national state and NGO initiatives), and which come to contribute to the specific matrix of differing place milieu. Places are, in part, dynamic outcomes of the coming together of local, regional, national and international cultural constructions, in co-present material, social, economic, and historical contexts. Cultural attributes are often particularly significant in the consideration of places where trees are characteristic of place milieu, as in Schama's (1995) telling of differing national-scaled cultural inscriptions of tree meanings, which influence the complex ways in which tree-places are constructed locally. Trees in Britain and elsewhere have become carriers of some people's environmental anxiety and love for nature, cropping up in various discourses on environmental crisis, countryside change and habitat loss, and quality of urban life. More generally, trees have long been symbols for all manner of key social meanings and practices (Rival, 1998b), for example being associated with fear and spirituality as well as with recreation (Cloke et al., 1996a). Within these broad but often very powerful understandings of trees, more specific variations occur. For instance in Britain, trees are commonly understood as native or alien; evergreen or deciduous; wild or planted; young or ancient. Each of these labels of understanding comes with a raft of meanings which will be influential in how a tree is regarded and understood culturally and, perhaps, acted upon. This coming together of local and national cultural constructions, with the particular presences and juxtapositions of elements making up particular places, makes for an extremely fine-grained set of relations, meanings and significances, which provide both potential opportunities and problems for the interpretations of, and the (environmental) management of, any type of site. This is particularly so where trees are involved, given the huge amount of cultural, emotional and even spiritual baggage certain trees in certain places can carry.

This book accesses tree discourses in various cultural locations which range through novels, poetry, and accounts of ancient spirituality to coverage of 'tree issues' in the press. It is through such representations that discourses circulate in an 'active process of cultural creation and destruction . . . moments in a cumulatively historical spiral of signification' (Thrift, 1981, cited by Crang, 1998: 46). Inevitably this gives the book a 'britanno-centric' form as it is (mostly) tree discourses of Britain with which we deal, although we do venture further afield in search of particular tree narratives which help us develop our account.

Such a focus is itself a reflection of arbori-culture in that national cultures do have their distinctive representations of trees, and woods (and wider nature).

Agency

Alongside the influence of cultural constructions, we aim to present a detailed reading of the agency which trees themselves bring to the continuous unfolding of places and landscapes. In contemporary understandings of nature–society relations it is recognized that nature is not merely inscribed upon by human culture and practice. Rather, nature 'pushes back' with its own vitality which is manifest in specific material processes. Whatmore and Boucher (1992: 167–8), in their analysis of social constructions of nature, emphasize that

> while nature cannot be (re)produced outside social relations, neither is it reducible to them. Rather, the biological and physical dynamics of life forms and processes need to be recognised on their own terms, conceptually independent of human social agency, such that social nature represents 'the outcome of a specific structure of natural/social articulation'.

In this way, agents of nature are now seen as palpably active, not only in terms of their own biological constitution, but also relationally when bound up in the construction of ecological, social, economic, cultural, political and material formations. Harvey (1996) deploys the term 'socio-ecological' processes both to encompass the non-dichotomous relations of human and non-human agency and to emphasize the need for careful consideration of non-human agency within such processes. He calls for a disaggregation of the homogenized term 'nature', into its various 'intensely internally variegated[,] unparalleled fields of difference' (Harvey, 1996: 183). Thus the agency of, in this case, trees and of differing kinds of trees needs to be taken seriously. Indeed Ingold (2000: 429) has recently made this point. He questioned the premise of Rival's (1998a) edited collection on 'the social lives of trees', saying that it

> paradoxically took as its starting point a question that would deny to trees any such life. Contributors to the volume were asked to consider 'To which symbolic ends have trees been used' . . . This is to suppose that the social life being symbolised is human, and that the trees have no part in it.

However, we are aware that to talk of trees having agency is to invite scepticism, or worse, although we believe that trees should be understood not only as active, but also as active in ways which are purposive (as a fulfilment of their embedded tendencies to grow in certain ways and to reproduce), transformative and even creative. These qualities are constituent parts of agency (Mele, 1997), and once we release ourselves from trying to squeeze all notions of agency through the very human grid of language and thought (Callon and Law, 1995), the capacity for agency can be redistributed throughout a heterogeneous set of actors, including non-human actors. Such understandings have particular relevance to philosophical debates within social theory (Latour, 1993), human geography (Whatmore, 1999), environmentalism (Plumwood, 1993) and, we suggest, environmental management (Cloke and Jones, 2000). When any site is considered as a milieu of physical and cultural elements, it can be expected that trees will play an active role, projecting themselves into political, cultural and economic fabrics, and through the historical geographies of these fabrics as articulated in the changing nature of places and landscapes. This is evident in Watkins's (1998a) study of the ancient oaks in Sherwood Forest which 'can be so long-lived that they develop several layers of meaning that can be documented through time' (1998b: 8), with these differing meanings contributing to shifting constructions of the Forest as a place over time.

So we argue in this book that there is a need to step back from a *purely* relational view of agency which, while disrupting established notions of exclusive autonomous human agency, might also be responsible for cloaking the creative effects of various non-human others. While we accept that relational agency must remain as the key conceptualization of practice, we argue at the same time that the creative input of heterogeneous actors/actants needs to be recognized within this relational framework. In our discussion of agency we show how the distinction between creative and routine agency is questionable, how differing aspects of agency can be attributed to trees, and how time may be a critical factor in redefining approaches to agency. We also consider how 'non-representational' theories – and, in particular, notions of floating signifiers – may be seen as 'ways into' considering aspects of non-human agency.

In so doing, we draw on emerging critiques of the supposed separation of nature and society to suggest that trees can, and should, be understood as non-human agents, with a potential to act, to bend space around themselves, to facilitate dependence and even to translate the will of others into their own articulation. Indeed, we argue that the non-human agency of trees can provide significant grounded contributions to the wider understanding of how agency transcends the social/human realm.

This claim rests on three lines of reasoning. First, we suggest that questions of non-human agency will benefit from being worked through embodied and emplaced particularities of being, rather than being confined to general realms of abstraction. Secondly, most of the pioneering discussions of organic non-human agency have involved animals (Ingold, 1995, 1988; Whatmore and Thorne, 1998, 2000; Emel and Wolch, 1998), and there would seem to be considerable scope for widening discussions of non-human agency to embrace beings or entities which are more markedly different than animals from the human. Thirdly, we contend that trees, both individually and especially collectively, present very significant narratives of non-human agency, particularly in terms of the complex and multi-faceted agencies they exercise in relation with other actors in a range of geographical settings.

Finally, as already indicated, we are also interested in the resonances that occur between representation and agency. David Crouch (2001) highlights the importance of these 'spaces' between representation and (embodied) practice: '"non-representational geographies" conceptualise the body as sensuous, sensitive, agentive and expressive in relation to the world, knowing and innovating amongst contexts and representations that become refigured in practice' (62).

We will show some of the key ways in which trees are imagined, and how trees may be encountered. This between-space hosts 'the creative tension between contextual representation and embodied subjective practice' (Crouch, 2001: 61), and in the case of 'trees' such creative tensions we argue are particularly dense and rich.

Place

The above considerations lead on to ideas of place as, in the end, they are talking about particularities in 'timespace'. Place is a fundamental aspect of existence: we (humans and non-humans) are all in place, in some way or other, at all times (Casey, 1998), yet the term *place* is one with an extreme range of (contested) meanings (Harvey, 1996). It is at once a very obvious yet very illusive notion. In our account we want to offer understandings of place in ways which have, in part, been vividly articulated by the environmental organization Common Ground. Their notion of place revolves around the idea of 'local distinctiveness', suggesting place to be some form of physical/imaginative space, such as a village, urban district, park, wood, forest, or region, identified as having some internal cohesion distinct from that around it. Such distinctions may be material or cultural, and will usually be a complex construction of differing elements. There may well be overlapping scales of distinctiveness involved, and any sense of place-identity will usually be subject to contestation, change, partiality, fading and reforming. Such places will also reflect complex interconnections between the global and the local (see Massey and Jess, 1995). Drawing on the work of the anthropologist Tim Ingold (1993), we view this notion of place as a manifestation of 'dwelling', where all manner of elements – people, artefacts, animals, plants, topography, climate, culture, economy, and history – are knotted together in a unique way to form an unfolding timespace of particular landscapes and places. Such an approach overcomes many of the epistemological weaknesses which have beset academic approaches to nature, the environment and landscape. For example, Macnaghten and Urry (1998) suggest that when nature is seen as landscape and conceptualized from a dwelling perspective, it offers exciting new perspectives which contrast both with the incomplete narrowness of three dominant views of the environment – 'realism', 'idealism' and 'instrumentalism' – and also with the great divide of nature and culture which still dominates many world views. This approach offers a way to deal with the 'richness' of place, where the ecological and the cultural, the human and non-human, the local and the global, and the real and the imaginary all become bound together in particular formations in particular places. It is this very richness which Common Ground has been attempting to defend from the homogenizing tendencies of industrialization, modernization and globalization.

There are, of course, ways of understanding place as a more malevolent force, such as that seen in Sibley's (1995) work which demonstrates how spaces and places can become variously purified, thus serving to exclude rather than offering democratic or egalitarian inclusions. We acknowledge that the treatment of place in this book is predominantly positive, but that this is in part because trees are often highly valued in places, and can render places as valued, and because trees are highly skilful place-makers and place enhancers. There is of course another side to this. Places of trees, as we will consider, can be places of fear (Burgess, 1993) as well as of exclusion. Trees will not always themselves represent positive socio-cultural or political vibes. The presence of 'alien' trees can make for alien places, rendering them, to use Cresswell's (1996) term, 'out of place' in the wider bucolic idyll of countryside or paradisal natures. In this book, our investigations of different tree-places tend to accentuate positive place characteristics, but the concepts we deploy appear equally valid in situations where more industrial, exploitative or fearful place characteristics apply.

Ethics

In many respects this is the most challenging theoretical aspect of our conceptual apparatus. If to talk about the *agency* of trees is to push at the boundaries of accepted stable assumptions about the human/non-human world, then to talk of ethical considerations of trees for most people will transgress the normal boundaries of ethical consideration, which rarely stretch beyond animals in the non-human world. There is an obvious difference here between consideration of broad ethical positions at large aggregate scales (opposition to the chopping down of rainforests might be an obvious example) and adopting similar ethical stances on behalf of specific individual trees. Different strands of environmental philosophy have presented important guidelines for the recognition of the 'intrinsic rights' of nature, and the ethical prerogatives which result from such recognition. However, when the focus switches to particular forms of nature such as individual trees, which are in complex relational associations in particular places, the general idea of 'intrinsic rights' becomes complex and is often lost. We pursue the issue of ethics in this book, first because there seems to be a link between understandings of agency and understandings of ethics. In many moral philosophies the ethical realm is equated to the human realm because humans are viewed as the only actors who possess some form of meaningful agency. Once we begin to ascribe meaningful agency (albeit of a differing kind to that which humans possess) to other actants such as trees, important implications for ethics follow. In particular, there is a prospect of developing a relational 'hybrid' form of ethics (Whatmore, 1997). Secondly, we are trying to interrogate various reticular pronouncements on ethics, in terms of their practical and political applications to particular places of trees. As we will demonstrate, there is a strong movement in environmental philosophy which emphasizes the importance of place, or home (see for example Cronon, 1996) as the locus for viable ethical formulations. We therefore seek to respond to writers such as Thrift (1996a) who stress the need for non-universalized, situated ethics of a neo-Aristotelian mould and Proctor (1998), who calls for a 'geoethic' of place.

We argue that a balance between generalized intrinsic value and an ethics of situatedness is required. The former derives from a reconfigured view of agency, but this can do no more than underpin the principle of 'an ethical precautionary principle' as in systems of understanding such as deep ecology, where trees as (relational) makers of our planet, and some of its places, are given their 'bioethical' due. However, those places or dwellings of differing actants and elements require a form of concrete relational ethics where the place itself is co-constitutive of how it is ethically configured. This entails, as Cronon (1996: 90) puts it, 'get[ting] on with the unending task of struggling to live rightly in the world'.

We therefore suggest that 'places of trees' – be they forests, orchards, woods, parks – need to be understood as the result of the 'dialectical unfolding of historical and ecological processes' (Rival, 1998b: 24) regardless of the tendency to consider trees and forests as 'naturally given categories'. Watkins (1998b: 1) suggests that 'the history of European woods and forests has long remained somewhat on the edge of academic study' and concludes that more contemporary approaches and studies 'contribute to an increasing *uncertainty* about woodland and forest history', because they show the particularity of each case, and bring ecological, historical, and cultural specificity to previously rather homogeneous categorizations:

> It is increasingly difficult to accept woodland as a simple category from which a settled landscape is wrought. Rather it must be seen as a complex type of land use which has varied dramatically in the density, age, species and forms of trees and shrubs of which it consists. The utility of woodland and the cultural values ascribed to it are also diverse . . . To explore this complex bundle of uses and values is no simple matter. (Watkins, 1998b: 1)

It is these place-related complexities which form a significant axis of our ethical discussions of non-human agents.

Four Tree-places

We devote the second half of the book to explorations of these conceptual themes in and through specific tree-places. A note of explanation is required here. It will appear strange to some readers that we have selected rather small, localized places for study. Nature in general is so often encountered and recounted in macro-spatial swathes – as wilderness, outback, industrialized agriculture, and so on. Even when our tree-emphasis is entertained, there will be a broad recognition of mighty forests covering very significant geographical spaces and, perhaps, not reflecting the 'place' characteristics discussed here. Therefore, our analysis of small, localized sites may appear insignificant against these wider perspectives.

While acknowledging the issues of scale at work here, our contention is that the non-human agency of trees can be affirmed as co-constitutive of place-making and remaking in practically any context. We have selected four initial sites for our research, and in many ways these locations are suggestive of aspects of idyllized, arcadian or civilized space as would be anticipated given cultural constructions of rural and urban landscapes in the south-west of England. Were we to have selected, say, the huge industrialized orchards of the American state of Washington, or the politically charged landscapes of South African agriculture or viticulture under apartheid, the political economy of labour relations and the cultural construction of landscape would certainly be different, but the agency of trees in their place would continue to be significant. Our four detailed studies, then, represent examples of conceptual approaches and research investigations which are not bound by the particularities of place and time.

Nevertheless, for the purposes of our research, we did purposefully select different types of tree-place where we anticipated that the non-human agencies of trees would contribute in an interesting way to the (re)production of nature–society relations and place milieu in the different rural and urban settings.

Chapter 6, 'Orchard', takes as it subject *West Bradley Fruit Farm*, a 65-acre orchard in the Glastonbury area of Somerset. Orchards comprehensively and vividly weave across any notion of a 'nature-culture divide'. Here we consider the central creative agency of the trees in the relational and quintessentially hybrid achievement that is 'an orchard'. We also reconsider the idea of place as dwelling in the orchard setting where the transitions, persistences and changes of 'orchard-ness' reflect a time-deepened dwelling of trees and people; where trees have had a physical active presence in the (re)construction of landscape; but where modern technologies and extending networks, among other factors, are challenging conventional notions of dwelling. The orchard can been seen both as a 'place' at a number of different levels, and also as a networked relational achievement which destabilizes the notion of it as a fixed place.

In Chapter 7, 'Cemetery', we consider *Arnos Vale*, a Victorian cemetery in Bristol. This is a truly remarkable place, with a rich and controversial history with trees being fully implicated in both the richness and the controversy. Here we present a reading which involves the themes of non-human agency, place-making, and dwelling. However, at Arnos Vale, these narratives take on a different character. In this context, the trees have been an unruly, even destructive force, whose relational agency seem more autonomous and 'other' to that of the orchard trees.

Here, we suggest, is a form of dwelling which is more ambiguous and problematic than is the case in our orchard place. Trees have both acted as socialized actors in the narrative of the changing nature of Arnos Vale and contributed significantly to the relational agencies involved. Trees have thereby been implicated in processes of resistance at the site, particularly through their incorporation in practices of monitoring and surveillance. The changing tree-presence at Arnos Vale has served to re-contextualize and resignify the site, and the monitoring of trees has made this bricolage known, prompting the construction of a significant site of resistance, where the privatization of public space has been contested.

In Chapter 8, 'Heritage Trail', we consider the story of the abandoned spoil heaps from the *Camerton* colliery in the now defunct Somerset coalfield. The spoils heaps are the last visible signs of the colliery which once dominated this rural village. They now play important new roles and carry considerable freights of local symbolism and institutional investment, and this is articulated by, or channelled through, the trees which have colonized the site. The spoil heaps are partially covered by conifer trees planted at the turn of the last century, partly by wild self-sown native trees, and partly by young hardwood trees, planted under a recent woodland regeneration scheme. The presence of the conifers, and the colonizing 'wild' native trees, has been bound into a process resisting redevelopment of the site. Indeed, these trees have been adopted in the promotion of conservation of the site as a Local Nature Reserve which reflects not only industrial heritage but also the role of trees in signifying local place character (known locally as 'Little Switzerland'). However, the appropriation of the site into institutional discourses and practices of 'woodland management', and the clearing of some of the conifers to make way for new broadleaf trees, has proved to be a controversial and contested issue. Here we are interested in the place-bound local inversions of broader cultural discourses and related management practices, and in how the trees have been incorporated again into complex strategies of resistance and identity development.

In Chapter 9, 'Square', we consider Victoria Park, a small square in Bristol where mature trees dominate both the architecture and the place milieu, and where issues of conservation are essentially interconnected with strong emotional sentiments of value extended to *individual* trees. Victoria Park offers an interesting historical narrative of how particular trees have come to define urban residential and civic space, and have come to be embroiled in processes of transition from 'private' to 'public' ownership. Residents of the area genuinely cherish some of the individual trees in the square, and the hybridity of these emotional or even spiritual relationships highlights a range of ethical potentials in the treatment given to the life-forms that are the trees themselves. Here, broad-scale ethical principles are brought down to earth, as lifestyles and management decisions become co-constituted with the sustained agency of increasingly 'veteran' trees.

Part I
Placing Trees in Cultural Theory

Preamble

> We love [trees] for their liveliness, for their changes through the seasons and our lives, for their ageing and persistence, for their individuality. Our attitudes to trees are full of … paradoxes. They are symbols of life, but also of wilderness, and all that stands in the way of 'civilisation'. They are the natural climax vegetation of most of the planet, yet they are obstinately viewed, even by their friends, as some kind of human benefaction. And, most ironically, they continue to be destroyed across the globe in barely credible quantities, just at the moment when we are beginning to understand their crucial role in regulating the climate. We say we love them but somehow we have not yet learned how to live together. (Mabey, 1990: 5)

In this first half of the book we look to place the non-human agency of trees into a range of conceptual arenas. We consider such conceptualization to be significant in at least three respects. First, we are keen to emphasize the sheer weight of presence which trees, individually and collectively, exert within cultural constructions of nature–society relations. Secondly, we argue that any seemingly homogeneous cultural reading of this tree-presence very quickly shatters into an often bewildering range of tree-meanings. Moreover, such tree-meanings are co-constitutive in the understandings reached about particular nature–society relations involving trees, woods and forests, and are thereby implicated in the formation of encounters and narratives of particular places and landscapes. Thirdly, the often vivid and rich nature of these narratives and encounters provides an opportunity to give consideration to three crucial areas of concern within nature–society relations – agency, place and ethics – and thereby contribute to the continuing project of developing social theory which (re)incorporates nature. Although we now deal with these four areas of concern in separate chapters, we recognize that important spaces and resonances occur between representation and place, and between place and agency, and we believe that these are opened up as we consider the four 'tree places' in the second half of the book.

–2–

Arbori-culture

> There is an inextricable link between people and trees, especially old trees. From all the thousands of uses we have put them to, and all the fears and desires we have projected onto them, human cultures around the world have emerged from the trees. Now that we know our abuse of trees has bought ruin to them and us, we turn again to the venerable ones, searching for some resilient spirit, eternal, or near as damn it.
>
> (Evans, 1999)

> The trees are coming into leaf
> Like something almost being said;
> The recent buds relax and spread,
> The greenness is a kind of grief.
>
> (Larkin, '*The Trees*')

In this chapter we begin to explore the cartography of the mutual implication of trees and culture. Our starting point is to reaffirm the tree as a category of life-form. As Atran (1990: 35) argues:

> The natural discontinuities apparent in the conception of tree pertain to processes of evolutionary convergence bound to ecological considerations in the competition for sunlight. People naturally tend to find trees phenomenally compelling because of their evident ecological role in determining local distributions of flora and fauna.

However, we argue that the assumptions and inferences made about trees are not solely derived from these evolutionary ecological principles, for trees also carry significant cultural baggage. Deep currents of meaning swirl around our culture(s) and brush through the branches of any tree or tree-place which is being encountered, experienced, narrated or imagined at any given time. Such meanings vary from the vaguest acknowledgement that trees somehow serve to 'breathe' for the planet, to deeply held and poignant appreciations in wider discourses, for example relating to socio-ecological sustainability, countryside conservation, and even political nationalism.

We tend to think of these mutual implications as 'arbori-cultures', and we should immediately recognize arbori-culture as a global phenomenon, with different societies and places offering often distinctive discursive narratives of tree-meanings (Franklin, 1999; Rival, 1998a/b; Schama, 1995). While we reflect this global nature to some extent in this chapter, our particular focus is on arbori-culture in Britain, where, for such a relatively small island, we encounter a complex cultural map of the overlapping positions and roles in which trees are placed.

This focus on arbori-culture chimes with recent work in human geography and cultural studies which develops new cultural engagements with landscape. As Cosgrove wrote in 1984, 'landscape has re-emerged in . . . writings as an important term because its affective meaning seems to allow for an escape from the outsider's position and for the incorporation of sensitivity to human engagement with particular places and areas (1984: 34). And in these writings trees have featured as integral components of landscapes. Thus in Meinig's (1979) discussions of symbolic landscapes and their iconography, he considers one of the most famous landscape depictions in/of America – a depiction of a New England village which comprised a 'scene of a village embowered in great elms and maples' (165).

The urge to read landscapes and people's interaction with them developed the notion of landscape as text that was loaded with ideological traces of power, class, gender, and ethnicity. As such, the term 'landscape' itself became problematized, with ideas of 'ways of seeing' being brought to the fore (Muir, 1999), while at the same time landscapes were seen as 'one of the central elements in a cultural system' (Duncan 1990: 17). It was argued that all landscapes carried symbolic meaning, and that the analysis of landscape was best done through an 'iconographic approach' which not only understood these symbols and their contexts but also, in a postmodern sense, understood how contemporary interpretation itself reconstructed and reframed this symbolic structure in its own context.

These critical advances from 'traditional' approaches to landscape and the cultures of landscapes included new concerns for place, space and landscapes from within cultural studies, a good example being Whitt and Slack's call for cultural studies to probe how communities are embedded 'in the material world (whether the immediate landscape be "natural" or "urban") . . . Geographical and ecological features of community are rarely incidental to political and cultural struggle: they contextualise – enable and constrain – relations of power' (1994: 6). This materialization and spatialization of cultural studies was itself informed by the spatial turn within social theory (see Crang and Thrift, 2000). Thus cultural geography in its most recent forms can be 'earthed' while still being 'attuned to difficult theoretical issues' – particularly those which question space in its Euclidian form (Philo, 2000: 36).

As we will show, tree-landscapes are bound up with all manner of powerful cultural constructions, not least national identity. The powerful material and symbolic character of trees can place them at the very heart of these new approaches to landscapes, as trees are woven into the material/imaginative fabrics of the world. Such weaving can take all manner of forms, some disturbing, as in the case of a large swastika (clearly visible from the air) formed of larch trees which stood out (golden in the autumn) in a forest of darker green conifers near Zernikow, Germany. These trees had been planted in 1938, had been felled after the Second World War but had re-sprouted and controversially became visible again in the 1990s (Karacs: 2000).

These aspects of the cultural turn and its re-emphasis of landscape have themselves been subject to critical review. For example Muir (1999), as others have before him (e.g. Daniels, 1992), questions the more 'extreme' treatment of landscape as text and symbol, which rests on iconography and semiotics alone, seemingly relegates the material as a meaningful presence, and discounts 'objective historical analysis' (as in the work of W.G. Hoskins). Muir sees a more fruitful approach in the work of writers 'who venture out into the field' and are still prepared to confront 'real landscapes' but in ways informed by theoretical developments. In this context, he cites David Lowenthal's (1979) work on burial grounds, and Catherine Nash's (1993) work on Irish landscapes and identity, where the very materiality of the landscape is an active component in such processes rather than being merely scripted.

Such valorization of the 'real' as well as the 'symbolic' in landscape studies is central to our approach to arbori-culture. We want to map out the cultural symbolisms and meanings which are associated with trees and tree-places, but we want to do so in a way which presents a 'grounded' narrative of particular places. Our purpose here is twofold. First, we argue that this exercise in cultural cartography represents an important step in the disaggregation of cultural constructions of an undifferentiated notion of 'nature', and of 'trees' themselves as a broad collective. The complex multifaceted, and inter-folding meanings associated with trees will have a major bearing on understandings of 'nature', landscapes and places where trees are present. As we have already said, Harvey (1996: 183) has expressed concern that there has been a tendency to 'homogenise the category "nature"'. 'Trees' are particular forms of 'nature' which bring all manner of particular resonances to considerations of nature–society relations, place, landscape and environmental philosophy and management. They also, of course, offer a 'field of difference' within themselves and this plays out in how humans construct, and act upon, different trees in differing places. As Watkins (1998a: 8) emphasizes, 'The ways in which trees are catalogued and categorised play an important part in their protection and survival'.

Secondly, a cultural cartography of trees is directly relevant to the understanding of different places and landscapes. Whether the approach to place be highly theoretical (see for example Casey 1998; Thrift, 1999) or more practically concerned with day-to-day environmental management (see for example Barrow, 1999), it will be important to reach an understanding of the broad cultural constructions of trees which are imported into those places, and which are then refolded and mixed into the unique chemistry of the local milieu. While this maxim holds for all culturally constructed narratives of nature, it seems to be of particular relevance in relation to trees, which have a commanding material and symbolic presence which is as subject to complex variegation as are trees themselves. The processes by which trees become culturally meaningful will have significant implications for understanding how places and landscapes are imagined, and for processes of environmental management, where those working with trees will be continually confronting the complex symbolic and emotional freight attached to trees in any particular place.

In what follows we set out a kind of typology of 'tree positions' within society. We would not claim this to be comprehensive, but we argue that these are some of *the key ways in which trees are seen*, and that these constructions feed through into how landscapes and places are seen and formed. Any such typology should be regarded as impressionistic rather than creating rigid or tightly-drawn categoric boundaries. Viewed from particular perspectives, distinct variations and forms can be seen within a cultural geography of trees, but close up, the brush strokes which constitute that geography become more abstract, arbitrary, blurred and uncertain.

Our discussion begins with a consideration of the different meanings which radiate from particular categories of tree-places – notably 'forests' and 'woodlands'. These aggregate descriptors convey very powerful iconography and symbolisms which contribute significantly to the cartography of arbori-culture. We then investigate two aspects of the relationship between biology and culture as manifest in trees and tree-places. First, emphasizing the botanical, we discuss the materiality of trees, and in particular the ways in which the biology of trees is culturally (re)constructed and (re)configured into popular dualistic motifs such as alien/native or ancient/young. Then, emphasizing the semiotic, we discuss the symbolic natures of trees, examining the ways in which spiritual and mythical constructs become translated variously into experiential and mythical meaningfulness for observers or consumers of trees and tree-places. Finally we look more closely at the involvement of trees in wider processes of production and consumption, noting with interest the roles which are allocated to trees, and the complex assumed meanings associated with these roles. In this way, for example, trees can be variously understood as 'working', 'conserved', or 'wild'. From the outset, though, we want to emphasize that trees will usually occupy multiple cultural places simultaneously, and indeed will migrate through different cultural spaces over time. These complexities and mobilities are integrally involved in the folding and refolding of nature–society relations in particular places at particular times.

Forests, Woodlands and Trees

Trees are often acknowledged and recognized in multiple categories rather than as individuals. Such categories produce key identifiers of tree-places, which in turn can shape popular conceptions of space and place, and can help to define the social spatializations (Shields 1991) which are produced therein. These categories often overlap and interpenetrate in complex ways, but they also carry distinct cultural resonances which relate strongly to the meanings which may be imported into encounters with, and knowings of, particular tree places.

Forests

The term *forest* has a complex and somewhat uncertain history (Watkins 1998a), but strictly defined it suggests tracts of land on which royalty has 'retained special hunting rights'. Forest areas were not necessarily highly wooded but, since some of the most prominent forest areas in Britain were wooded (such as the Forest of Dean and the New Forest), the term forest came to be synonymous with such areas. From these specific roots, the term forest has translated into a wide range of international contexts, taking with it the general meaning of 'a large wooded area' (Broad 1998). Such areas have become associated with a suite of culturally constructed meanings which vary spatially and temporally, and variously intersect with other constructions of the individual trees to be found in the places and spaces concerned.

At a deep symbolic level, 'forest' can be interpreted as being the 'other' to Western civilization – a historical and geographical 'sylvan fringe of darkness' which plays a significant role in the 'cultural imagination of the West' (Harrison, 1992: ix). At the national scale, too, forest-meanings are pertinent to the interpretation of landscape. Schama's (1995) *Landscape and Memory*, for example, presents compelling evidence of how forests have embodied particular meanings in different nations: a militaristic spirit in Germany; a passion for order in France; a transcendental connection with the 'Creator' in America; a struggle for national freedom in Poland. In the English context, he points to histories of human liberties in the 'greenwood' which translate into mapped-on meanings of forests as places in which to find one. Schama also highlights the continuous flow of analogy between the character of timber and the character of the nation ('hearts of oak'). He warns, however, that 'There have always been two kinds of arcadia: shaggy and smooth; dark and light; a place of bucolic leisure and a place of primitive panic (ibid.: 517).

We can therefore expect different and frequently contradictory or ambiguous social meanings to be associated with forests. Equally, we can expect these national consciousness(es) to be deconstructed by particular individualized relationships with wooded landscapes. For example, Cloke et al. (1996a) have shown how intimate and detailed constructions of forest can emerge from broad (and sometimes stereotyped) national symbolic forms. Their list is intended to be illustrative rather than exhaustive:

Forests as paradisal landscapes. Hecht and Cockburn (1989) suggest that, for the tropical world at least, there is a perception of forests as divine virgin-nature, unmodified by human nature and therefore the subject of virtuous contemplation. In the temperate world too, forest suggests natural habitus and forms part of rural pastoral paradises whose benefits can be shared by all. Such meanings, however, can give rise to opposite sentiments of paradise 'lost' and paradise 'invaded' (Ellen, 1993).

Forests as spiritual landscapes. The postmodern era has increasingly seen the reclamation of nature and spirituality (Matless, 1991) and, for many, the notion of tree and forest is not only paradisal but spiritual. In New Zealand, for example, the symbolic practice of 'hugging a kauri' denotes spiritual bond as well as a conservation ethic directed at rare indigenous tree species.

Forests as mythological landscapes. Along with ideas of primordial paradise and natural spirituality, forests also conjure up mythological suggestions (Harrison, 1992). For example, in the Western world, many of the fairy tales learnt when young and sustained through parenthood are located by Grimm, Anderson and others in forest settings. The 'forests' are thereby imbued with notions of danger, mystery and lack of light, and with a clear sense of the risk to women and children of becoming lost, far from home (see below). We should also contest ethnocentricity here by stressing the importance of challenging the scope of Western conceptions in this respect (see Shiva, 1989). Mythology is also interconnected with modern reproduction of paradisal pastoralism. D. Curry (2000) discusses in detail how trees are a central theme in one of the great 'new' mythological creations – that of Tolkien's Middle-Earth. Hecht and Cockburn (1989) talk of Disneyized forests in which, with the coming of the nature documentary, Eden has been born again as the élan which is the key to genteel television.

Forests as gendered landscapes. The very productive linking of environmentalism and feminism (see for example Monk, 1992; Nesmith and Radcliffe, 1993) has shown not only how social, cultural and political meanings have been inscribed on landscapes but also how these meanings are gendered. One important outcome of this has been to define the dominant masculinist characteristics which have been transposed as distinctively 'human' in relation to nature – for example rationality, transcendence and intervention in, domination and control of nature as opposed to passive immersion in it (Plumwood 1993). Another outcome has been to recognize the other to predominantly masculinist landscapes by identifying those landscapes where women do not fit, do not belong or are forbidden. Forests are thus likely to be important as areas of women's fear.

Forests as landscapes or 'orthodox' gaze. The work of Urry (1990) and Wilson (1992) in particular has been influential in demonstrating how the gaze of visitors to a landscape is often mediated and directed by tourist representations and educational materials. We are invited to inspect and photograph the landscape from clearly signed viewpoints, to traverse the landscape on way-marked routes and to understand the landscape via punctuations on those routes where interpretative information is provided. Such experiences will often have been preceded by idealized representations of the landscape in advertising brochures and thus the imagined geography sparked by representations of, say, a forest can be reinforced by the interpretative gaze provided.

There are of course differing forms of 'forest' such as old growth or primary forests, new commercial forests, temperate rainforests, and the tropical rainforests which are held up to be 'the lungs of the world' and spaces of pure nature and indigenous people as part of that nature. All these identities bring cultural baggage with them which may well be fiercely contested, and which will affect how trees, people and places are understood and acted upon. For example, Slater (1996) suggests that the construction of the forests of Amazonia as 'Edenic Rain Forest' results in policy decisions which 'wreak havoc on the lives of both trees and people' (115). Similarly, Goin (1996: vii) tells of the sudden realization that 'the virgin forests' (as labelled by a logging company for political expedience) he saw when driving in the United States were in fact commercial plantations, and that this had felt as if someone had 'punched [him] in the gut'. This revelation led him to reassess his view of the American landscape from one based on Romantic/Transcendental views of 'Nature' to a position which he terms 'Humanature' – an outlook which parallels Wilson's (1992) approach to the culture of nature.

Such reactions suggest that moral geographies will emerge from observations of, and reactions to, arbori-cultures. For example, Proctor (1996: 288) asserts that American forests have long been 'a contested moral landscape'. Here understandings of the old growth forests and trees as economic resource, habitat, recreational amenity, or wilderness came into sharp confrontation. It is important to note that the meanings of differing landscapes seep into each other. As Proctor relates, references to the destruction of the Amazon rainforest were deployed in the disputes he studied in the United States, as they have been in the direct actions against tree clearances in Britain.

Continuing concern for the fate of 'the world's forests' feeds into public discourses on forests, woods and trees via the media and NGO campaigns. For example, Radford's (2001) report on the recent UNEP's (United Nations Environment Programme) satellite survey of forest loss between 1990 and 1995 predicts, 'the earth's remaining closed canopy forests and their associated biodiversity are destined to disappear in the coming decades'. The Global Trees Campaign, run by a coalition of NGOs and the UNEP (Gates, 2000) claims 'more than 8,000 tree species, representing 10 per cent of the Earth's tree flora are threatened with extinction through woodland and forest loss and forest destruction' (1) and that 'almost half of the original forest cover of Earth – 3 billion hectares – has been removed' (4). Such claims and concerns for the 'world's forests' set up, we suggest, key cultural contexts and environmental and arboreal anxieties which resonate through other tree–human relationships which operate at differing local scales.

Woodland

In many ways the terms *woodlands* and *forests* are interchangeable, and woodlands will carry associations similar to those outlined above. But in other ways they do carry distinct resonances that vary across cultures. The idea of forest is often about large spaces, wilderness, wildness, habitat, nature and landscapes other to civilization and modernity; landscapes where the human is enclosed, dwarfed, concealed and/or lost. These factors have constructed forests as contradictory places: of refuge and threat; of retreat from modernity and as a tool of the state; as savage and noble, as well as savage, backward and uncivilized.

The category of woodland suggests a more intimate, culturalized space than is the case with forest. This is so particularly in Britain, but such a distinction is highly dependent on national cultural contexts. For example, Henry Thoreau's (1972) sojourn in the *Maine Woods*, and Bryson's (1998) account of a *Walk in the Woods* show that the distinction between 'woods' and 'forests' in the United States may have differing dynamics. Muir (1999: 91–2) discusses the difference between woodlands and forests in American and English landscapes, and quotes Williams's (1990) conclusion that 'the forest is still a dominant feature of the American visual scene'. In Britain however, where the overall tree cover is low and large tracts of forests are now rare, woodland has developed a particular cultural niche. Watkins (1998a) shows that precise spatial definitions of woodland are problematic, and that such problems extend, for example, to the calculation of historical changes in woodland cover. Our concern here, however, is with more fuzzy, but nonetheless significant cultural mappings of woodland.

Woodland is a key component of the notion of the idyllic and picturesque British landscape. The patches and ribbons of woodland that contribute to the mosaic of such landscapes are of a more localized scale than that of forest. The woods of Britain occupy a wide range of imaginative positions, ranging from spaces of utter innocence and freedom in children's literature, through spaces of authenticity and traditional culture, to the landscapes of liberty, as described earlier in this chapter. Again our purpose is not to try to provide an exhaustive account of such constructions, but rather to illustrate how woods as imaginative entities do come with freight of associations which entangle with imaginative constructions of particular trees, and which affect both understandings of particular landscapes and the ways in which those landscapes are encountered and performative meanings and agencies constructed.

Woodland is often constructed as a place of freedom and refuge in British culture, as famously depicted in the Robin Hood stories, and in lines from Shakespeare's *As You Like It* where any dweller, 'Under the greenwood tree . . . shall . . . see/*No enemy*/But winter and rough weather'. Daniels (1999) points out how this contrasts with some European constructions of woods and forests:

> The greenwood has exerted a powerful hold on the English imagination. It is not the dark forest of howling beasts and tribal bloodshed that haunts the folklore of and literature of mainland Europe, but rather a golden world of sunny glades and leafy trees where the living is free and easy. (298)

In his earlier excellent political iconography of woodland in later Georgian England, Daniels (1988) shows how tree symbolism was deployed in both the 'conservative' and the 'radical' imagination, and how the great landscapers such as Repton deployed both political ideas and those associated with the 'English Picturesque' in their re-imagining and redesigning of landscapes using trees as a principal medium of change. Such literal and symbolic constructions and ideologies of woodland and landscape are explored by Tsouvalis (2000) where she shows medieval feudalism, Crown sovereignty, the state, capitalism, and scientific rationalism being articulated in woodland landscapes. The changing everyday lives of communities in these landscapes are charted in novels such as Thomas Hardy's *The Woodlanders* and *Under the Greenwood Tree*, and more recently in Edward Rutherford's historical novel *The Forest*, set in the New Forest. Here the life portrayed is far from idyllic, but is characterised by a unique culture and an authenticity which resonates of dwelling and community, in which labour, power, trees and landscape fold together. The details of the cultures with their crafts and custom have also be documented by writers, particularly as they were seen to be in decline over the last century or so (see for example Seymour, 1983).

Often on a more idyllic note, woods also feature prominently in children's literature. Croom Wood, in Richmal Crompton's forty or so famous *William Brown* stories, is a place of freedom and sanctuary for William and his gang in their on-going skirmishes with the stultifying adult ordering of the world. The poignant innocence of A.A. Milne's *Winnie-the-Pooh* stories has the 100-acre Wood as its blithesome, innocent narrative territory. More recent examples of woodland-set childhood stories are the highly successful series of books and television programmes *The Creatures of Farthing Wood*, and *Oakie Doke*. Yet in contrast to all this in one of the quintessential classics of children's literature, Kenneth Grahame's *The Wind in the Willows*, the Wild Wood is a place of danger and disorder on the edge of the bucolic, genteel countryside of Ratty and Mole.

Forests and Woods as places of fear. We should recognize, then, that the freedom and refuge of woods will often be counterpointed by the association of woodland and forests with landscapes of fear. Two strands of fear can be recognized. First, there is a fear of what woodlands might contain or conceal, which can range from the mythic to very real fears of personal safety. Many common fairy tales use woods as a place where dangers lurk for those who have to venture into them, or who stray into them. But the fear has another more elusive dimension, as Denes (2000) argues, 'In fairy tales . . . living besides a wood denotes "living on the edge of mystery", getting lost in the wood, on the other hand, is a more dangerous business, a sign that one is losing one's mind, one's self'. Stevie Smith's poem 'Fairy Story' gently captures exactly this loss.

The European woods which were the settings of many scary fairy tales (*Little Red Riding Hood, Hansel and Gretel*) were also the place of war atrocities, mass graves, and 'buried memories', as in Powers's novel *In the Memory of the Forest*, which charts a post-1989 Polish community dealing with the legacies of the Second World War, for whom the struggle is way-marked by a forgotten overgrown Jewish cemetery in the woods near the village. In America, when Bill Bryson (1998) decides to do his *Walk in the Woods* along the Appalachian Trail through the forests of the eastern United States, the list of reasons why it is a scary, bad idea lasts for three pages, and includes, 'fire ants', 'lightening strikes', 'snakes', 'bears', 'wolves', 'diseases lurking in the woods', 'loony hillbillies destabilised by gross quantities of impure corn liquor and generations of profoundly unbiblical sex', and the threat of becoming 'the tenth hiker to be murdered on the trail since 1974' (15).

There is also a clear gendered dimension to woods as landscapes of fear. Kaza (1993: 141), for example, gives a powerful account of the woods she loves becoming a place of fear at night. 'All the fear comes up together. Fear of getting lost, fear of enemies, fear of attack . . . fear of the dark, fear of death . . . I can no longer see the beautiful forest.' More generally, there is a recognition that woodland is perceived by women to be a 'dangerous place at dangerous times' (Valentine, 1989) – an association which has been investigated and confirmed by Burgess (1993) who identifies a clear need for countryside policy-makers to take steps to respond to these perceived safety issues.

In a second strand of fear, woods themselves can be constructed as sinister brooding presences (see Perlman 1994: 100). The trees in Disney's *Sleeping Beauty* anthropomorphize into grabbing malignant forces. In Holdstock's novel *Mythago Wood*, an area of ancient English woodland is a forceful and brooding presence within the narrative, as well as being the setting for it. The same can be said for David Lynch's seminal television drama series *Twin Peaks,* where the woods provide a claustrophobic, ambivalent (part brooding) contribution to the story. Such fears tap into Harrison's (1992) notion of forests being the dark other to modern civilization, and into the idea that trees themselves can be powerful presences. Images of 'Green Men' – Celtic pagan figures of men formed from tree elements – also tap into Christian-derived anxiety about such dark traditions, and are being redeployed to reclaim the spirit of trees and woods as a positive rather than negative symbolism.

Trees

In addition to forests and woodland tree-spaces, we should acknowledge that individual trees themselves have attracted a huge array of imaginative attachments and cultural roles. According to Mabey (1996: 71), 'Trees have size, longevity, economic usefulness and a profound impact on the landscape – which means that they have entered our culture more thoroughly than most smaller flowering plants'. For trees to be seen as individuals, they somehow have to stand out from the crowds of their own kind. They can of course literally stand alone and thus be a visually distinct landmark within the landscape. They can also stand out through features such as rarity, size, form and age, as recorded by Packenham (1997) and Boyer (1996). Sometimes trees can even, by some means or other, become 'visible' even within forests or woodlands, as for example in the case of the great oaks in Britain in Sherwood Forest (Watkins, 1998b). Along with such 'remarkable trees' (Packenham, 1997) there are of course all the 'ordinary trees', the 'anonymous', each of which has, however, 'its own harmony, its own history, and its own strangeness' (Boyer, 1996: 10).

It follows that the felling of a single tree standing in some prominent position in a landscape may be highly contentious, but a similar tree being felled in a forest management programme goes entirely unnoticed. Individuality in trees comes through both their characteristics and their position. In the case of the Newbury bypass protests in Britain, for example, it was *woods* which were being cleared and campaigned for, but in the end *trees* were individualized as they were occupied, fought over and finally felled, one by one (Merrick, 1996).

These cultural constructions of forests, woods and trees interact in complex ways. For example, the positive associations people may have with trees can either be enhanced or overshadowed by constructions of the woodlands they form. Loved trees as woodland, as we have seen, can become landscapes of fear. But equally, certain trees such as veteran oaks, when placed in esteemed landscapes such as ancient woodland in Britain, build up layers of positive association which make them key cultural icons and conservation projects. However, just as negative constructions of woodlands can usurp positive constructions of trees, the reverse is also possible. For example, a forest can be the subject of negative cultural construction, and acted upon in markedly differing ways depending on whether it is considered to be formed from native trees in natural formations, or alien trees in artificial formations.

But often, such linkages of trees, forests, places and culture can spiral together into powerful formations, and this sometimes even to the extent of evangelical arbori-cultural ambitions, as in the proclamation by Baker (1944: 256),

> Man (*sic*) is the most advanced example of animal evolution, whereas his brother tree is the highest phase of vegetable progress. The fruits of trees, rather than the carcasses of lower animals, should constitute the ideal food for man, for they represent the last state of all the cosmic energies in a form available to human vitality.
>
> Trees and forests are the ideal environment for man, and he should study how to help his brother tree or communities of trees and forests. The evolution of the animal and vegetable kingdoms of earth has culminated in men and trees, and they are interdependent.

Biology and Culture: the Materiality of Trees

A number of recent theoretical developments relating to nature–society relations – particularly critical developments of social nature (Whatmore and Boucher, 1992), nature–culture dialectics (Harvey, 1996), Actor Network Theory (Whatmore, 1999; Thrift, 1996a) and some ecofeminist stances (Cheney, 1994; Haraway, 1992; Merchant, 1992; Warren, 1994) – have asserted that nature cannot be seen as a passive, blank sheet on which cultural formations are simply inscribed. Nature clearly 'pushes back' and injects its own materiality and dynamism into what Harvey terms 'socio-ecological processes'. These positions (discussed more fully in the next chapter) form the background to what we want to discuss here: that is, the complex coming together of tree materiality and the cultural constructions of trees, in the formation of what we are calling 'arbori-culture'.

As Proctor (1996: 194) suggests, understandings of how landscapes are complex interweavings of subject and object – the material and the imaginative – is still rare, but is an important trajectory in approaches to landscape. The materiality of trees, particularly their form, nature, habits, and spatial distribution, present complex, dynamic, material formations into which cultural constructions fold and which have become potent symbolic markers operating within society. Such markers relate to trees being alien or native, to differing species of trees, and even to differing ages of trees. There is a need, as Mabey (1996: 76) puts it, to understand 'the way that trees and woods 'work', socially and ecologically' if we are to understand the richness of human–nature interactions.

Native and Alien

On the British Tree website (www. British-Trees.com) 33 trees are listed as being native, with native being defined as those trees 'that colonised the British Isles after the last ice age and before they were cut of from the rest of Europe by rising sea levels'. The implications of native status are considerable. First, in ecological terms, the length of presence of a particular tree-type in the landscape means that the ecosystems into which they are integrated may have developed greater variety and complexity; second, they will have equally deep cultural ecologies. It is these 'natives' in particular (e.g. common oak, ash, holly, yew) which can be established symbols of landscape, and deeply embedded in various economic, technological and cultural formations. Many other trees which have also been long present in Britain (for example those which arrived with the Roman occupation) represent similarly evolved and embedded presences. However, the 'alien' status of some trees, particularly when set alongside other bio-cultural identifiers such as 'invasive', or 'ecologically poor', means that such trees can be regarded as *arbores non gratae* in certain settings. This was evident in a recent press release by the Forestry Commission in regard to clearing alien trees from the New Forest:

> More than 440 acres of the area's most historic woods are threatened by the spread of invasive trees and shrubs including rhododendron, Turkey oak and sycamore. Foresters fear that left unchecked they could damage the landscape, ecology and historic character of England's largest expanse of ancient woodland. (Forestry Commission, 1996)

We touch again upon the hostility that alien trees can attract later (see also Tsouvalis, 2000). But it should be noted that such negative constructions of alien species can become highly politicized and contentious, as highlighted in the work of Julian Agyeman (1993) who equates the social construction of 'alien' and 'native' trees with similar constructions of race, colour and nationalism in human society. The idea of *alien*, then, goes well beyond understandings of landscape and place, and sometimes seeps out from these arenas into wider constructions of human society.

Deciduous and Evergreen

This is a further broad classification of tree which has clear links to ideas of alien and native, but which diverts significantly into other sets of meanings. Most of the native or long-resident trees in Britain are deciduous, but this is not exclusively so (yew, holly, Scots pine, are evergreen native trees). The very different nature and life patterns of these two categories of trees are appropriated and developed culturally in a number of ways.

Perhaps most obviously, the seasonal cycle of deciduous trees is deeply embedded in our cultures of landscape and seasonality. For example, we are told that '[D]eciduous trees keep us in touch with the seasons and with the brevity of our own mortality' (Common Ground, 1991: 1). The glory of certain trees in the autumn is repeatedly celebrated in a thousand glossy calendars and 'higher' art. People are inspired to take vacations in New England in order to witness the colours and textures of the fall. Arboreta, such as that in Britain at Westonbirt near Bath, organize special floodlit 'autumn extravaganzas' to celebrate this seasonal display which has become a time-marker for much of British society. Equally, spring – when trees come into leaf and flower – is a repeated theme in poetry as in (perhaps most obviously) Shakespeare's 'darling buds of may', Housman's reflection that 'about the woodlands I will go, to see the cherry hung with snow', and Larkin's 'The Trees'. Less obviously, evergreen trees have been associated with the geographies of burial grounds, from the ancient association of yews and churchyards to the planting schemes of Victorian cemeteries which we consider in Chapter 7.

Evergreen trees, such as the conifers deployed in the now notorious early afforestation policies of the Forestry Commission, have generally been constructed in a negative light in Britain, as exemplified by Massingham's (1988b) analysis of 'The Curse of the Conifers'. As Wright (1992) put it,

> We British . . . have looked at those coniferous plantations and decided we do not like them. We have brewed up a frantic symbolism of revulsion around them. We deplore the dark world beneath the coniferous canopy . . . those wretched fir trees are as deprived of individuality as people under communism.

Interestingly, the dislike of conifers is often accompanied by further political or ideological discourse. The martial ranks of conifers marching across hillsides (Fairbrother, 1970) invoked scarcely settled fears of invasion as well as of cold war communism. Such invocations produce strong instinctive and stereotyped reactions, as Bosanquet (2000) suggests: 'I know the feelings people have about the serried ranks and so on. It's a bit like Animal Farm – hardwoods good conifers bad'.

The mixing of ecology and culture which forms the basis for such views is seen when Condry (1974) compares walking in an oak wood and in a coniferous forest, where woodland as habitat, as aesthetic and cultural experience merge together:

> To be in an oakwood where all the birds are singing and the wildflowers are gay in the dappled sunlight of a spring day, is a beautiful experience. Then if you walk . . . into a mature spruce plantation you get the full impact of what a gloomy, flowerless, silent and depressing place a conifer forest can be. (132)

Ironically, the conifers which have become so disliked, despite their usefulness as the staple resource of twentieth-century forestry, were originally introduced as novelties and rare specimens in the great plant-collecting movement of the nineteenth century. Planting and collecting such species became something of a craze. For example, in 1850 'The Oregon Association' was formed which was 'an association of noblemen and gentlemen . . . for the purpose of promoting the botanical exploration of north-west America, and the introduction into Great Britain of plants and trees, especially Coniferae, indigenous to that region' (Hadfield, 1967: 160). Trees types such as the Douglas Fir have thus shifted in their cultural location from rare exotic novelty to commonplace alien intruder as their biological characteristics have led them into particular economic and land-use relationships in Britain.

More recently another alien evergreen, the Leylandii tree, has also acquired a notorious reputation, becoming a symbol of an overbearing urge for privacy and property demarcation. Their speed of growth (up to six feet a year, Mabey, 1996), size and density of year-round foliage make them ideal for fast-growing hedges. Amazingly, according to Evans (1998), '20% of the trees in Britain are now Leylandii', and more often than not they are viewed as 'monsters running amok, sowing discontent among neighbours'. So the tree categories deciduous and evergreen carry cultural associations along with notions of native and alien, and these combine with each other and with yet further categories.

Young and Old

In many contemporary Western societies youth is valorized. Children and young animals receive particular emotional and symbolic attention, and youth 'lifestyle' is culturally dominant in many domains, while old age in humans and animals is often accompanied by a lack of interest and empathy. This age-related valuation is often reversed in society-tree relations. The older a tree is, the more likely it is to become the focus of particular attention and value. Lewington and Parker (1999) have recently produced a lavish and loving book entitled *Ancient Trees* which is devoted to the celebration of 'veteran trees'. All the 'Remarkable Trees' Packenham

(1997) meets 'are of great size and age, and consequently striking form'. There is also a Veteran Trees Initiative in Britain, the supporting publicity for which claims that 'Veteran Trees are important as part of our cultural and historical landscape. An individual Veteran Tree can create a place with beauty, atmosphere and myriad cultural and historical associations'.

As Evans (1999) asserts, 'there is an inextricable link between people and trees, especially old trees'. This belief in the special quality of aesthetic value of old trees leads Sinden (1990: 10) to suggest that 'All old trees and ancient woodland are priceless and should be jealously guarded. Old trees are more important than young trees, culturally, ecologically, and aesthetically'. These observations are evident in many facets of the planning system, which places considerable emphasis on the retention and conservation of mature trees. For example, the layout of new developments such as housing estates has to accommodate large old trees into the new landscape formation. Indeed, such trees add value to, and often become a focal point of the new development (Figure 2.1).

Even so trees which may be of a considerable size can be cleared if they have not grown old enough or 'remarkable enough'. For example, a number of mature plane trees were cut down to accommodate a new road layout in the Temple Meads area of the city of Bristol. If these trees had been much older and more distinctive in form, their felling and the subsequent redevelopment would have been much more problematic for the authorities. As with other tree characteristics, different

Figure 2.1 New housing development planned to accommodate existing old oak trees (Owain Jones)

meanings can fold together to form powerful bundles of associations. For example, old *native* trees – particularly oaks – will attract more attention than old conifer trees, and of course the place in which they stand and the relations which bind them to other materialities and symbolisms add yet further to the depth and power of these associations.

Individual Species

As we have already hinted, the tree type itself can also be accompanied by complex cultural associations. Accordingly, as Mabey (1996: 71) suggests, 'oaks, elms, and willow especially – could have whole anthologies of poetry and paintings collected about them'. Perhaps the most obvious example of a tree type with a powerful range of cultural associations which attach to the tree itself, the landscapes it inhabits, and all the economic production cultures which are associated with trees is the 'common oak'. As Simon Schama (2000) points out 'Ancient Britons were thought to have worshipped them; righteous outlaws are sheltered by them; kings on the run hide in them; hearts of oak go to sea and win empires' (341). The oak is thus a symbol of freedom, strength and refuge (See also Morris and Perring, 1974), as in the Major Oak – the huge hollow tree Robin Hood and his associates supposedly hid in. It also represents the longevity and resilience of the English state, as seen in the Royal Oak (witness many a pub name and sign), which refers to the longstanding narrative of an ancient oak near Boscobel in which Charles the Second is reputed to have hidden on 6 September 1651. Such narratives rely in part on fanciful myths, but oak *was* used extensively in the building of the ships which led to England becoming a marine super-power, and thus the powerful symbolism of England's 'heart of oak' grew out of the quality of the timber and the skills and technologies which deployed that timber in shipbuilding.

Other types of tree have similar ranges of ecological, technical, economic and cultural traces radiating from them, leading to a weaving of those trees into landscape, craft and culture. For example, Wilkinson (1979) charts not only the botany of the elm, but also its history in the British landscape. The account emphasizes not only the uses of elm timber, but also the 'Elm in the Landscape of the Mind' recognizing its presence in the paintings of Constable, in prose and poetry, and in its folklore reputation as a tree of ill fortune.

The woodlands formed by different trees can also become culturally distinct. For example, Tansley (1968) considers the biological make up of British oak-woods and British beech-woods, and how these translate into different landscapes of aesthetic appeal:

> While the oak-hazel coppices provide the finest shows of spring flowers, there is nothing more beautiful and satisfying than a beech-wood at all times of year . . . The very emptiness of the wood caused by the dearth of shrubs, combined with the striking grace and beauty of the tree trunks, gives a unique simplicity and dignity to the scene. For their loveliness alone we ought to preserve our few beech woods with jealous care. (114)

Many common trees have corresponding cultural niches bound up with their production and consumption in both economic and symbolic terms and those in turn rest upon the material characteristics of those trees; the conditions they will grow in (e.g. the willow as a wetland tree, the London Plane as a tree of the city street) and the timber, fruit and other products they may produce. For landscape architects and gardeners, different trees offer different properties in terms of size, shape, foliage type, durability, and adaptability to certain conditions. Thus the materiality and the cultural 'feel' of trees become combined in a planned way on various scales.

Culture and Biology: the Symbolism of Trees

Cross-cutting with but also extending beyond some of the above categorizations, based on the materiality of trees, are cultural edifices which emphasize various psychological realms of human identity and imagination. Trees have been and remain the focus of spiritual attention, the ground of myths, and the fabric upon which other aesthetic and symbolic concepts are built. As a consequence 'trees are used as major symbols all over the world' (Bloch: 1998: 39). Our purpose here is to suggest the range of symbolisms, and the *symbolisms of symbolisms* that cling to various trees in various places in various ways. The precise ways in which such attachments occur will often be contested and fragmented, but they do bring with them further baggage of imaginative substance which folds into emplaced tree meanings. Ancient tree symbolism has – to considerable extent – eroded away in modern society, being reduced to blunt and vague protrusions into popular culture (as in the idea of dancing around the maypole). However, other symbolisms have been reinvigorated by 'new age' cultures which renew links between spirituality and tree-culture, and by discourses of nature and landscape conservation and celebration, as in the work of Common Ground. From this matrix, new tree symbolisms have emerged which often relate to an anxiety about the environment and to individual and collective alienation from nature.

The revival of spiritual movements associated with pre-Christian European cultures has (re)produced religious structures much more embedded in and focused upon the natural environment than are their Christian equivalents. In these now favoured passages of spiritual history, nature was seen to extend seamlessly into other spiritual and sacred dimensions of being, and elements of nature offered gateways to those other dimensions. Trees, given their dominance of much of the pre-modern landscape, became central figures within these spiritual structures (see Frazer, 1993; Bates, 1997). They were seen as meaningful entities in themselves and creators of sacred places where devotion to the other world could be made. For example, there is a such a tree in one of the tales of *The Mabinogion* (a collection of ancient Welsh folk tales) which, 'from root to crown one half was aflame and the other green with leaves', thus representing a link between this and the other world.

Robert Graves (1961) argues in extraordinary arcane detail how tree symbolism was a key resource in the poetic and spiritual language which emerged from this world, and suggests that these coded symbols were used as sites of resistance to the imposition of Christian culture, as in the Welsh myth 'Cad Goddeu' (The Battle of the Trees). Graves also shows that the early Irish 'Tree Alphabets' (the Tree Oghams) are replete with biological characteristics rendered symbolic. For example, the first tree in the first alphabet he considers is the birch, the twigs of which 'are used throughout Europe in the beating of bounds . . . The birch is the tree of inception, it is indeed the earliest forest tree, with the exception of the mysterious elder, to put out new leaves' (166). But, as mentioned, many of these symbolic associations have faded in the modern Christian era. Frazer (1993) shows that there are 'relics of tree-worship in modern Europe', but rituals such as the maypole dance, which echo in differing forms across Europe, are so symbolized now as to lose any obvious connections to the trees which were their genesis.

More recently the notion of 'tree hugging', and 'talking to the trees', has often been used as a derogatory short-hand for people who relate to nature in a spiritual or mystical way beyond the expected norms of society. However, this view has been challenged to some extent by the emergence of 'new age' spiritualities which draw on Celtic pagan symbolism. The direct-action campaigns of the 1990s, which often had trees as a focal point of resistance, made an attachment (in many cases literal attachment so as to prevent felling) to trees more acceptable. Not only do trees continue to be components of a threatened countryside and icons of beleaguered national and global environments, but their status as meaningful entities has (re)emerged significantly. The arts and environment organization Common Ground has (re)mobilized certain tree myths and traditions in an effort to raise public awareness and interaction with their local trees. Events such as 'Tree Dressing Day' and 'Apple Day' have sought to revive ancient customs through which to (re)discover appropriate cultural frameworks for celebrating the variety, vitality, beauty and natural and cultural ecology of trees.

Beyond these ancient mythological foundations, and across cultures, an incredible range of symbolic constructions build upon the image of the tree (Rival, 1998a). As powerful, varied, material presences in many societies, they are a key substrate on which imaginative edifices are constructed. As Rival points out, 'Trees are used symbolically to make concrete and material the abstract notion of life' (1998a: 3). Why this may be so in one respect is set out by Davis (1988):

> The tree presents itself as a medium of thought in a direct and obvious way through its possession of a trunk, roots and branches. Other factors such as type of bark, flower, fruit, and colour all add subsidiary themes, as does the fact that the tree is habitat for many creatures. (34)

Indeed, tree symbolisms are so embedded in Western thought that Deleuze and Guattari (1987) feel moved to say that they are 'fed up with trees' and turn to the rhizome as alternative biological symbolic substrate. Rival (1998b) considers how, in differing cultural settings, trees are symbols of life-cycle rituals, the human body, environmental efficacy, green politics, vitality, strength, cultural identity, history, and self-generating power. The very otherness of tree-being, particularly the apparent deadness of wood (as opposed to leaf and fruit) and trees' ability to be both partly alive and partly dead, also form the basis of further symbolic edifices. Rival also draws some distinction between the symbolism associated with individual trees, and that associated with woodlands, which, for example, can be symbolic of community and community struggle. In some of the anthropological studies collected in Rival (1998a), and in the extensive survey of tree symbolism conducted by Frazer (1993), the focus is on 'primitive' cultures, picked out because of their more immediate, intense symbolic relationship with trees. But Rival (1998b) and Zelter (1998) both also explore the symbolism embedded in what the former terms 'Western Tree Activism'. This includes the direct actions against tree-felling for development in Britain and logging in North America. Trees in these cases 'stand not only for life, but also for social justice and public space' (Rival, 1998b: 16). Thus in today's climate of anxiety about environmental and social integrity trees can not only be key iconic symbols of nature, but also of 'natural community' and social hope. This is something that the novelist John Fowles argues, saying that trees 'seem to be the best, most revealing messengers to us from all nature, the nearest its heart' (cited by D. Curry, 2000: 283).

An interesting example of this representative role can be found in Zelter's (1998: 221) account of how her direct-action tree protests felt like responses to the 'lack of respect for all living beings on our planet' and were attempting to deploy the message 'wake up[,] the planet is dying'. The trees which protesters try to protect are not just individual entities of ethical, aesthetic, or spiritual note, but symbols of wider nature and the landscape. In modern societies, which have in many respects moved a long way from direct spiritual or symbolic connection with trees, this symbolism of trees as icons of nature is of the utmost importance. The destruction of the rainforests has long been at the forefront of discourses of global environmental despoliation. In Shoard's (1980) *Theft of the Countryside*, losses of hedgerow trees and woodland constitute key casualties of the onslaught of industrial agriculture. Such environmental losses have demanded a response, and the response often involves tree planting. In Britain there is now a plethora of programmes and schemes – for example, the Community Forests, the National Forest, Woods On Your Doorstep, Trees of Time and Place, the Work of the Woodland Trust, The Tree Council, Trees for Life, Esso's Living Trees Campaign, and myriad local opportunities associated with Millennium projects – which promote tree-planting of various scales. The fact that the planting of trees so often constitutes the symbolic as well as the material response to environmental issues represents a significant manifestation of the pivotal position of the tree in lay, popular, professional, and political discourses of nature–society relations.

National, Regional, and Local Identity

We have already discussed how forests have become bound up with imaginative interpretations of national cultures, and how certain tree types have particular national-level cultural associations. However, it is also important to recognize that such cultural constructions also occur at regional or even local levels, serving both to reinforce national symbolisms and sometimes to subvert them. Mabey (1996: 7) states that 'plants can be powerful emblems of place and identity . . . not just of nations, but of villages, neighbourhoods and even personal retreats'.

Thus, while there is a sense in which any suitable tree planting conforms to positive global and national instincts of environmental action, there can be contexts in which such planting will not be deemed to be appropriate. A number of commentators, notably Rackham (1996) and Mabey (1980), are critical of some tree-planting initiatives, which they consider can be ill-conceived knee-jerk reactions, or politically expedient 'solutions' to environmental concern about over-productive agricultural land, and a panacea for problematic urban fringe areas. At the heart of these objections is that planting can undermine regional variation in tree populations and this in turn emphasizes the importance of local and regional identity, and the desire to construct appropriate nature-society linkages in city and countryside. As Rackham argues,

> Tree planters seldom understand, still less respect *the meaning of trees*. The countryside is urbanised no less by introducing trees with urban associations – horse chestnut, weeping willow, Norway maple, etc. – than by erecting urban buildings. Every oak or alder planted in Cambridge (traditionally a city of willows, ashes, elms and cherry-plums) erodes the difference between Cambridge and other places. (Cited by Common Ground, 1989b: 14, our emphasis)

These local and regional distinctions are often carefully charted. For example, Morton's (1991) study of the *Trees of Shropshire* and other such local accounts not only recount the presence of trees in these regions by type but also in terms of local history and culture. Similarly, the Common Ground 'Save our Orchards' campaign has produced an apple map of Britain which identifies the local varieties and cultures of fruit production and consumption, thus adding (and indeed cementing) a further layer of cultural variation. Certain species of tree, particularly fruit trees such as apple, pear and plum, will have intricate and intimate local variations such as the Blaisdon Red plum which 'flourishes' in a five-mile radius around the village of Blaisdon in west Gloucestershire (King and Clifford, 1993: 74).

Harrison (1991: 139) argues that we 'have a need . . . for parochial monuments, landmarks, milestones and other points of reference by which each person can take his or her own bearings in place and time'. Trees, particularly those large and old, have a prominent role within this establishment of reference points and Harrison recounts the place-making impacts of the large old trees near his home. Ley's (1995) account of 'the missing sequoias' similarly offers a strong picture of how powerful such associations can be. Here, in reaction to the felling of two mature sequoia trees in a residential area of Vancouver, he describes how

> an extraordinary effusion of topophilia, love of place, stands bare . . . The trees are an extension of the self, the social self, the confirmation of an identity shared with like-minded others . . . a collective *neighbourhood* loss that is announced in this arboreal obituary. (203)

Casey's (1993, 1998) pursuit of the centrality of place to being in the world leads him to consider how 'colour, texture, and depth, are known to us only in and by the body that enters and occupies a given place' (1998: 204). Trees, given their size and material form are major generators of sensations, spaces and perspectives with which, through our senses, we engage with place and with nature (these issues are considered in more detail in Chapter 4). These engagements once more represent to us a very significant elision of materiality and culture, bound into everyday encounters of local places. The symbolic power of trees floats through our senses and our emotions, seasonally acting as scene-changers to the stage of our everyday life in locality and landscape. However, to these frameworks accentuating the materiality and the symbolic value of trees, we would add a third, emphasizing some of the specific roles in which trees are cast, or which trees cast for themselves.

Production and Consumption : the Roles of Trees

Just as trees play a wide range of imaginative roles in society, they also perform a similarly rich range of roles in various production and consumption networks.

Stuart Franklin's (1999) remarkable photographic essay *The Times of Trees* show just how diverse these roles can be, and how trees are often fulfilling more than one role at once. Trees are consumed as food, material and as the object of tourist gaze or wilderness experience. They form habitats around themselves, they offer shade, blossom, fruit and dappled light. They yield timber which can be put to diverse uses – firewood, charcoal, paper, craft, construction, sports equipment or warships. These positionings in processes of producing and consuming can be illustrated with reference to a number of key roles which add further complexity to the place of trees in material and symbolic terms.

Working Trees

Trees are put to work in many ways, but we suggest an interesting distinction in the ways in which they are cropped, harvested and deployed. **Cropped trees** are those which are planted (or were self-seeded) for the production of timber and other raw materials. This role entails the felling of the tree, and produces timber for building and artefact-making, wood pulp and many other forms of material. The differing qualities of the wood and materials produced by different trees have been exploited for many particular purposes. For example, pearwood has been used for making cogs because of its strength and fine grain structure; elm, which resists splitting and resists rotting when wet, has been used for making chair seats, wheel hubs, pipes, lock gates and waterwheels; coppiced lime poles have provided fibre for rope-making and lime wood was favoured for decorative carving; maple wood has traditionally been used for making harps; ash, due to its strength and flexibility has been used in the production of various items of sporting equipment such as oars, hockey sticks and billiard cues; and walnut wood has been used for producing decorative veneers. This list could go on and on. Some of these associations, such as the use of willow for cricket bats, become incorporated into wider cultural representations, reflecting in this case the 'sound' of leather on willow, as much as the visual culture of cricket.

Harvested trees are those which produce a crop of one kind or another. Most obviously, the crop comes in the form of fruit, nuts and other foodstuffs of various kinds, but trees are also harvested for building materials and fuels using production systems such as coppicing and pollarding and the leaves, bark, resins and other parts of the trees are also used. The roles of harvested trees are also many and detailed. Miles (1999) in the section of *Silva* entitled 'Tree Culture' lists the main tree types in Britain and details the parts of the tree used for food, materials, medicines and ritual. For example, the parts of the Scots pine used are listed as 'needles, bark, resin, cones, buds, kernels' (254). Similarly, Vitale (1997) catalogues the use of leaves in 'myth, magic and medicine'. Other writers such as Rackham and Edlin have charted in detail differing aspects of the production of timber and produce from British trees. Edlin (1948) for example, details the timber gained from British forests and the 'minor produce' which comes from systems such as coppicing and pollarding, showing how the wood from different trees was used for different products such hop poles, fencing, firewood, charcoal, turnery poles, basketwork and hurdles.

Deployed trees are those planted for landscaping purposes of one kind or another. These are trees which are working not through the production of timber, fuel or crop but through their presence in the landscape. Trees are now essential ingredients in the landscaping of everyday and special places. Their importance can be traced back at least to the English landscape parks of the eighteenth century, where the estates designed by Lancelot 'Capability' Brown and others provided a model of pastoral style that has endured in a multitude of scales and settings. Brown's style has frequently been formally revived as in the 'rural cemetery movement' in the United States which started in the nineteenth century and was subsequently popularized by the likes of Andrew Jackson Downing and Frederick Law Olmsted. However, the informal influence of the pastoral style of landscaping, including the focal influence of trees, has endured into more prosaic modernist forms of landscape architecture.

As Wilson (1992: 89) emphasizes, the notion of landscape design now encompasses a range of new modern areas:

> Throughout the twentieth century, landscape design ('landscaping' as opposed to landscape) has expanded into new spheres. Regional planning agencies have built new towns and reorganised entire watersheds, all of which require landscaping. In addition to traditional sites such as public parks and private estates, landscaping is now done alongside freeways and in industrial parks. We see landscaping at airports and outside restaurants and shopping centres, as well as inside buildings.

The role of trees in these processes and practices of landscape design should not be underestimated. Design guides governing the planning of new supermarkets, housing estates, pedestrianized civic spaces and so on, all dictate a tree-planting programme for the site concerned. Ironically, the Tesco supermarket development at Golden Hill, Bristol (see our discussion in Chapter 1) which necessitated the highly contested felling of mature lime trees, now displays the results of an intensive tree-planting programme both to screen the development from the road and to landscape the car park. In these kinds of arena trees provide an essential aesthetic. They represent nature in built-up space; they also bring colour, height, movement, sound and sometimes even scent to developments which might otherwise be lacking in such qualities. In this way, trees have been deployed as part of the blurring of urban–rural distinctions in a conscious attempt to bring nature into the city and the suburb in a planned and landscaped fashion.

There are, of course, a variety of other situations in which trees are deployed. For example, the use of trees to stabilize slopes and edges, to provide windbreaks and to form visual screens is now a very familiar even if often unnoticed aspect of our everyday landscapes. Each deployment is part of an application both of scientific process and of cultural significance, guided by handbooks such as *The Arboriculturalist's Companion* (James, 1990) which informs the processes of planting and maintenance of trees in rural and urban settings, and which details the appearance, sizes and suitability of trees for differing locations and roles.

Therapeutic Trees

There is a close interconnection between the deployment of trees for aesthetic enhancement of landscaping and the idea that the presence of trees can be therapeutic to landscape and to people. Chris Arnot (1999) says of the trees planted on derelict coal-mining land under the National Forest initiative that 'native hardwood saplings growing out of the spoil tip are symbolic of renewal springing from dereliction'. The Urban Forestry Unit in Britain represents both a recognition and an institutionalization of the ability of trees to restore such derelict landscapes, rendering 'brownfield sites' commercially attractive again. The unit has been established specifically to use trees in derelict urban and industrial places, relying on the therapeutic value of trees to reclaim old mine and quarry workings, to purify the soil of contaminated land, and to breath fresher air into polluted roadside or urban industrial environments (Brown, 1998).

Another example of the formal recognition of the therapeutic value of trees can be seen in the network of Community Forests which is being built up in and around Britain's urban centres. The forests are a mix of existing and newly planted woodland, and have multifaceted roles ranging from producing environmentally friendly materials to the creation of habitats and arenas of amenity. A key theme in the development of Community Forests is that trees can be a 'cure' for many city ills and for problem areas of land on the urban fringe. This idea is demonstrated in an extract from the Forest Services website which extols the virtue of urban tree planting, claiming that

> Trees reduce air pollution
> Trees fight the atmospheric greenhouse effect
> Trees conserve water and reduce soil erosion
> Trees save energy

Trees modify local climate
Trees stabilise economic stability
Trees reduce noise pollution and create wildlife and plant diversity.

In similar fashion, trees are also believed to be good for people, particularly in stressed, polluted urban environments, but beyond that in modern lifestyles more generally. A publicity leaflet for Esso National Tree Week (Tree Council, Esso Living Tree Campaign, undated), proclaims:

> Trees not only look good, they make you feel good too. They are one of the most important natural resources for a healthy mind and body. A walk in the woods is one of the healthiest forms of exercise. Trees give you extra oxygen which is invigorating. Trees help us relax from our stressful urban lives.

Commenting on tree planting in the Spitalfields area of London, organized by Trees for London, the novelist Jeanette Winterson (2000) writes 'planting these trees is about hope . . . how do we ever cost the pleasure of birdsong or the sudden relief of a tree-lined street'. This perceived therapeutic value of trees is an important if neglected and perhaps often intangible issue. One important contribution has come from Perlman (1994) who presents a lengthy treatise on 'the psychological vitality and beauty of trees' (157). What emerges is that trees perform both general and specific therapeutic roles. Their general contribution is to exude an atmosphere of peacefulness, tranquillity and well-being. This ability to invoke such feelings can also be put to specific use, for example in the design of hospital gardens and the views from hospital windows so as to present people recovering from surgery with beneficial tree-related therapy (Perlman, 1994).

Conserved Trees

One further role for trees that deserves brief consideration falls under the headings of conservation and collection. Miles (1999: 333) has suggested that

> Trees are seldom conserved or preserved for their own sake: their conservation usually depends upon their contributions to the conservation of something else. It might be a landscape, or the shelter they provide for birdlife, animals or insects. It might be the fungi and invertebrates they directly support. Likewise tree habitats are not usually managed just for the benefit of trees. The trees simply form a framework for everything else.

This idea that the conservation of trees is usually concerned with the place of trees in other networks of concern clearly offers some purchase on the roles played by trees in wider issues of landscape and conservation. However, we would also suggest that it is important not to underestimate the level of direct concern for trees as individuals that drives some forms of tree conservation. This is particularly so in the case of veteran trees, champion trees or landmark trees whose 'individuality' is in some way prominent.

It is this mix of individuality, and contribution to wider networks or place milieux, which underpins the planning mechanisms which are used in Britain to regulate the felling of particularly valued trees. The principal mechanism concerned is the Tree Preservation Order (TPO), the purpose of which is to 'protect trees for public enjoyment and the environmental (principally visual) benefit' (CPRE, 1996: 23). TPOs can apply to individual trees, groups of trees and areas of trees (such as avenues), and prohibits the cutting-down, topping, lopping, uprooting, wilful damage or wilful destruction of trees without first obtaining permission. There are also Woodland Tree Preservation Orders to protect areas of woodland. Trees can also be protected under Conservation Area status in Local Plans where they are seen to contribute to the character of the area. Felling Licences need to be obtained from the Forestry Authority (FA) if larger areas of woodland are to be felled. The FA 'must be satisfied that applications . . . are sensible in terms of silviculture, landscape, nature conservation and other environmental concerns' (CPRE, 1996: 33). More broadly, the Forestry Commission's policy aims are to prevent the loss of areas of broad-leaved woodland to agriculture or other land uses; to protect ancient woodland; to try to ensure that Felling Licences have replanting conditions built into them; to encourage natural regeneration and appropriate use of existing broadleaf woodlands and to prevent their transformation to other forms of woodland. All of these mechanisms suggest a crucial role for trees in conservation and a tightening of the ambition of society to protect trees.

The Migration of Trees Through Cultural Space(s)

In concluding this chapter we want to (re)emphasize that trees will occupy multiple cultural positions at any given time. These positions may be harmonious, as with the oak that is valued for its spirit, its ecological richness, and its visual aesthetic qualities; but equally, multiple constructions may be contested, as with the tree as crop or timber, or with woodland as place of fear, or conserved nature reserve. In addition, we need to recognize that because they have the ability to grow, survive and reproduce independent of human management, and because of their potential longevity, trees will often migrate through different cultural spaces during their lifetime. Such migration is apparent in Tsouvalis-Gerber's (1998) account of the emergence of the woodland category 'ancient woodland' throughout the 1970s and

1980s, and of how policies were put in place to try to define, manage and conserve them. These processes led to particular areas of woodland being culturally reclassified and revalued, and the policies relating to them shifting markedly. As a further illustration, Watkins (1998b) demonstrates how the ancient oaks of Sherwood Forest have migrated through various cultural locations and how the space and places, and wider forest around them, are reconstructed accordingly. The oaks

> have been ascribed a catalogue of changing values and meanings. They have been prodded and probed, lopped and pollarded, exploited and felled. They have been designated status and power and caused legal disputes. They have been the subject of archaeological experiment and aesthetic experiment. They have been categorised as fuel, timber, picturesque, dead and habitat. (112)

One final example, and one to which we return, is that of orchards. These too can be seen as examples of trees which have migrated through the cultural spaces mapped out above. In past decades they have been cropping, working trees and as such of little interest to conservation gaze. However, in areas such as Somerset, orchard cover has been lost; and now, particularly through the work of Common Ground (1989a), orchards and especially traditional orchards have migrated into the spaces of conservation. Although not truly native trees they are seen as quintessentially part of the traditional English landscape, and are a constituent of local distinctiveness within it.

Given growing public concern about environmental issues on a scale which ranges from the local to the global, all trees may be said to have undergone a certain degree of cultural migration. Common Ground in their 'tree manifesto' deploys the slogan 'every tree counts', and this reflects the heightened political and emotional baggage now attached to trees. It is this general cultural frame folded with all the particular frames of tree types, tree places, tree symbolisms, tree roles which we feel make up the vital (in two senses of the word) field of 'arbori-culture'.

–3–

The Non-human Agency of Trees

> Once nature is reconceived as capable of agency and intentionality, and human identity is reconceived in less polarised and disembodied ways, the great gulf which Cartesian thought established between the conscious, mindful human sphere and the mindless, clockwork natural one disappears. (Plumwood, 1993: 5)

> Heterogeneous geographies . . . imply a radically different understanding of 'who' (what) constitutes the worlds 'we' inhabit. Such an understanding . . . decouples social agency from the logocentric assumptions that restrict the capacity to act or to have effects to human beings, admitting other players to the networks of social life. (Whatmore, 2000: 267)

> It would be hard to say that trees are not pulling their weight. Even in their depleted numbers they are still the planet's lungs, converting sunlight to living tissues and doing their best to absorb the carbon dioxide with which we are drenching the atmosphere. They will grow entirely by themselves, stabilise soil, purify water, spring up again when blown down or cut down – all without any assistance from humans. Over the centuries they help shape the character of the places where they grow, and it takes very determined action to wipe out their traces. (Mabey, 1990: 6)

In this chapter we now turn to issues of agency, which in some ways represents the most challenging and potentially problematic topic of discussion in the book. Thinking through the 'agency' of trees leads to an immediate confrontation with some very important questions within social and environmental theory which need to be addressed if new ways of understanding and even practising nature-society relations are to be achieved. Non-human agency has in recent times become rather a fashionable concept. If an earthquake is responsible for damage to buildings or freeways, and thereby influences human behaviour or even well-being, then it is a reasonable supposition that an agency is present in the earthquake that can be regarded as non-human. Equally, the practice of foxhunting with hounds, over which serious political conflict has broken out recently in the British countryside, involves the non-human agency of the foxes, the horses and the hounds as well as the human hunters. By recognizing agency beyond the human domain, albeit usually interrelated with human agency, it is possible to contest, fragment and dissolve the nature-culture divide which has to date dominated Western thought and action.

In this chapter we advance two principal arguments. First, while it is relatively straightforward to present discussions of non-human agency in generalized ungrounded terms, if the intention is to make a serious attempt to 'give others their due' (Thrift, 1996a: 26) then there needs to be a more detailed and grounded account of the non-human agency of particular beings, things and materials. Trees represent to us a particularly rich research arena in this respect. As Mabey says in the opening quote, they are key players in the functioning of a viable atmosphere, and in the creation of habitat, landscape and materials. Moreover, their agency, like themselves, may be unruly and intensely variegated in its nature.

The second argument relates to the first. While some conceptual approaches (particularly those associated with Actor Network Theory – ANT) have adopted a serious approach to non-human agency, there remain some significant gaps in the types of non-human agent that have been subjected to serious study. Overall, there has been a distinct preoccupation with technological materials as non-human agents, and an under-emphasis on organic non-humans whose rather more unruly agency has been neglected by comparison. Those studies which are now considering the agency of non-human life-forms in very constructive ways still tend to focus on animals rather than plants (for example see Peterson, 2001). A key objective of this chapter, then, is to redress this balance in a discussion of the non-human agency of trees.

Re-viewing the World; Re-placing the Human

The need for more serious recognition of non-human agency in social scientific enquiry into nature–society relations is becoming clearly recognized. For example, Wolch and Emel (1998: xv) suggest 'Nature has remained a largely undifferentiated concept, *its constituent parts rarely theorized separately*'. And as we have already quoted, Harvey (1996) also calls for 'nature' to be disaggregated into the multifarious and active cast which forms it. By considering the roles of trees, their agency, and their connections with place, we are seeking to respond to these calls for recognition of 'nature's' different active capacities.

To begin with, we will review recent discussions of the interconnectivity of human and natural worlds, noting how the notion of agency has been translated across a previously disabling binary distinction between human and non-human. Here, we immediately encounter different understandings of agency based on what theoretical questions are being posed. For example the development of Actor Network Theory (ANT) (Callon, 1986, 1991; Callon and Law, 1995; Latour, 1993; Law, 1994; Law and Hassard, 1999; Murdoch, 1995, 1997; Thrift, 1996a; Whatmore, 1999) has explicitly valorized a perspective on agency which accentuates the *relational*, subjugating the importance of particular actors per se within networks in favour of a focus on the multiplicity of mutually constitutive and positioning 'actants' which together serve to hybridize agency. ANT has, therefore, both emphasized the 'non-humanness' of agency and declined to categorize it as such because to do so might jeopardize the overall project of deconstructing the antinomy of nature and society.

Our concern with the *agency* of non-human actants leads us to ask some different but related questions. In one sense, we are seeking to give others 'their due' by exploring different forms of non-human agency in the context of trees. While relational agency is crucial to the project of hybridity, there remain very significant questions about the potential contribution of non-human agents such as trees to hybrid relations. Our discussion of varying types of agency confirms that trees act upon as well as being acted upon. Indeed, it can be argued that forms of transformative, purposive and non-representational agency may be enacted by trees (and other non-humans). The argument is not that trees possess the particular and extraordinary capabilities of humans in these respects, but that they do possess very significant forms of active agency, which have usually been assumed to exist only in the human realm.

This view of non-human others as active agents is important for a wide range of ontological, epistemological, political and ethical reasons. However it also begs further questions about a purely relational view of nature–society in which processes, flows, fluxes – and the networks which are their fabric – render notions of autonomous separated individuals as untenable. In particular, to what extent are what we might commonly consider to be individual entities (such as trees) destabilized and reassembled in hybrid bodies, or networks? As Lee and Stenner (1999: 110) state, if we 'render everything "networky" we will become insensitive to complexity and heterogeneity'.

In addition to this, much of the illustration of this hybridity seems to have been biased towards technological rather than organic non-human entities (see for example Woolgar, 1991) – a manoeuvre which somehow makes it easier to deny the specific non-human contribution to hybrid agency, and perhaps continues, implicitly, to value human authority in the shaping of hybridity and relational networks. If, as Whatmore (1999: 26) suggests, agency should be seen as 'a relational achievement, involving the *creative* presence of organic beings, technological devices and discursive codes' (our emphasis), what is the nature of that 'creativity' which these 'beings' bring to the relational process? This, in association with ideas about place, forms the crux of our approach. What kinds of creativity do trees bring to the achievements of relational agency? Our argument, as developed through this chapter and the book more generally, is that trees are not just passive recipients of human interventions. Rather, they bring their own creative abilities and tendencies to various equations.

Agency: Human and Non-human

> Agency . . . is the other side to structure, the materiality of the social world which is to be changed by the human subject. In this approach, agency is a characteristic of a consciousness adequate to the social world, and which thus puts change into motion. (Game, 1991: 12)

> It has been commonplace in social theory to ignore the specific 'agency' and materiality of nature, or, where that agency has been admitted, to conceive of it within the disabling binary logics that have for so long organised modern thought. (Fitzsimmons and Goodman, 1998: 194)

Over recent years there has been a significant re-viewing of the world by social theorists who argue that previous ideas of 'agency' have been far too narrow. By defining agency in terms of 'the human subject', much social theory has tended to ignore the agency and materiality of nature, leading to the social and scientific construction of nature in human terms. In Latour's (1993: 138) words, 'modern humanists are reductionist because they seek to attribute action to a small number of powers, leaving the rest of the world with nothing but simple mute forces'. The major stumbling block to acknowledging agency beyond the human sphere has been the attribution of apparently unique characteristics of purpose and communication to human beings. Callon and Law (1995: 491) suggest that in contemporary Western cultures 'something is treated as an agent, or at any rate, as a candidate for agency, if it performs, or might perform, two great classes of condition: intentionality and language use'. These agency 'thresholds' have previously dictated that agency be regarded as a human process. Whatmore (1999: 29) highlights that it is 'a refusal to equate agency (the capacity to act or have effects) with intentionality, premised on narrow linguistic competences' which has been 'the point of greatest tension between ANT and conventional social theories'.

Such a restricted view of meaningful agency has now become untenable in many different streams of social theory, in which it is argued that differing forms of agency need to be recognized and understood. Four such streams are particularly important here. First, a significant theoretical prompt for non-human agency has come from ecofeminism. Warren (1994: 4) for example suggests that 'acknowledgement of the world's active agency seems to be necessary to the deconstructive process of dismantling totalising and essentialising discourse, and it is something eco-feminist philosophy can and does do well'. Thus Donna Haraway's seminal writings have brought ecofeminist concerns to the sociology of scientific knowledge, concluding that 'nature' is a multidimensional tangle of the political, economic, technical, cultural, mythic and organic which 'collapse into each other in a knot of extraordinary density' (Haraway, 1994: 63). Her work 'envisions "feminist theory . . . with actors who come in many and wonderful forms"' (Cheney, 1994: 170–1, citing Haraway, 1988), and the agencies of nature have been spotlighted as a consequence.

A second stream of influential social theory has emerged from critical development of ideas about 'social nature' (Fitzsimmons, 1989a, 1989b; Harrison and Burgess, 1994), where radical geographies of political economy have become increasingly reconciled to the need to regard nature as an essential third theoretical arena in addition to those of society and space. The initial argument that nature cannot be (re)produced outside of social relations was quickly tempered by the equally significant argument that nature is not reducible to such social relations (Whatmore and Boucher, 1992).

Indeed, Castree (2000: 539) has summarized that social nature without such a development was 'drastically anthropocentric' and '*underplay[ed] the material powers and capacities of the "natural" entities* supposedly constructed [and] ignore[d] the power of nature at its peril' (our emphasis). And that it also may cut the ground away from under attempts to allocate intrinsic non-anthropocentric values, qualities and rights to nature.

These theoretical trajectories are taken up and emphasized by David Harvey (1996) who has lent his considerable personal standing to the task of understanding how fundamental physical and biological conditions and processes work together with social, economic and cultural projects to create tangible historical geographies, and to do so in ways which do not position the physical and the biological and banal and passive contexts within which dominant human processes occur. He too, then, argues that non-human organisms should be seen as 'active subjects' capable of 'transforming nature' and 'adapting to the ecosystem they themselves construct' (186). And in charting this theoretical territory, he too argues that the 'artificial break between "society" and "nature" must be eroded, rendered porous, and eventually dissolved' (192).

A third and more recent theoretical development in the re-placing of the human has come from socio-anthropological writings. For example, Macnaghten and Urry (1998) have recognized the significance of non-human agency through their development of Ingold's (1993) notions of 'dwelling' and 'taskscape'. They argue that landscape and 'nature' are complex spatial and temporal achievements and that 'relationships with what is taken to be "nature" are embodied, involving a variety of senses and that there are "physical" components of walls, textures, land, plants and so on, which partly constitute such "dwellings"' (168). Ingold (1997: 249) has suggested the need to dissolve the 'category of the social, so as to re-embed (human) relationships within the continuum of organic life'. In other words, dwelling is a complex performative achievement of heterogeneous actors in relational spatial/temporal settings. We take up this idea of dwelling, and how trees have been narrated within it, more fully in the next chapter.

It is, however, the fourth theoretical strand – ANT – which has been most influential in proposing and drawing together fundamentally new ways of understanding the relations between nature and society. The development and substance of ANT has been critically reviewed elsewhere (see Braun and Castree 1998; Law and Hassard, 1999; Murdoch 1995, 1997; Thrift, 1996a; Whatmore 1999). For our purposes here, it is sufficient to underline two aspects of ANT. First, ANT has recognized the agency of non-humans as an essential element in how the natural and the social flow into one another. For example, Callon's (1986) classic discussion of scallop-fishing treats the scallop as an active agent, rather than a passive subject of human activity. In so doing he dismantled the existing protocols which confined agency to the social sphere, and set in train a move beyond socio-biology into terrains of agency in which the human and the non-human were networked together.

The second and key contribution of ANT has been to provide what Demeritt (1994: 183) refers to as a 'new metaphor . . . for framing nature as both a real material actor and a socially constructed object'. In fact, at least two metaphors are employed. A drawing together of Haraway's (1991) 'Cyborgs' – partnerships between human and non-human actors in the mutual construction of artefactual nature – and Latour's (1993) 'hybrids' – mixtures of nature and culture – provides the metaphor for *hybrid geographies* (Whatmore, 1999). Here, agency is viewed as being spun between different actors (or 'actants') rather than manifested as solitary or unitary intent, and it is decoupled from subject–object distinctions. These hybrids are then seen as mobilized and assembled into associative networks in which agency represents the collective capacity for action by humans and non-humans. The inherently collective nature of this networking – or the 'hybrid collectif' (Callon and Law, 1995) – retheorizes the notion of agency:

> The notion of the hybrid collectif implodes the inside/outside binary which discerns social action as an individual property of discrete, unitary individuals (including collective individuals). Agency is reconfigured as a relational effect generated by a network of heterogeneous, interacting components whose activity is constituted in the networks of which they form a part. (Whatmore, 1999: 28)

Thus ANT has championed non-human agency while at the same time it has rejected the non-human/human distinction. To pose nature and society in dialectic terms, even with an inherent purpose of dissolving nature–society dualisms, is seen as an unacceptably risky strategy, which 'seems still to reproduce the dualism which we are seeking to resolve' (Fitzsimmons and Goodman, 1998: 207). By employing metaphors of hybridity and network, social theorists have sought to dismantle the binary logic which poses nature and society as opposites and which champions the social over the natural. In so doing, the further investigation of non-human agency per se becomes a necessary casualty of the manoeuvre toward networked hybridity. In effect, in questions relating to the nature of non-human agency, its potential contributions to various hybrid geographies have become regarded as theoretically dubious – a return to the bad old days of modernistic separation of nature and society.

We believe that to rule out notions of non-human agency in this way may be both to lose out on significant understandings of the ways in which non-human organisms and materials contribute to the networked agencies of hybrid collectifs, and to obscure assumptions about the relative significance of different forms of hybridity. On the latter point, for example, there are strong preconceptions in social science about the hierarchy of agency potentials among the 'components' of hybrid collectifs:

> We tend to think that human agents are only true agents because of the essential link we feel exists between thought and action, properly so called. Thus animals are regarded as simply behaving when they 'act' because we regard them as incapable of thought and therefore somehow governed in their 'endeavours' by internal drives whose status as 'thoughts' is moot. Again, sticks and stones, considered as agents, are one step lower and 'behave' in strict accordance to the laws of nature which are regarded as determining their 'endeavours' as if they themselves contributed nothing at all to what happens to them. (McPhail and Ward, 1988: 72)

Such preconceptions seem to identify animals as the 'obvious' first step in considering non-human forms of agency, and indeed there has been a surge in 'animal studies' in recent years (Ingold, 1988, 1995; Whatmore and Thorne, 1998; Wolch and Emel, 1998) in which the agency of animals has been a focus. The level 'below' animals in the above quote is 'sticks and stones' where, presumably, other living entities such as trees are also classified *without distinction* in terms of agency.

Is it possible that these preconceptions about differentiated 'tiers' of agency have sometimes found their way into our thinking about hybridity and networks? Although ANT theorists have been keen to destabilize anthropocentric views of agency, it does seem that actors from 'nature' – organic non-human others of one kind or another – are sometimes curiously absent from some ANT considerations. At the same time, there does seem to be an overemphasis on the relational agency of artefacts and technology. Thrift (1996a: 24) for example, suggests that the 'intermediaries' which Callon and others involve in actor networks are 'usually considered to be texts, technical artefacts, human beings and money' (despite Callon's early focus on scallops!). Latour's (1993) claim to have 're-established symmetry between two branches of government', is with reference to 'that of things – called science and technology – and that of human beings' (p138).

Woolgar's (1991) cry of 'let's hear it for machines, for a change' is echoed in Callon and Law's (1995) concern to study machines and devices, reflecting debates about 'whether computers, robots, *or for that matter animals* are 'really agents' or 'not' (282, our emphasis). Note here that while Callon and Law do gesture towards 'natural' non-humans, they venture only as 'far' as animals, which appear as something of an after-thought, and the wider realm of organisms is absent.

Can it be, then, that there is a danger that the agency of organisms such as trees will be obscured or even forgotten within the ANT framework? We suggest not only that there is a need to move away from treating the human realm as separate, privileged and ontologically unique in terms of agency, but also that there is a need to disaggregate the notion of agency itself. In the remainder of this chapter, we show how it is possible to conceptualize agency in different forms, and to show how such different agencies are employed or exercised by non-humans.

Trees are a fertile territory for the grounding of such conceptualizations. As we have shown in Chapter 2, collectively they have a bewildering range of skills and/or uses, and they are embedded in a plethora of relationships, both with humans and other non-humans. Equally, with humans they are embedded in a vast range of cultural, social, technological and economic networks, as well as being highly visible in local, national and global disputes over the 'environment'. They operate in their own ecological time which is rather different from the typical time-scales of human-centred analysis. Finally they offer interesting examples of how floating signifiers transfer between human and non-human codes, contributing significantly to the hybridities which result.

Agency and Routine Action

Our argument, then, is that trees are associated with forms of agency – transformative, purposive and reflective – which are traditionally associated with the human realm. To reiterate, we are not seeking to argue that non-human organisms are the same as humans, or that they employ or exert the same agency. Rather, non-human agency in its own way transcends the passive role often allocated to nature's subjects. Part of the task of clarifying what is meant by 'in its own way' is to pose questions about orthodox typologies of agency. One key differentiation is discussed by Harvey (1996) who distinguishes between 'transformative' action and 'routine' action. While routine action is seen as that which maintains the ongoing processes of existence, it is transformative action that Harvey looks to for a more devolved view of agency. Transformative actions are seen to be 'creative'. They are actions which can somehow disrupt, divert, create and destroy within the contexts of routine processes. Thus agency is bound up with transformative action and Harvey suggests that such action 'arises out of contradiction, [so] it follows that it can in principle be *found anywhere and everywhere in the physical, biological and social world*' (55, our emphasis). Harvey adds that the theoretical and empirical task is to identify moments and things (and potential moments and potential things) which constitute such transformative action, and also that which can create conditions of relative stability within these dynamic fields. He concludes that, 'the question of "agency" in social and biological as well as in physical systems has to be formulated broadly in such terms' (55).

To some extent, Harvey's search for the transformative chimes with the direction taken by other notable theorists of agency. For example, Thrift (1996a) sets out a focus on agency as 'the production of action and of what counts as action (and the production of actors and what counts as actors)' and he adds that in particular his interest is, in 'the "wellsprings" of active participation in new beginnings' (2). Again, then, agency is built around the notion of *creative* action and is, in these instances, recognized as a capacity of both the human and non-human realms. One starting point for a discussion of non-human agency would, therefore, be to map out the kinds of transformative and creative agency associated with non-human organisms. However, before doing so we wish to deconstruct the seemingly clear distinction between routine and transformative action, suggesting instead that some of nature's routine actions need to be regarded as creative and transformative.

In some ways we argue that it is unreasonable to formulate an understanding of agency which is based on separating out routine action from creative action. Indeed, if routine action underpins and sustains creative action, it may be regarded itself as creative. Scale and time are crucial here. On the cosmic scale, and in geological time, human activity and agency produce little by way of transformative or creative agency. Within its own realm such human activity is vitally significant, but that realm is itself constituted by and dependent upon other vast fields of non-human (routine) action. Natural processes of cosmic creation, evolution, atmospheric sustainability and so on do not so much as make human things happen, as being rather, the very tissues of existence into which human action is faintly and locally woven. These 'natural' processes create and dissolve humans, and everything else. Humans are actors in stories and processes which they did not start and will not finish. As Ian McEwan (1998) puts it, 'the biosphere made us what we are and sustains us'.

So if, for example, we were seeking to understand the agency of trees and other plant organisms, their routinized involvement in the evolving fabric of existence would be an important starting-point. As Peattie describes:

> The green leaf pigment, chlorophyll, is the one link between the sun and life; it is the conduit of perpetual energy to our own fragile organisms. From inert and inorganic elements – water and carbon dioxide of the air, the same we breathe out as waste –

> chlorophyll can synthesise with the energy of sunlight. Every day, every hour of all the ages, as each continent and, equally important, each ocean, rolls into the sunlight, chlorophyll *ceaselessly creates*. Only when man (*sic*) has done as much, may he call himself the equal of a weed. Plant life sustains the living world – more precisely, chlorophyll does so. (Donald Culross Peattie, cited by Vitale, 1997: 12–13, our emphasis)

Such 'routine' processes are creative in at least two senses. First, the routine is an ongoing process of repeated yet shifting creation in a technical sense. Secondly, the routine serves to create itself, and all that which depends on it. Therefore, to focus exclusively on the creative (as opposed to routine) action of non-human agency is maybe to establish yet another untenable 'meta-dualism', this time of action, and thereby to ignore or obscure important relational agency which hybridizes the human and non-human.

In these ways, and as reflected in Lovelock's (1988) radical theorization of Gaia, the creative agency of the world is embedded in the world in a relational sense. Thus as Naess (1989) suggests, in the relational view of deep ecology, the world is 'construed' as networks of relations within which things participate to become themselves from which they cannot be meaningfully isolated (see Harvey 1996: 169 on Naess). Equally, Whatmore (1997) considers how spatially embedded relational (as opposed to individualized) ethical frameworks may be conceived as 'a world of fragile heterogeneous networks in which equality (in the sense of *an equivalence of being* rather than a universal rational ideal) remains the common premise of emancipatory subjects or movements' (50, our emphasis). In these approaches, the view of the individual as separate and autonomous is unsustainable, and therefore the notion of separate autonomous creativity is equally so. Creative agency is to be found collectively and relationally embedded. As Grange (1997: 9) observes,

> An environment is a very special mode of togetherness, since it drives towards the creation of the new even as it sustains itself through the appropriation of the past . . . Environments are regions where many things go on simultaneously. Inhibitions, enhancements, eliminations and casual influences are but some of the activities to be found in environmental domains. They can be stable or ephemeral, enduring or fleeting, fatal or life-giving.

Within these broad/deep space-time-scales, routinized non-human agency may be seen as creative, and integrally related to myriad human activities occurring on different timespace scales. Whatmore (2000) states that 'the mutability of organisms in terms *of their intrinsic organisation and morphological plasticity* has been somewhat overshadowed by the heady talk of their malleability in the socio-technical networks' (268). Here we can bring attention to the creative, powerful and active morphologies of trees.

Agency and Transformative Action

So far we have questioned whether the sharp distinction between routine and creative action is legitimate, and suggested that the so-called routine actions of trees are in fact creative and transformative actions particularly on the larger timespace scales of ecology. But clearly some distinction has to be made between these different forms of agency. Some actions, as Harvey and Thrift state, are ones which transform, convert – make *new directions and formations*. This is a type of agency which has long been considered to exist in the human realm alone. It could be argued that all 'natural' actions are in some ways routine, and that the locus of non-routinized creative action is exclusively the human realm. Many theorists, however, now argue that 'organic life [is] active rather than passive' (Ingold, 1997: 243), not least because of the 'creative unfolding of a field of relations within which beings emerge and take on the particular forms they do, in relation to each other' (ibid.). It is therefore pertinent to consider how non-human agents such as trees can produce actions which transform in the creative way discussed by Harvey and Thrift.

We examined in Chapter 2 how trees are used to transform environments, and in Chapter 4 we will see how trees are bound up with transforming places. Often, for example, in the practice of planting trees to prevent desertification, it is 'human' agency which is at work in that it is human actors which have enrolled the trees into a network dedicated to a particular end. However, in line with ANT, it seems more appropriate to suggest that the agency is relational in that trees bring to the process skills which humans could not otherwise acquire and deploy. Therefore the creative, transformative achievement comes from an agency spanning between the human and the trees and other actants in the process. This transformative agency is often harnessed by planned human agency, where tree-related policy relies on the positive cultural impact of the creative capacity of trees as non-human agents. For example, Cloke et al. (1996a, 1996b) have demonstrated in the case of the new National Forest in Britain how the transformative action of trees is enrolled by forest planners to produce both material and cultural effects on local and visiting populations.

However, trees can, of course, act autonomously, outside the confines and expectations of human actions. They frequently seed themselves; they grow in unexpected places and in unexpected forms. These actions, when remixed with the social, have what can only be described as creative transformative effects. For example, Brown (1997) tells how the 'Black Country' region of Britain, after the de-industrialization of the 1980s, had large tracts of contaminated wasteland, which merely added to the already established reputation of an industrially degraded environment which was 'celebrated' in the name. However,

> to the locals' surprise, even where there was nothing but rubble, trees began to grow and woods were springing up on ground that was considered too contaminated to be redeveloped. Although the Black Country was collectively taken aback by this unexpected side-effect of de-industrialisation, the citizens do have a reputation for innovation, and suddenly here was the opportunity to transform the image of Tipton, Dudley, Walsall and Wolverhampton. The Black Country Urban Forest Project was born. Old railway sidings, coal and waste tips and demolished factories have been turned into tree plantations over the last five years. The effect, and the intention is to make unattractive areas look like green belt. And the immediate effect has been a rise in the letting rates of empty offices and factories . . . Additional benefits have also become obvious. It was discovered that the ever-present air pollution from the overcrowded M5 and M6 was considerably reduced where there were trees. The trees trapped the dust from vehicle exhausts. The forest was therefore extended for the full 16 miles of the motorway through the Black Country. So successful has the urban forest become that the Department of the Environment and Transport has transformed the Black Country scheme into a National Urban Forestry Unit with 15 staff.

Here the trees as well as contributing to the routine agency of constructing a liveable biosphere, have intruded into a non-'natural' sequence of spatial transition, even overcoming toxins left in the soil by human activity. In one way the actions of the trees are routine in that they are only going through 'normal' processes in terms of seeding, growing and spreading, and because the physical parameters of the sites they colonized were within their tolerance horizons of successful growth. But these actions also must be seen as creative and transformative in terms of the physical, cultural, social, economic reproduction of the spaces in question. If humans have not initiated these processes, yet the spaces have been transformed, where else can the creative agency lie but within the capacities of the trees? The trees here not only colonized these spaces in terms of material spatiality, but they have also grown, sent 'roots' and 'branches' into the social, cultural, and economic world, and become agents therein.

Trees collectively have a bewildering range of capacities, and engage in myriad relational processes with both humans and non-humans (see Rival, 1998a; Rackham, 1996, 1997; Schama, 1995; Sinden, 1990; Edlin, 1948, 1970), but within these processes they have a transformative agency which is reflected in their individual characteristics of form and substance, their growth, ability to spread, and their seasonal cycles. This transformative agency can be seen in the grounded discussion of particular sites in Part II of the book. In particular on the Camerton Heritage Trail, and at Arnos Vale cemetery, the planted trees have slipped the leash of the initial cultural constructions under which they were planted, and have projected themselves into new cultural reconstructions of these places with very particular consequences. Also on these sites, self-seeded trees have become key actors in the ongoing formation of *places*. Trees have played a distinctively creative role in the dynamic unfolding of place characteristics. The agency of trees is not merely subordinate to a more powerful and distinct form of human agency; it can also be an unruly other force. As Eisenberg (1998: 7) states 'trees are among the few creatures on earth that really compete with us'. As soon as persistent human enrolment of spaces stops, and of trees in spaces stop, (then) trees begin to transform and create (see Kaza, 1993: 239–44). Trees are the climax vegetation for much of the world.

Agency and Purposive Action

One of the key issues in seeking to understand the non-human agency of organisms such as trees is to address the question of whether trees are capable of *intentional* transformative action. It is intentionality that is the key threshold by which agency has traditionally been tied to the social realm. As Callon and Law (1995: 503) suggest, 'the agents we tend to recognise are those which perform intention'. Any attempt to ascribe intentionality (as understood in human agency) to non-human agents immediately raises the ghost of naturalism with attendant reductions of agency to physiological or genetic constitution. Such attempts in socio-biology are at times recognized as being associated with essentialism, reductionism and use of over-simplified taxonomic devices, to the extent that they have been linked with eugenics and even fascist politics (see Shilling, 1993; Evans, 1996).

Issues of intention have often dominated philosophical approaches to agency, and have tended to exclude the possibility of intentional non-human agency (see Mele, 1997). Intentional action, or meaningful agency, is usually thought to rest on 'psychological notions of plan, intention, evidence and skill' and agents satisfying such notions are 'markedly different from the windswept sand' (Mele and Moser 1997: 225). According to these markers, humans are seen as the only meaningful source of creative agency because of their particular capacities. There is little room for the non-human in this view of agency, but it is interesting that in order to draw a conclusive comparison between the human and non-human, Mele and Moser opt to use the example of 'windswept sand', thus avoiding the realms of animals and plants.

Yet there is a developing strand of theorization which is willing to ascribe the idea of intentionality to non-human agents. For example Rachel (1994) suggests of the scallops which Callon (1986) considers, '[T]heir resistance to pass in terms of the biologists' representation might help to construe them as actors in their own right, with their own intentions' (812). A similar suggestion is made by Ingold (1997) who claims that animals are 'social' because they are thought to reveal, in their actions, the same qualities of intentionality, feeling, memory and speech that humans do (243). Here, animals are receiving greater attention because they are seen to be more like humans than previously considered, and have other competences also (Peterson, 2001); although this is an important step in breaking down any artificial nature–culture divide, in effect it merely shifts the divide a little further away from the anthropocentric epicentre. It certainly does not allow for intentional agency on the part of organisms such as trees.

In order to avoid essentialist naturalisms we want to argue that non-human agents exercise not intentional but *purposive* agency at a certain level and in a certain way, which may become creative or transformative in particular circumstances. By this we mean that there can be some direction and purpose in the being and becoming of agents such as trees which reflects a certain course of future action. An acorn, for example, has some form of future plan embedded within it, and is purposive in acting on that plan. This purposive action involves a growing and a living in a very specific way. The acorn has a degree of adaptability built in, and some latitude in terms of the conditions to which it can successfully adapt its actions. The actions of the acorn/oak tree, then, include the purpose of reproduction in both spatial and temporal terms.

Attfield (1981), using trees as an example, adopts this embedded purposiveness as a key point in his theorization of non-human ethical considerations and, in particular, uses purposive qualities to circumnavigate questions of consciousness, which have been a significant stumbling-block in attempts to extend ethical consideration of the non-human. He suggests that

> all [individual plants and animals] *have latent tendencies at some time or other, all have a direction of growth*, and all can flourish after their natural kind. There is no need to hold that trees have unconscious goals to reach the conclusion that trees have interests; indeed, where nothing counts as a conscious goal it is hard to see how anything counts as an unconscious one either. The growth and thriving of trees does not need to be regarded as a kind of wanting, nor trees as a possible object of sympathy, for us to recognise that they too have a good of their own. (39–40, our emphasis)

We take up this linking of agency and ethics more fully in Chapter 5, but for now we want to pursue this idea that there is some form of purposeful agency in the beings of nature.

Within the nature of living organisms it is possible to detect some form of each of the four requirements for agency – plan, intention (or as we argue, purposiveness), evidence, skill – set out by Mele and Moser (1997). The DNA of plants and animals clearly entertains a form of plan, which by its very nature is purposive, intending particular forms of being and becoming for the life-force concerned – 'it contains an implicit "blueprint" of the morphological structure of the organism and "instructions" for its construction and physiological functioning' (Gordon, 1997: 91). In Mele and Moser's analysis, intentional action must involve evidence that the intended delivery of some plan is likely to succeed – intentions are not mere hopes, wishes, or guesses. For many non-human organisms such as trees, that delivery system is born of experience. The existence of a tree represents evidence that the purposive action from whence it came has worked. In processes of natural selection and ongoing existence, the survival of a tree in a certain place is evidence that the seeds it will produce have at least some chance of succeeding and continuing to develop. But what about 'skill' as a necessary element of agency? According to Mele and Moser, not only must agency be based on a plan, an intention to deliver that plan, and evidence that there are workable means of doing so, but there must also be skill with which to execute the plan. We would argue that successful non-human organisms do have the skills required to deliver a purposive plan of being and becoming. Moreover, such skills can be developed so as to act effectively in diverse situations.

It is not some pointless abundance which leads a tree to launch many thousands of its seeds. The scale of seeding is necessary for some seeds to fall where circumstances are favourable for growth, and to compete with others using similar tactics. Heinrich (1997) describes such a process in a forest setting when new light hits 'the seed leavened earth' due to the felling of an established canopy tree.

> Where the forest was cut selectively . . . in one mixed stand of red spruce, balsam fir, hemlock, white birch, white pine and maple, I counted the following seedlings: fourteen spruce, ten birch, six hemlock, two red maple, one cherry, and one poplar. All were packed into one two-foot square area. They were by no means maximum numbers. I counted up to eighty inch-tall tree seedlings per square foot. If the environment is suitable, suitable trees will grow there . . . I do not know which amongst these potential trees will become a real tree, but in the forest the land will select the best one for every square foot of ground. It has much 'choice' in the naturally provided rain of native tree seeds, and can hardly fail to pick the best tree for each slot. (14)

In the cases of Arnos Vale cemetery and The Camerton Heritage Trail considered later, it is these abilities, within the context of the particular circumstances of those places, which have enabled trees to transform them. In the former many of the ash and sycamore have 'taken' advantage of the joints in the stone masonry as a 'safe haven' in which to get established (this is why they are so ruinous of the grave monuments). In the latter case the trees have colonized the apparently unpromising and possibly 'toxic' 'soil' presented by the mining waste (Moffat and Buckley, 1995). The skill, then, is to have a means of executing embedded 'purposeful agency' which is capable of exploiting a wide and contingent variety of circumstances. Through such means trees can force themselves into hybridized processes of place production.

One of the principal stumbling blocks in the recognition of non-human agency is that these active elements of plan, purpose, evidence and skills are not articulated through language, or as Mele and Moser (1997) have it, 'psychological notions'. Callon and Law (1995) reflect that it is very difficult to translate the active positioning of an artefact, or a non-linguistic organism, into human language narratives, because to do so is to try to press representation or translation through 'the grid of language', but this has a speciesist bias in favour of humans. 'Cats, catflaps, computers, and fax machines – not to mention X-ray sources, safety interlocks, and keys – all of these order and organise, create paths and links. *All* of these signify, but they do so in their own ways' (502).

For some it is possible to read nature as text. Dawkins' (1996) discussion of DNA, for example, suggests that 'genes . . . are long strings of pure digital information. What is more, they are truly digital, in the full and strong sense of computers and compact discs' (19). He adds, 'every cell in your body contains the equivalent of forty-six immense data tapes, reeling off digital characters via numerous reading heads working simultaneously' (21). The same goes for plants and trees, and elsewhere Dawkins portrays the seeds raining down from a tree as kinds of floppy discs. These ideas introduce the notion of some form of 'language' into the purposive equation of non-human agency, and suggest the presence of text in such agency, thereby chiming with the significant role ascribed to texts in ANT accounts of relational agency.

Within ANT, texts and information are regarded as key 'intermediaries' which cannot merely be interpreted as 'passive tools'. Latour stresses the importance of, and long-running fascination with what he calls 'immutable mobiles' which 'can be carried around and resist(s) deformation despite transformation' (1997: 180). These entities, numbers, texts, and so forth, are critical in the building and extending of networks because they can transport intentions. We suggest that seeds, and the 'text' which they carry, are seminal examples of immutable mobiles. As Whatmore (2000: 270) illustrates, they have become adapted to transport their encoded intentions intact in many ingenious ways, and to resist deformation or destruction as they transform. For example, 'plant seeds journey long distances in the bellies of animals', and have also travelled in 'the socio-technical networks of humans for well over 30,000 years'. This relational ability has been critical in the formation of life on earth. Ridley (1930) writing before an understanding of DNA had been developed, noted

> that the dispersal of plants – whether by seed or vegetative portion – is one of very great importance in its bearing on the distribution of plants throughout the world, the causes

> of their presence or absences in different localities, the changes of floras at differing periods, and that which goes to make a local flora. It has also been an important factor in the evolution of species, genera, and, in some cases, even of orders. (ix)

In other words, the ability of seeds as immutable mobiles is at the heart of the historical geography of the biosphere. Ridley shows in amazing detail how seeds are dispersed by wind (floating, flying), water (sea, rain-wash, ice stream, river, flood), and animals (birds, reptiles, insects, fish, batrachians, humans), and how seeds are differently adapted to float, fly, adhere, hook on to, attract by colour, and to survive the various often arduous passages that result, such as through the gut of a bird, or floating across sea reaches, with their DNA intact.

Clearly, this appreciation of the purposive texts in non-human agency needs to be tempered by a concern over the over-deterministic nature of some genetically-based neo-Darwinist approaches to explaining socio-ecological life patterns. Ingold (1995) for example, stresses that on its own, DNA 'specifies nothing' and argues that an organism is the outcome of the coming together of environment and a genome, which together 'constitute a developmental system' (76). This suggests that there can be no 'reading' of the genetic code which is not itself part of the development of that organism within its environment, but there remains a sense of purposive agency within the complement of DNA in the genome. Therefore, to suggest that DNA specifies nothing is to ignore the plan, purpose, evidence and skill embedded in the seed of any given tree or equivalent organism.

Clearly, the agency at work here is relational, but such agency reflects the need to acknowledge the significance of contributory non-human action. These processes and their outcomes are not intentional in terms which are equivalent to human agency, but they are purposive processes involving a plan and the choice of best means with which to deliver the purposive outcome.

Agency and (Non-)Reflexive Action

It is in considering reflexive agency that the human realm of action appears to differentiate sharply from the non-human. Callon and Law's (1995) consideration of agency as 'reflexive teleology' (491) reflects a form of action in which agents can choose, set goals, prioritize those goals, and rework their intentions through those goals. The notion of 'choosing' here suggests the kind of free will which is unique to humans. Indeed, it is simply not arguable that humans have a number of uniquely developed competencies which grant them extraordinary capacity as agents (although the status of humans as 'free agents' has been itself long disputed: see Hornsby, 1997). However, acknowledging the power of human agency does not require a conclusion that such power is the sole significant form of agency at work in the world.

So while it is obviously problematic to suggest that organic others such as trees (but perhaps less so for higher animals – see Mahner and Bunge, 1997) have any capacity which equates to the kind of reflexive, intentional and transformative action which has been seen as the essence of human agency, we suggest that more recent critiques of reflexive agency do open up more scope for parallel forms of non-human agency. Here, we refer in particular to recent developments in non-representational theories of agency.

In search of a view of agency which captures the 'dynamics of emergent creativity' (Goodwin, 1994: 184), Thrift (1996a, 1999) has outlined a theoretical redirection which acknowledges the inherent difficulties of extracting a representation of the world when we are busily co-constructing that world with numerous others from various beginnings and to various ends:

> Non-representational theory is anchored in an irreducible ontology in which the world is made up of billions of happy or unhappy encounters, encounters which describe a 'mindful connected physicalism' consisting of multitudinous paths which intersect. (Thrift 1999: 302)

This ontological frame is matched by an epistemology

> which recognises very strong limits on what can be known and how we can know it because of the way human subjects are embodied as beings in time-space, because of their interconnected position in multiple social relations, and because these are numerous perspectives on, and metaphors of, what counts as knowledge. (ibid.: 303)

From this viewpoint, human action-competencies and agency-capacities are not seen as bound by the intentionalities of reflexive choice. Human action is entangled with the unconscious, the subconscious, the habitual, the accidental and the spontaneous. Such entanglements produce much of what we regard as human agency, but are difficult to define as the product of fully reflexive intentional decision-making. Following this theoretical redirection, then, some of the seeming certainties about what sets human agency apart from its non-human counterpart – freedom to think, to make choices, to represent a world of our own making, to contain our knowledge and capacity in language – seem somehow less certain. It is not that human agency is rendered equivalent to non-human agency, rather that these categories are brought together in compatible surfaces of complexity, with 'certain macroscopic phenomena . . . becoming the result of the non-linear interaction of microscopic elements in complex systems' (Thrift, 1999: 306)

Two important nuances for non-human agency follow from this. First, the socio-ecological world exhibits incredible creativity, and creative potentials, and non-human agents fully participate in creative becoming and being. Grange (1997) sees this 'creativity' as the most important dimension of environmental cosmology. It is the creativity of the always ushering into being, and of the always unique present of existence:

> The never-ending freshness of the world . . . announces the meaning of the universe. The creative march into novelty . . . This creativity works silently and secretly. It is around and within us. It does not necessarily show itself in big surprises. It is the astounding fact that the world is never the same once. It is the obvious fact that we cannot stop the world. It is a reminder that we live in a universe larger than our own interests. It is a sign too that we, too, shall pass. (15)

Secondly, non-representational theory suggests that creative complexities of agency involve practices of what Thrift calls 'haunting'. It is here that things, emotions, newness and performances come together in an embodied, emplaced and entimed fashion to bring about practices which defy conventional expectations of agency-in-place. The 'haunting' of a place, or by a place, may reflect passion, spirituality, imagination, dreaming, the valuing of anomaly; exchanges between the visible present and the starkly absent – in other words multiple and incomplete becomings of agency. Such agency, although clearly relational, will draw on complementary relations between signifiers and signifieds, some of which will be related to codes such as human/non-human, but others of which will be hidden, floating between such codes.

Gil's (1998) discussion of Metamorphoses of the Body is helpful here. He argues that we identify living things and objects by attempting to establish precise relations between signifiers and signifieds. However, these systems of correspondence between signs and things will only ever be partial; meanings will be imprecise and the strict interconnections between signifiers and signifieds will be unclear. Moreover, some signs will be free-floating, seemingly not anchored by particular signifiers. It is these floating signifiers which we argue offer an interesting window on human and non-human agencies. Gil suggests that

> these floating signifiers do not designate anything in particular, they would simply have a 'zero symbolic value', but they would have a basic function in that they allow 'symbolic thinking to operate'. In this case one can imagine that the zone of the signified that the floating signifier corresponds to is found in the space that separates the codes, or it is their hinge – because . . . when it is filled with content, it always belongs to these semantically disordered zones, straddling two or several codes, two classes of objects, or two worlds. (94)

The space separating human and non-human codes of agency will be replete with floating signifiers, which designate energies and forces that cannot be signified in either code. These floating signifiers will function as mediators and interchangers between the codes, and may demarcate many of the hauntings which intertwine human and non-human agency.

Such an understanding poses two problematic questions for our discussion of non-human agencies. First – is it possible to understand the significance of floating signifiers without reference to the codes concerned? As Gil asks,

> How can we understand the transfer of signifiers from one code to another, how can we make sense of this passage from difference to identity with its gaps and redundancies? Especially since each code keeps its secrets, its principle of untranslatability and its separate individuality? (95)

Where codes cannot be translated into a similar language (as in the human and non-human) they will need to be translated 'among each other'. This suggests to us that the hauntings of non-representational agency will require both human and non-human codes of agency to yield their secrets, and their untranslatable separate individualities in order that hybrid relations may be more fully understood. In other words, relational networks of agency may need to be founded on an appreciation of the contribution of different codes of agency to hybridity.

A second and related question concerns the irresistible dominance of the human code. After all, this language is directly shared by human analysts, and problems of untranslatability and discovering secrets relate more to the deconstruction of 'obvious' representations of action, and to the opening out of performative natures of language. There can be little doubt that the non-human other presents many more difficulties in terms of translation and coded secrecy, and that accounts of relational hybridity will therefore tend to be human-centred. Until the lions have their historians, history will always glorify the tales of the hunter. Until non-human agency is more directly championed, accounts of relational agency which claim to transcend human–non-human divides will always be magnetically attracted to the human core. Non-representational theories of agency, though inherently relational, do point to the hauntings of coded and floating signifiers which designate many of the forces which put power, possibilities and life into objects and living things. Non-human agency will float in and out of human lived experience, just as human agency will similarly float in and out of the lived experiences of non-human agents such as trees. In this way non-representational ideas attribute yet fuller significance to the multiple but discontinuous creativity of nature's agencies.

Agency and Relational Agency

E.O. Wilson has claimed that 'insects are the little things that run the world' (cited by Hubbell, 1993) and Peattie (in Vitale, 1997) has forcefully suggested that it is 'the green leaf pigment, chlorophyll' which effectively runs the world. Such claims about the particular unique functional significances of non-human agency need to be taken seriously, but only with the proviso that any segment of agency when looked at in isolation can create the impression of discrete vitality. Our point in this chapter is not that non-human agency should be viewed discretely, as such agency will always be relational. Rather, we argue that attempts to understand the complexity and multifunctionality of particular non-human agents will both help to destabilize chronically anthropocentric views of agency and contribute toward more balanced and nuanced perspectives on hybridity. Any claim to a critical position within one or another network of agency is only credible as long as the critical positions of others are recognized also, and in the end it is the network itself which is of paramount significance. This is not, therefore, an argument about how nature would cease to exist without insects, or photosynthesis, or trees, but rather that the contributions of non-human agents have shaped and been shaped by the evolving existence of planetary dwelling.

Grange (1997) (following Whitehead) uses the notion of coherence to emphasize the mutuality of agency:

> The quality of coherence presupposes the fact that in an environment the becoming of every being is woven into the becoming of all its members. There is no isolated fact, value, achievement, expression or perspective. Because of the interrelatedness of concrete environments, a complete abstraction is a theoretical impossibility. Once together, always together: so it goes in any environment whatsoever. (5)

In such a view it is the whole which is creative and the whole in which agency is ultimately situated. Within this wholeness, subsections or smaller fields of agency also have to be conceived of in a relational way. In response to the rejection of the ontological stratifications of modernism and in recognition of interconnectedness, Haraway stresses that she is pursuing 'a concept of agency that opens up possibilities for figuring relationality within social worlds, where actors fit oddly, at best, into previous taxa of the human, the natural, or the constructed' (1991: 3). This relationality of agency is where ANT has made a very substantial contribution, making a significant break from previous approaches which have regarded agency purely in human terms and have privileged the social over the natural. Moreover, there is a politics to relational agency.

Latour (1993), for example, voices the hope that recognizing relational networks will allow us to expose and confront the 'monsters' represented by malevolent networks which have grown hitherto unforeseen under the modernist constitution. Equally, a broader view of agency might destabilize the anthropocentric weightings within ethics and politics and might lead to a shift which will alter the alarming course of modern capitalist/industrial society (Guattari, 2000).

The actor–network perspective, of relational symmetry between the human and non-human world, as Fitzsimmons and Goodman (1998) suggest, 'has much to contribute to the articulation of political projects to overcome the environmental despoliation and social asymmetries of late modernity and create more ecologically sensitive, egalitarian societies' (217).

Given these political hopes, it is easy to see why the role of human agency – as enroller, weaver, connector, severer and so on – might be seen as crucial to relational networks and therefore deserving of special attention. We argue on two sets of grounds, however, that equally special attention should be given to non-human aspects of agency.

First, there is the need to recognize the mutually constitutive role of humans and others. As Ingold (1997) suggests:

> Farmers [in] the work that they do, in such activities as field clearance, fencing, planting, weeding and so on, or in tending their livestock, do not literally make plants and animals but rather establish the environmental conditions for their growth and development . . . Instead of thinking about plants or animals as part of the natural environment for human beings, we have to think of humans and their activities as part of the environment for plants and animals. (244)

Within such processes the user is clearly configured in a way which was initially conceptualized into contexts of human technology relations. Woolgar (1991) suggests that the processes of design which went into a new range of microcomputers not only socially construct the user, but also 'by setting parameters for the user's actions, the evolving machine attempts to configure the user' (61). The same could be said about many relationships, not only between humans and machines but also between organic entities and humans. The pruning of apple trees which occurs in orchards is a case again where the user has been configured. Pruning is not an arbitrary process imposed on the trees. It is an accomplishment which has evolved over a long period of time, where the desire to control the tree is shaped by the biology of the tree. Pruning is shaped by the innate disposition of the tree to grow in a certain way at certain times. Pruning has been adapted to best work with this disposition. Trees have shaped pruning just as much as, in the end, pruning shapes the tree.

There are also other circumstances in which non-human agency plays a distinctive role in the mutual constitution of relational agency. These might include those networks which are not enrolled by or acted out in terms of human ambition, such as the self-seeding trees which are operating outside human-enrolled networks; those human-enrolled networks which are commonly blocked, disrupted or subverted by non-human agents, such as the sycamores which when chopped down only grow back more vigorously; and networks where the role of non-human agents is generally unrecognized, for example, where the production of a cultivated apple is vaguely and wrongly attributed to purely human action.

Secondly, there is a need to recognize the blurring influence of time in appreciating non-human contributions to hybrid collectifs. Macnaghten and Urry (1998) suggest that 'social time is different from and opposed to the time(s) of nature, including the temporal processes and rhythms that inhibit or order the natural world' (135). Thus, non-human agency operates on time scales which make it hard to recognize within the framework of social time. These scales can involve glacial time and the agency of say, plate tectonics, and ecological time in which the agency of trees will often span many generations, or much shorter lifespans which can appear momentary in relation to social time.

This issue of time is particularly significant when tracing the agencies exercised by trees. Trees produce action not only through their overall growth and development but also in their seasonal cycles. A wood or city park, say, are deeply different places in the winter, spring, summer and autumn. When considered in flashes of instantaneous time as we pass them, or in the odd hour or more of clock time when we visit them, this difference will mostly be lost. But, as time-lapse film shows, the trees in their own time are extremely active, producing buds, flowers, leaves, fruit and so forth. Also tree time is complex because of the spiralling coming together of the annual development and seasonal cycle. Again the agency of such a process can only be fully appreciated by longitudinal photography. Trees can hide buildings, cut off views, fill spaces, make skyline features. As Bail (1999) says, 'It is trees which compose a landscape', but they do so in their own time, a time which humans generally find hard to recognize. Therefore it is vital that hybrid collectifs are not simply defined in terms of social time, for fear that our understanding of agency relations will in this way simply revert to the study of those networks which centre on human agency.

In this chapter we have gone, at least in part, against the grain of the exciting new theorizations about actor (or actant) networks. We have done so not out of any lack of affinity with the framework being proposed by ANT, but rather because we believe that its understandable haste in deconstructing the binary divides between nature and society, and human and non-human, has left unquestioned a number of significant issues about non-human agency. ANT suggests that hybridity is the optimal model for incorporating the agency of non-human actants. However, hybridity is approached with the baggage of long traditions of focusing on human agency, but with very little prior appreciation of the roles of different non-human agents. There are, then, some in-built tendencies toward an emphasis on collectif hybrids which are human-centred, which assume social time rather than ecological or organic time and which may stretch as far as non-human organisms, but rarely to other organic non-humans such as trees.

So, it has been our goal to retrace these steps in order to ask pertinent questions about non-human agency and its contribution to the relational agencies of hybridity. We have briefly illustrated these questions from our research on trees, although the questions clearly transcend the specific capacities for action contained by trees. We have shown that trees have the capacity for routine action in their being and becoming. Moreover, we have argued that the apparent distinction between routinized and transformative agency needs to be deconstructed, as routine action typically underpins and sustains the complex creativities displayed by non-human action. Thus routine action can be regarded itself as creative. Further evidence of transformative action is also apparent, both in contexts where trees are enrolled as part of planned processes of planting, and where trees seed themselves and transform places, habitats and ecosystems without planned human intervention. The subject of the intentionality of non-human agency is a difficult one, particularly given the discursive connotations of essentialism and reductionist naturalism which are so often wedded to intentionality. We prefer to claim that trees have the capacity for purposive action, in that particularly within the processes of reproduction there is evidence of a plan and purpose for being and becoming and of the skills with which to deliver that purposeful plan.

Finally, the distinctiveness of human reflexivity in agency is acknowledged, but significant themes from recent non-representational theorization are used to suggest some key parallels between human and non-human creativity and performance. In particular we suggest how both human and non-human agencies participate in the practices of 'haunting' and 'being haunted' and act as codes between which floating signifiers designate energies and forces as mediators and interchangers which may demarcate many of the hauntings which intertwine the human and the non-human.

In each of these respects, non-human organisms demonstrate the capacity to act. Such action will be relational, but the focus on relational hybridity will be enhanced by a more detailed acknowledgement of these capacities for non-human agency. Moreover, this framework does permit further investigation of questions such as what are the different agencies currently attributable to trees (or any other non-human organism) and how do these agencies intersect with geographical theorizing of, say, place or landscape. It is these intersections where ANT is currently at its weakest, and so for geography there may yet be value in seeking to ascribe particular contributions of competence to particular parts or places within networks.

It can be argued strongly that it is Descartes' now (in)famous dualism(s) between mind and matter, fact and value which have 'for far too long stalled the process of getting on with a viable environmental philosophy' (Grange 1997: 11). These conceptualizations have rendered animals and nature as 'mechanical automata', devoid of thought, and thus of agency, and thus from membership of the 'ethical community'. This view of animals means that forms of nature which are even further away from any conceivable notion of mind-thought-agency-morality, for example trees and plants, have no chance of consideration in such a system.

As environmental futures become more and more uncertain, and as the claim for animal rights grows stronger, the possibility of recognizing the 'agency' of plants and even other components of nature will be or should be a complex, unpredictable future narrative. Imagining the implications and formations which may spring from this is difficult, but we attempt to do so in the next two chapters by weaving the idea of 'the agency of trees' through notions of place and ethics.

–4–

Tree-places

> Trees locate us in time and place.
>
> (Sinden, 1989 cited by Rival, 1998b: 19)

> This much is true for place: we are immersed in it and could not do without it. To be at all . . . is to be somewhere . . . We are surrounded by places . . . Nothing we do is unplaced.
>
> (Casey, 1998: ix)

> I was born here, my father and mother lived here, and my grandfather too, and I love this house – I can't conceive life without the cherry orchard, and if it really is to be sold, then sell me with it.
>
> (Chekhov, 1959: 375)

Ideas of place, and the places which are occupied and co-constituted by trees, are fundamental components of our thesis in this book. In Part II, we explore four tree-places in detail, asserting that the meanings and agencies associated with trees are performed in particular situations and locations. In this chapter, however, we focus on a range of conceptual issues relating to place, and in so doing we make connections with current themes in human geography, anthropology and landscape studies which address the theorization of nature-society relations and environmental discourse. We want to consider how trees are makers of place(s) and how place(s) are makers of trees. The first consideration is about how the physical, active, creative presence of trees in differing locations can play key yet shifting roles in the production of places and landscapes. The second consideration is about how trees are culturally constructed in a complex milieu, which depends both on their physical location and context and on their symbolic and imaginative locations within local and wider cultures. Together these forces combine and recombine in rich, dense formations in particular spaces contributing to the production of place and thereby constituting the places concerned.

Our concern, then, is to highlight the powerful yet often unnoticed roles which trees play in the construction of places and landscapes, and therefore to talk back to theoretical considerations of place which have had a prominent yet uneven status within human geography and beyond. Ideas of place, culture and agency are essentially interconnected. In Chapters 2 and 3 we discussed both the power of culturally constructed symbolism, which attaches meanings to trees, and the powerful contribution which trees as non-human agents bring to relational agencies in nature–society relations. Both culture and agency are mobilized, folded and refolded in the context of particular tree-places. Place therefore becomes a key focus for the understanding of nature–culture. So it is in terms of arbori-culture that we can suggest that trees make places, and places make trees. Such a suggestion raises many issues.

First there are trees themselves, which represent a massive presence in many forms of place and landscapes, encompassing the global, the national and the local, the urban, suburban and rural; the public and private; and the domestic, industrial and the agricultural. Just as 'animal geographies' have come to be a vibrant and vital part of 'human geography' (Philo and Wilbert, 2000; Wolch and Emel, 1998), so should the presence of flora within human cultural spaces become an integral element in the understanding of places. This is particularly so for trees, given their significant material presence and hugely variegated cultural and economic articulations within society. Trees are culturally constructed representing a form of social nature, but they are also living, active, creative, physical presences. This mix of the cultural, the material and the living presents interconnected agency and performance wherever trees are to be found.

Secondly, we are concerned with place. Place is a fundamental aspect of everyday life, but the meaning and forms of 'place' are manifold and constantly shifting (Casey, 1993, 1998; Creswell, 1996; Harvey, 1996). The continuing geographical engagement with notions of place, along with important conceptualization from anthropology and landscape studies, suggest five main themes which not only illuminate the places of trees and nature, but also are in turn illuminated by the nature of tree-places:

1. the significance of place in the construction of the everyday world and including how trees, because of their nature, are 'players of place' par excellence
2. the recognition that places are dynamic and shifting phenomena which somehow retain threads of meaning (or narrative) which sustain them as places
3. the interrelationships between place and the alternative foci of new conceptual approaches drawn from post-structuralism and Actor Network Theory – approaches which can challenge the notion of place as commonly given
4. the importance of non-human actors (in this case, broadly nature and more specifically, trees) playing active, *creative* parts in processes of place-formation, rather than being blank canvasses onto which ideas of place drawn from human practice and imagination are painted
5. the deployment of the concept of dwelling to consider landscape, place and environment, which is with certain provisos an effective means of approaching place and nature roles within place.

These five themes are explored throughout this chapter in order to pursue the notion that trees should be considered in relation to the geographical and cultural places they occupy and the place and spatial formations which result. Such places are always in transition, but (can) remain in some ways coherent and knowable in ways which sustain them. Trees are implicated both in transition and in the enduring coherence.

Ideas of Place

Place has of course (almost by definition) been a central concern to geography, but not consistently or unproblematically so. Often place has been subordinate to the analysis of space which appears in some ways to offer deeper insights into and understandings of the patterns of society. Ideas of place have often been thought to be problematic because of their subjective and humanistic associations, which have tended to subsume place with 'community' (Agnew, 1989). This patchy regard of place in geography may be reflected in Casey's (1993: xiv) assertion that in 'the period of modernity – place has come to be not only neglected but actively suppressed'. Some geographers (e.g. Gregory, 1989) have seen such suppression as a 'betrayal', a denial of what seems to be an incredibly powerful, common and somehow spatial concept at once embedded in and embedding people's everyday lives. Accordingly, concern for place as a key subjective experience has continued to flourish within geography (Adams et al. 2001; Agnew and Duncan, 1989; Daniels, 1992; Entrikin, 1991). Johnston (1996: 73), for example, asserts that 'understanding places is fundamental to understanding the world', and Smith, Light and Roberts (1998), while appreciating the difficulties of conceptualizing place, point to the essence of why it is important to do so:

> Place is difficult to theorise because of its confused and intractable qualities. It also arouses suspicion because it is undeniably associated with exclusion and xenophobia. Nevertheless, place remains an incorrigible philosophical problem, if only because it so fundamentally structures human experience. It is deeply human to make places, and to think in terms of places. (6)

Recent conceptualizations of spatial formations, actor networks and geographies of difference have brought with them a renewed sense of the significant but problematic nature of place. For example, Curry (2000) has argued that the increasing reference to the philosophical writings of Wittgenstein allows geographers and other social scientists to 'cut through the welter of spatial metaphors in which we live – level, scale, container, hierarchy – and see the extent to which all arise out of a human life that is carried out in places' (110). For others, however, the idea of place is too rigid and static, too bound up with Euclidean space and time. Thus Doel (1999: 7–9) sees many geographical attempts to define places as 'solidification(s)' of 'sedentary thought' which are 'always slower, more earthly, more concrete, more grounded, and more real than space'. In splicing together notions of place, space and time, Doel suggests that place is only an acceptable idea if 'places are [seen as] events' and as 'what take place', rather than any kind of fixed territory. Thrift (1999: 295) likewise confesses a complete mistrust of such 'solidifications' – 'the more you think about place, the less it seems to offer' – and, like Doel, is only happy to consider places if they are seen 'as dynamic, as taking place only in their passing' (310).

Such views are informed to some extent, by the ways in which Actor Network Theory has radically challenged Euclidean notions of place, space and locality (Murdoch, 1998; Thrift, 1999). Murdoch (1998: 358) considers that the recasting of time and space into networks has 'profound implications' for 'traditional' geographical endeavours which have orbited around ideas of space and place in various trajectories. Curry's (2000: 110) invocation of Wittgenstein's 'deep appreciation of the nature of places and their role in everyday life' also regards place in a performative way – far from being carved out of a pre-existing spatial container, places are created and maintained through the everyday actions of everyday life.

Place, then, emerges as 'local condensations and distillations of tremulous global processes' (Gregory, 1994: 122) – more topological than topographical. However, more commonplace discourses of place have proved durable. In studies of everyday life, the use of place to convey some kind of ubiquitous characteristic of being seems to endure. The popular power of place, as identifier, as sensory category, as conveyor of socio-spatial meaning, as focus for the grounding of complex networks, seems to demand sustained attention. As Thrift (1999) acknowledges, while Actor Network Theory does provide a convincing account of how all manner of things constantly combine and recombine in the formation of the functioning social world, it does not recognize how these coming togethers can have qualities, or have qualities brought to them, which can seem as forms of place formation. In his view, 'Latour and other actor network theorists . . . fail to see the importance of place because they are reluctant to ascribe different competencies to different aspects of the network or to understand the role of common ground in how networks echo back and forth, often unwittingly' (313). To some extent, then, an emphasis on place may be seen as counter to some actor network theorization. It is, however, possible to suggest that some actor networks are constituted out of local embedded entities and, in so doing, a local distinctiveness is generated which can become a key component in the construction of place identity. Such local distinctiveness can represent actor networks recruiting local actors and generating local expertise in order that the network be maintained. With the increased capacities of acting at a distance brought about by modern communications and transport, these localized networks have increasingly been colonized or displaced by remote and more powerful networks, leading to fears about the loss of local distinctiveness and about the potential destruction of place.

An example (with trees) serves to illustrate these suggestions. In Les Landes, in south-west France, there is a tradition of hunting wood pigeons which fly over the pine forests as they migrate south in the autumn from more northern regions. A very distinctive method of hunting these pigeons has developed over time. Live decoy pigeons are loosely tied onto small wooden platforms which are fixed into the tops of the trees. These platforms are see-sawlike, and can be rocked up and down by the pulling of wires attached to them. These wires lead to huts where hunters sit and watch for flights of migrating pigeon passing overhead. When a flight of approaching pigeons is spotted the wires to the platform are pulled and the decoy pigeons flutter their wings as they try to balance on their shifting perch. The flapping decoy pigeons in the trees tops are intended to attract the attention of the overflying pigeons and to tempt them to break their migration flight for food and rest where others of their kind are apparently active. Each hut has a whole series of wires running to a whole series of platforms and decoy pigeons, and there is a considerable expertise in luring the overflying pigeons to land in the pine treetops by orchestrating the movements of a number of decoy pigeons across the top of the wood. On the forest floor meanwhile, there is a labyrinth of tunnels made of cut brushwood. This permits the hunters to move from their huts to where any successfully attracted pigeons may have landed in the trees without alarming them. Once the hunters are in place the pigeons are then shot and gathered.

We see this very much as an actor-network. Here the hunters are enrolling a number of technological artefacts (wire, planks of wood, string, fulcrum, gun, gunpowder) and a number of organic entities (treetops, decoy pigeons, brushwood) to achieve the goal of enrolling the prey pigeons into the network, in a rather drastic fashion. This pigeon-hunting network is strong, and the various entities are (literally) tightly tied into it. In other words, it works well. The 'translation is perfect' (Murdoch, 1995). The components of the network, human, non-human and artefact, are 'translated' into a collective which has a specific aim which depends on the mobilization of various skills. The hut, human hand, wire, plank, pivot, string, decoy pigeon's foot, balance awareness, wings, brushwood tunnel, gun, gun powder, lead shot, all work together as one. The whole network employs the skill which string has, and the skill that gunpowder has. The string becomes killing-pigeon-string, the gun powder, killing-pigeon-gun-powder, and so on. The techniques of the construction of this network are a matter of local expertise and there has been an ongoing refinement of the enrolling of the artefacts into a stronger network. The building of such networks is a process of trial and error, of evolution. Despite this, often the wild pigeons ignore the decoys and fly on along their migration route, thus avoiding being enrolled and thus remaining in their own 'wild network' which is their life pattern. The *killing of pigeons* (for consumption or sale, and more recently for recreational and cultural currencies), which has to be initiated in this complex way through an actor network, is the point of agency. A would-be hunter without gun or wire or decoy would have no chance of catching an overflying pigeon.

We want to make the point in terms of place, in this example and in a myriad others, that the *local* resources – such as the trees – which happen to be present in a location are those recruited in the forming of an actor network. Other resources are imported, but the network or sub-network is embedded in the material and culture of a location, and this intimately bound up with what place is. There is a process of response to local situations. This will involve spotting opportunities to exploit, such as the pigeons which fly overhead, and then the use of local resources to devise a way of exploiting this opportunity. A local *expertise* develops as this process is refined. Other resources are brought in to make up the network, but it is the localness of the convergence of opportunity and resources which leads to a spatial uniqueness and thus a potential for place identity to emerge. By seeing such relations in terms of actor networks, the local connectivity of place may be understood as a network configuration which is enrolling actors who share a proximate location, as well as more remotely located actors in the network. Construction of place, then, will be influenced by the degree to which a network, or multiple networks, enrol locally situated actors. Such an understanding permits the recognition of *locally distinctive* places, and suggests a durability for the concept of place. The power of the idea of place, it seems, cannot be totally denied. In the example cited above, the need to hunt pigeon for economic reasons has faded, yet the practice is now retained as a process of local culture and place identity.

The Power of Place

In further pursuit of the 'power of place' in relation to trees, further illustration is provided by the organization Common Ground (see Chapter 2), and the emphasis placed in their work on the notion of 'local distinctiveness', and on trees and 'local distinctiveness'. The agenda promulgated by Common Ground is about the rich intimate mixing of the natural, the cultural, and the technological, which are co-present in particular landscapes and particular places. Here (as in the above example) place is formed by some *local distinction* which separates it out from that which is around it, and forms 'a subtle dance of detail and patina' (Clifford, 1996: 4). According to this view it is the unevenness of socio-ecological formations (Harvey, 1996) which renders the world as a series of places. Clearly these places should not be oversimplified as some kind of fixed patchwork. Rather they suggest much more ghostly, blurred, flexing entities which have multiple forms, which are contested and in flux, which have multiple depths and scales, yet which also retain some form of coherence which sustains them as places.

Within these persistent and powerful ideas of place, there is an acknowledgement that nature plays a significant creative role. Nature's role in place has long-standing pedigree; Sauerian cultural geography and cultural ecology, for example, emphasized nature–place relationships. However, the place of nature in these accounts did not acknowledge non-human agency but rather presented nature as a variable context or ground in which differing cultures evolved distinctively in dialectic relationships with the ecology of the land. Partly as a result, the recognition of nature's role in the power of place became dogged by the accusation of environmental determinism. Thus 'the natural' somewhat faded from theoretical focus to the extent that Daniels (1992: 319), when reviewing the fate of 'land' in recent geographical accounts of place, is able to argue that the physical has been 'largely ignored in recent writing about place, indeed in much human geography'. Here he echoes that call from some physical geographers to reinstate the 'physical' into the 'human' geography:

> geographers have forgotten – it is extraordinary to say so – that some parts of the Earth are high, others low; some wet, others dry; some desert, others covered in forest and grassland and ice ... These are the elemental categories of human existence in which geography must deal. (Stoddart, 1987: 331, cited by Daniels, 1992: 320)

Other theorizations have emerged which 'bring nature back in' and give it a creative relational agential role in the production of 'society'. As we have discussed, this has been the thrust of the developments of social nature (Whatmore and Boucher, 1992) and Actor Network Theory-derived positions (Fitzsimmons and Goodman, 1998). But as we have already said, in these developments, particularly in perspectives derived from Actor Network Theory, place has not been a readily acceptable concept.

Other approaches have been more willing to consider place favourably. Such a formation has been powerfully advocated by Whitt and Slack (1994) in the context of calling for stronger linkages in cultural studies, between ideas of culture, community and the environment.

> What we are proposing is that, for both theoretical and practical purposes, communities be approached as conjoined to and interpenetrated by particular environments which they transform and partially construct and which in turn transform and partially construct them. Far from being mere passive backdrops or props in an essentially (or exclusively) human play, environments so conceived are the embodiment, or material extension of communities . . . such environmental construction and transformation is a feature not

> just of the human constituents of a mixed community – [sites where the human and other than human are drawn together in multiple articulations] – but of its entire biotic constituency. (22)

Here there is a call for nature to be seen as a *creative* co-player in the production of communities embedded in particular physical contexts, the identity of which has to be, in the end, bound up with ideas of place.

The re-emphasis of nature in place has also drawn on other theoretical manoeuvres spearheaded by Donna Haraway and others. Haraway (1992) calls upon the 'topick gods' which were 'local gods, the gods specific to places and people' and asserts that we need these spirits 'in order to reinhabit, precisely, common places – locations that are widely shared, inescapably local, worldly, enspirited' (296). Although Haraway is anxious to destabilize the very term *nature*, particularly in its enlightenment formation, she is also anxious to recognize the creative roles, 'the witty agency,' of diverse actors in these processes. She writes, 'The commonplace nature I seek . . . has many houses with many inhabitants which/who can refigure the earth' (297).

Haraway's ideas, emphasizing diverse actants living together in many houses, chime with other theoretical strands which have focused on the idea of dwelling. One such strand has emerged, almost ghost-like, from post-structuralist writings about the environment. For example, Conley (1997) suggests that Felix Guattari, in his work *Les Trois Ecologies* (1989), is in fact arguing that ecological problems can be solved through 'sagacious use of technology towards humanity, when ecology is redefined as the art of dwelling, of occupying a mental and physical space, and of mapping out a territory' (96). This emergent idea of dwelling appears to us to be a fruitful approach to the understanding of tree-places. Trees, by virtue of their ubiquitous presence in different types of place, and their physical and symbolic dynamism, perform significant roles in the occupation of space and the mapping of territory. It is instructive that trees have been an important focus of the work of Common Ground (see for example Common Ground, 1989a/b; Sinden, 1990) as they chart and support how local places have (rich) distinction. Trees can be makers of landscapes and places in very powerful ways. Trees can also be distinctive prominent things, or can be arranged in distinctive and prominent formations, combinations and relations, and they also have distinctive imaginative identities thrust upon them.

Dwelling Places

This notion of dwelling can be traced back at least to the later thinking of Heidegger which, as Crang (1998) suggests, has been a useful source of ideas for considering how humans are always embedded in the world; how they are, in other words, embedded in place. Heidegger's ideas have more recently been reworked by Ingold (1993, 1995), and these two sources of writing about dwelling have been drawn upon by a number of commentators on place, landscape and nature. Bender (1998), Casey (1993, 1998, 2001), Harvey (1996), Macnaghten and Urry (1998), Malpas (1998), Marshall (1992), Relph (1989), Seamon and Mugerauer (1985), Tall (1993), Thrift (1999) have all used the notion of dwelling to address issues of nature, landscape and places. These accounts are variously dependent on the notion of dwelling, and more or less critical of some aspects of it. For example, Seamon and Mugerauer's (1985) phenomenological approach to place and the environment flows directly from the work of Heidegger, whereas Macnaghten and Urry advocate that the dwelling perspective, as (re)articulated by Ingold (1993, 1995), be taken up as an appropriate theoretical concept for new approaches to landscape and nature.

Dwelling is about the rich intimate ongoing togetherness of beings and things which make up landscapes and places, and which bind together nature and culture over time. It thus offers conceptual characteristics which blur the nature–culture divide, emphasize the temporal nature of landscape, and highlight performativity and nonrepresentation, and as such it is attractive to those trying to (re)theorize the nature of nature, and the nature of landscape and place. In particular, the understanding of dwelling provides a route for those who seek to move away from dichotomous realist and idealist approaches to place, environment and landscape (Macnaghten and Urry, 1998; Muir, 1999).

In his work on dwelling, Heidegger emphasized how people were always embedded in the world. It is this recognition of an embodied experience of the world – and the consequent challenge to the Cartesian split of mind from body, and culture from nature – which has been seen as hugely important in the understanding of landscape (Bender, 1998; Crang, 1998; Thrift, 1996). Recognition of dwelling implies a shift from seeing the relationship between people and the environment as a 'building perspective', where ideal human mental constructs are imposed (built) upon the world, to a 'dwelling perspective', where any act of building, living or even thinking is formed in the context of already being-in-the-world which, in turn, affects that forming. For example, Harvey (1996) considers the contribution of 'dwelling' in terms of its emphasis on how repeated encounters with places, and complex associations with them, serve to build up memory and affection for those places, thereby rendering the places themselves deepened by time and qualified by memory. Dwelling is thus *potentially* bound up with ideas of home, the local, and concern or affection for nature and the environment. To dwell, according to this kind of interpretation, is to become rooted by the act of accommodation in place (Tall, 1993).

Heidegger's notion of dwelling, however, is complex and obscure. Vycinas (1969) summarizes it as the process of sparing or preserving the unity of earth, sky, gods, and mortals (four things key to Heidegger's vision). Thus, 'to dwell is to spare the earth, receive the sky, expect the gods and have capacity for death' (15). This sparing of the earth is sharply contrasted to the modern domination of things. A respectful 'sparing', rather than rule or control, will allow the earth to appear in its gifts. Heideggerian dwelling, then, is to be rooted emphatically in the heavens and the company of the gods, and also in the concrete nature of the everyday. It is these last aspects which have been developed geographically as theories of place and landscape, and which are drawn upon by some environmentalist thinkers (Marshall, 1992; Zimmerman, 1993).

For being-in-the-world, or dwelling, *things* are critical. To illustrate this, Heidegger, in different instances, discusses dwelling through the examples of a bridge and a house.

> A bridge built across a river 'assembles' the banks and the countries lying on both sides of the river; . . . A bridge is a thing not only by its 'assembling' of the foursome, but also by its assembling of the places. A bridge throws a variety of places into certain distances in respect to itself, and thus they become places. Such an 'assembling' of places actually is breaking into the space or spacing-in . . . of space. (Vycinas, 1969: 16)

Here the bridge makes a place, or places, making anew that which it connects, but this quite literal example should not obscure the idea that all things are connectors or, as in a translation of Heidegger's Old German, 'assemblers'. Here are some pre-echoes of an ANT vision of assembling of the world via things, but in Heidegger, unlike in much of ANT, place survives, and is in fact essential to his view of the world. This is demonstrated in Heidegger's most celebrated illustration of dwelling, a description of a peasant's cottage set harmoniously in the Black Forest. Here 'authentic' rural life is embedded in the land, articulated through the material of the house, and the craft and toil of those who work, build, and *dwell* there. It follows that some concepts of dwelling can be adapted to describe the connected hybrid materiality of the world without losing a sense of place (see Smith et al. 1998: 7–8; Malpas, 1998).

In effect, dwelling is 'the manner by which we are on the earth' (Vycinas, 1969: 15), and incorporates both a spatial and a temporal dimension. This philosophy of 'being-in-the-world' has been related more formally to landscape by Ingold (1993; 1995). He argues that it is always contextualized lived practices which create spaces, time, places, and landscapes which are 'not so much the object of our thoughts as the homeland(s) to our thoughts' (1995: 76, citing Merleau-Ponty, 1962: 24). Ingold tells us that landscape is the world formed by those who *have* dwelt there, who *do* dwell here, and who *will* dwell here, as well as those whose practical activities take them through its manifold sites and who journey down its manifold paths. Landscape is where the past and future are copresent with the present-through processes of memory and imagination. Past, present, and future are continuously reprocessed while the materiality of landscape is worked by, and marks, this process. Moreover, the practices of dwelling are articulated by a *taskscape,* where the habitual practices of humans form familiar patterns which can become landscapes or places.

These notions of dwelling, although complex, are closely related to the idea of place. As Von Maltzahn (1994: 116) states, 'dwelling implies the presence of place'. From our perspective, dwelling offers a number of conceptual advantages. First, it positions non-humans as active players in the 'performance of place'. It also offers scope for the sympathetic inclusion of and commitment to organic non-human agency, in contrast to ANT which, as Whatmore and Thorne (2000) assert, retains its leaning towards the technological and artefactual – very much extensions of the human. Secondly, dwelling takes a temporal as well as spatial view of place. The temporality of place, and its unfolding variation in form and character are essential emphasis in the transformation in place theorization called for by Doel, Thrift and others. Casey (1998: 286) lists a range of contemporary thinkers, from post-structuralists to environmentalists who do not conduct 'a definitive . . . eidetic search for the formal structure of place. Instead, each tries to find *place at work, part of something ongoing and dynamic*' (our emphasis). Dwelling emphasizes the temporal dimension, and envisions ensembles of characters (people, things, and animals) producing places and landscapes over time. Thirdly, the idea of place(s) as dwelling(s) does not negate a networked view of the world. Indeed dwelling can coexist with networks by describing hybrid ensembles – or hybrid collectifs to use Callon and Law's (1995) phrase – and by postulating the notion of place as interwoven with other places and networks at multiple layers and scales. Seamon and Mugerauer (1985: 8) hinted at such an open, connected view of place in their suggestion that 'Dwelling incorporates environments and places but extends beyond them, signifying our inescapable immersion in the present as well as the possibility of reach beyond to new places, experiences and ideas'.

So places are dynamic, and yet they entail some sort of coherent familiarity or identity often feeding a sustained narrative over time. Place is therefore rather like a whirlpool or eddy in a flow of water. It is made of that which surrounds it and so, in that sense, is undistinguishable from its surroundings. Instead it is formed from a persistent pattern of flow, so becomes an entity with some form of stable identity, even though it is made of nothing but dynamism. Places may be seen in this way, as some sort of holding pattern in the flows of materiality which swirl together as space-times. But these patterns are formed of a vast variety of actors twisting together, dwelling together, in rich formations. These ideas – of places being formed by diverse actors, in some form of connection, in an ongoing temporal freshness – suggest a sense of performance as well as of dwelling, so before going on to consider tree roles more closely, we turn to the notion of performance in more detail.

Places as Performances

As Nigel Thrift (2000: 225) has emphasized 'performance, at this moment, is one of the most pervasive metaphors in the human sciences'. Even in those performance studies related to performance art 'there is no doubt that performance has moved beyond the theatre' (231) and is clearly present in all manner of everyday life. In short, Thrift suggests, performance is 'the art of producing the now' (see also Phelan, 1993). In many ways, we regard performance as an entirely relevant gateway to the conceptualization of place. Consider, for example, Schechner's assertion that

> Any event, action, item or behaviour may be examined 'as' performance. Approaching phenomena as performance has certain advantages. One can consider things as provisional, in-process, existing and changing over time. (Schechner, 1998, cited in Thrift 2000: 232)

These ideas appear particularly applicable to ideas about place. Places slip away as they form, as did the room in which you read this a minute ago, for instance. They are never entirely static, yet they can remain identifiable as themselves. There will be comings and goings, twists and turns, excitements and calms. Like a performance, a place can never be represented or reproduced fully; to be fully appreciated they have to be experienced 'live'. Just as there is concern over the re-presentation of performance in this media dominated age, there are concerns and controversies over trying to represent 'place'.

An illustration is helpful here. William Least Heat-Moon's amazing book *PrairyErth* is over 600 pages long and sub-titled 'a deep map'. It describes in great detail Chase County, Kansas. According to Buell (1995: 256) it is 'the most ambitious literary reconstruction of a small portion of America ever attempted in a single volume', yet Buell also points to Heat-Moon's admission that 'ninety-nine-point nine to the ninth decimal of what ever has happened here isn't in the book'. Literary representations of place, like some (perhaps many) performances, do not go beyond the everyday; they are trying to move towards the everyday in all its richness. It is the place itself, or the event itself, which is the extraordinary living performance.

In addition, place, like performance, requires some form of audience. As well as the production of the now, there is the consumption of the now, even if audiences are performers and vice versa. Such consumption of course may involve the memory of the past as well as images of the future, but these are always made in the now. We should emphasize here that we are not trying to close the gap between the ideas of place and performance in any complete or final way. Rather we feel that considering places as performances can freshen and sharpen our understanding of them and of their dangers and potentials. We also acknowledge that place and performance have been linked by others as in David Seamon's idea of 'place-ballet' (see Von Maltzahn, 1994, for an account of this). Here place is seen as having rhythmic temporal dimensions performed by bodies individually and collectively. It emphasizes the phenomenological embedding that is place, this is important and we address it further, but it is centred on routine performance – we want to add a further dimension of developing, shifting performance.

Performance is clearly a process; an on-going, a becoming. And it is process which has attracted writers such as Guattari (2000: 36) because of its counter-position to system and structure. It offers the possibility of escaping in 'lines of flights' which 'set to work on their own account, gradually superseding the referential totality from which they emerge, and manifesting themselves finally as their own existential index' (in Conley, 1997: 101–2). Places in their ongoing freshness and unruly mixing can be seen in this light, particularly in the context of the intrusion and spontaneity of both human and non-human actors.

Trees are restless life-forms, growing slowly, maybe really slowly, but ever so surely, if they can. Exhaling oxygen, inhaling carbon dioxide, sucking up nutrients from the soil, engaging with the sun, they are continually growing or shedding buds, leaves, flowers, and fruit, maybe bark. They die over time. They move and make sound in the wind and reflect and filter light as they do so. They play host to other beings and of course they constantly aspire to propagate themselves, by seed or by sucker. Their place-making qualities can in these kinds of way be read in performative terms, and in doing so they become susceptible to further understandings of place in terms of embodiment.

Casey (1998) in his painstaking exploration of the *Fate of Place* draws on the work of Merleau-Ponty to source understandings of place through understandings of embodiment. Grange (1985: 72) similarly asserts that 'If place is ever to be seen in its concreteness, the implicit, subconscious prose and poetry of human flesh requires specific articulation'. For Merleau-Ponty the body is itself a place, but more importantly here, it is the way in which we mesh with place (and space) – '[T]he instrument of experience is our whole body subject' (Von Maltzahn, 1994: 76). Within this, the knowing of movement and the senses are critical. According to Casey 'Merleau-Ponty accorded full scope to the role of the lived body – above all to its actively expressive movements, its orientating capacity, and its inhabitational powers' (1998: 238). Thus as Casey (1993: 29) has it, 'place is what takes place between body and landscape'.

Movement then, constitutes a knowing, sensitive encounter with place and space. For example, Lippard (1997) suggests it offers an unparalleled way to open oneself to 'the spirit of place'. Your senses are in direct contact with that around you, you feel the hill, or the hardness or softness of the ground. Lippard explains that 'motion allows a certain mental freedom that translates a place to a person kinaesthetically . . . 'the erotic communication of body and place combines elements of desire and risk with those of time and space' (17).

If, as Casey says, we and everything else 'are always "in place"' then we are so via our bodies, which are always somewhere, always knowing things; sensing (hearing, seeing, touching, smelling, tasting); moving (breathing, pulsing, sitting, walking, crawling, climbing, orientating), and remembering (consciously, subconsciously and through the body). Trees offer a very significant part of this rich fabric of the world in which we move/act, sense, imagine and, in short, live.

Trees and Place

The interconnections between trees and these conceptualizations of place are many and various. Trees can construct places and vice versa. Many of the attributes of trees form common currencies in our understandings and appreciation of place; their size, rich materiality, their interconnectivity, their longevity, their life cycles and seasonal cycles all offer qualities which are readily and vividly drawn into the concepts of place we have discussed. No account can do full justice to these interconnections, although key authors have contributed fully to particular themes, such as trees and the British Landscape (e.g. Edlin, 1970; Miles, 1999; Rackham, 1996, 1997) or trees and people and places, (Franklin, 1999). We pursue our thesis of arbori-culture by discussing just some of the principal ways in which trees contribute to the making of places.

Trees and Dwelling

There are a number of examples of how trees are employed and understood in accounts of dwelling, either explicitly, as in the work of Ingold, or more implicitly, as in the work of other writers who talk about trees, time and place. Ingold's (1993) celebrated illustration of dwelling is partly based around an analysis of Pieter Bruegel's painting '*The Harvesters*'. In the foreground of the painting, and pivotal to its composition, is a pear tree; around it people are harvesting a field of grain, and in the background a vista of landscape stretches away from the high-on-the-hill vantage point of the painting. Ingold immediately gives the tree an active role in the construction of the place portrayed. He says of the scene depicted,

> the place was not there before the tree, but came into being with it. And for those gathered there, the prospect it affords, which is to be had nowhere else, is what gives it its particular character and identity. (1993: 167)

Speaking of the tree itself, Ingold states that

> no other tree has quite the same configuration of branches, diverging, bending and twisting in exactly the same way. In its present form the tree embodies the entire history of its development from the moment it first took root. And that history consists in the unfolding of its relations with the manifold components of the environment, including the people who have nurtured it, tilled the soil around it, pruned its branches, picked its fruit, and – as at present – use it as something to lean against. (167–8)

The tree, like the church and the path through the corn also depicted, is a marker of time, of circumstance, of ongoing embedded interconnections of things and people mixing together in ways which mark each other and bind each other. This 'taskscape', which Ingold considers carries marks of itself, becomes distinct, and therefore becomes a place.

Harrison's (1991) consideration of time, nature, place and landscape also turns to trees as iconic markers and makers of places. Talking about the huge old trees in his local landscape he says, 'To stand beneath one of these maimed colossi is to be overwhelmed by its powerful, resonant presence' (135). These oak trees are 'the living tissue of time' (135) and therefore (as do other trees, to differing extents) they meet a need which Harrison says that he 'believe[s] to be indispensable, for parochial monuments, landmarks, milestones and other points of reference by which each person can take his or her own bearings in time and place' (139). The oak tree in the churchyard which he describes is part of the material and cultural nexus through which 'the continuities of time and place are made visible, immediate and above all, tangible' (139).

This kind of understanding of trees has led to campaigns such as the Veteran Trees Initiative (see Chapter 2), which claims that '*An individual Veteran Tree can create a place with beauty, atmosphere and myriad cultural and historical associations*'. It has also led to the 'Trees of Time and Place' initiative which, through the encouragement of collecting seed from existing trees in particular places and planting them in nearby locations, emphasizes local ecology and tree presence and tries to expand the presence of trees and public awareness of them in local landscapes.

These examples (and many others we could have drawn upon) show how people consider that trees can make a place, or can 'gather places around themselves' through their growing/changing physical presence/permanence over time. Indeed trees chart the flow of that time in their very body and through the associations which build around trees as they continue to dwell. As we now explore, trees do this for all manner of reasons associated with their own being, and the meanings grafted upon them via free-flowing cultural construction in society.

Trees as Makers of Places

Trees stand out through their size and form, a characteristic which prompts Murray Bail (1999: 16) in his novel *Eucalyptus* to say 'It is trees, which compose a landscape'. Casey (1993: xv) also acknowledges the physicality of trees when he says '[A] tree stands in its own place . . . Not only is a tree in its place; it actively contributes to its place, filling it up with its own organic substance'. Trees as bodies, as groups of bodies, and as settings for bodies (ours and others), senses, and movement seem particularly vibrant, powerful makers of place. There are many reasons why this is so. Mirroring the conceptualizations of place discussed earlier in this chapter, our focus falls mostly on the rich resonating dwellings which can form between people and trees, and our aim is also to suggest both how trees are culturally constructed and how they are active material presences in themselves. We are thus anxious to ascribe some form of creative agency to nature, and to set trees in a framework of dwelling which addresses issues of place. Accordingly we now discuss some of the characteristics of trees which make them such powerful performers of places and resonant dwellers in places.

Sheer Presence. The presence of trees in a place contributes to and adapts the physical character of that place. As Sprin (1998: 138) has suggested,

> A tree modifies habitat to sustain itself and nurture its seedlings. Not only a context, not only a participant in, but a shaper of context, a tree modifies and orders environments to suit its needs and ensure survival.

Different types of tree enact this modification in different ways according to location. For example, Bail (1999) illustrates the sheer presence of an Australian gum tree:

> The gum tree has a pale and ragged beauty. A single specimen can dominate an entire Australian hill. It's an egotistical tree. Standing apart it draws attention to itself and soaks up moisture and all signs of life, such as harmless weeds and grasses, for a radius beyond its roots. (16)

This is a powerful picture of the physical and symbolic effects of a single tree. The ability to adapt and create habitats is hugely amplified by trees as collective presences. Such issues stretch right up to the scale of global dwelling as exemplified by Lovelock's (1988) notion of Gaia. As Rolston (1999) argues, the earth itself must be considered as *a place* creatively constructed by trees (and others) in processes of deep relational agency. On a more recognizable scale, tree presence can also be acknowledged at national and local levels. For example, H.E. Bates marvels at the harmonious quality of wild tree blossom in Britain, how it seems that as one tree ceases to flower, another starts and how their colours blend:

> how is it that this current of cream and white and pink goes on and on through the wild trees of Britain almost without break or variation? The chestnut and the crab . . . are white and pink. The dogwood and the elder and the lime are cream. The rest [cherry, blackthorn] are white . . . We have no wild exotic blossoming trees of scarlet or blue or purple. There is a sort of northern delicacy, almost fragility, about them all. (in, Mabey, 1997: 189)

On more local, intimate, everyday levels, trees are present in our everyday lives in many ways and places. Moving from where we live to where we work, or moving around the city and surrounding countryside, trees are nearly always part of the scene. The presence of trees may be dramatic and central to a place, or muted and incidental, but trees will play a part in nearly all the material contexts we move through and dwell in.

Sheer Size. In part the presence of trees is articulated through their size. The sheer size of (many) mature trees has a range of implications in the formation of place. Trees are often much bigger than people. Although the psychological, ethical and aesthetic effects of the size and scale of differing nature beings are extremely complex and in some regards understudied, there is no doubt that the size and scale of things and beings has implications for the way we react to them. To be dwarfed by another being, even if non-human, can invoke all manner of resonances from awe to comfort to fear. The popular references to large trees as 'noble giants' echoes with these impressions of their size. Packenham (1997) acknowledges that some of the trees he has encountered were 'stunningly large'. His photographs such as that of the weeping beech at Knap Hill vividly depict this.

There has been, and remains, a fascination with large trees, with the largest types of trees, and the largest specimens of tree types (champion trees). For example, in the nineteenth century a kind of 'sequoia fever' hit Britain as the seeds of this giant tree from the West Coast of America became available to gardeners and landscapers (Webb, 1997: 63) Within a decade of their introduction 'virtually every estate in England' had planted a 'Wellingtonia', as they were named, and the tallest was eventually recorded at 174 feet (52 metres). The presence of beings such as these, and the many other types of tree which grow to a large size in a landscape or place, is almost inevitably dramatic in visual and other ways.

Trees often present themselves as dominant in our field of vision for 'our eyes are so fixed that the space in front of us dominates our consciousness. The world appears before us, elicits our attention, demands our concern, beckons or discourages participation' (Grange, 1985: 72). So trees can fill our visual field, tower over us, enclose us. And it is this impact of size which is critical. As John Meehan argues 'Trees don't really make an impact until you start looking up at them' (cited in Nicholson-Lord, 2000). In other words sight-lines can be altered to accommodate and appreciate the scale of trees, changing the angle of view until the trees are bigger than we, until they dominate the view and enclose us. The psychology of being enclosed is again powerful and complex and, as we explored in Chapter 2, this connects with constructions of tree-places within geographies of both refuge and fear.

The size of trees means that they can produce meaningful quantities of materials, become habitats both as individuals and collectively as woods, but – more importantly, here – they can block views and make vistas, avenues, whole landscapes and places, in both rural and urban contexts. In towns and cities trees stand out among buildings, line streets, mark parks and squares, soften new development and car parks, mark key buildings and populate grand and ordinary gardens. Trees are large enough and strong enough to climb and even build tree houses in, the obvious but crucial stuff of many a child (even adult) tree encounter (Figure 4.1). It is through these endless ranges of potential contributions that trees can contribute to places and landscapes.

Figure 4.1 Tree house built in an old ash tree by children on a farm near Bath, Southwest England (Owain Jones)

Trees and the Senses. Their size, nature and form mean that trees are capable of exuding very substantial streams of 'data' which engage our senses. The sights, sounds, smells and touch of trees and woodlands are celebrated in a myriad ways, and these reflect the fantastic range of 'output' which trees emit. This range comes from the variation of types of trees (how they flower/fruit, their colour, leaf shape, canopy density, quality of form and so forth) cross-cutting with the shifting weather and light conditions that are constantly articulated by these variations. Trees, because of their nature, are capturers or players of weather and light *par excellence*. And this, linked to their other place/landscape making qualities we have touched upon, is why they have featured in painting to such a great extent, perhaps most obviously in the work of John Constable (see Daniels, 1999). Differing trees sound different as (differing) winds blow through them and thus form part of the intimate (often background) patina which embeds us in landscapes and places. The sounds of differing trees are described by Thomas Hardy in the opening paragraph of *Under the Greenwood Tree*:

> To dwellers in a wood almost every species of tree has its voice as well as its features. At the passing of the breeze the fir-trees sob and moan no less distinctly than they rock; the holly whistles as it battles with itself; the ash hisses amid its quiverings; the beech rustles while its flat boughs rise and fall. And winter, which modifies the note of such trees as shed their leaves, does not destroy their individuality. (1978: 39)

Trees also capture and reflect light differently. Different types of leaf flicker in different ways in different wind speeds. In sunshine, ash trees seem to turn a glimmering silver when a steady breeze lifts their leaves so the underneath surface reflects the light. It is such density and variation of detail that pours into our senses, and then memory, that can be so important in the formation of 'place perception' – 'it is the sounds and smells and sights of places which haunt us' (Gussow, 1971, cited by Mabey, 1997: 150).

Ordinary, everyday trees produce stunning acoustic and visual performances which are often taken for granted, but also often and passionately appreciated. They can also be articulated in all manner of artistic expression. We have mentioned painting, but people also explore the sights and sounds of trees through other art forms such as music, photography and sound recording. For example, John Blakemore's (1984: 94–5) 'Wind Series' – which are photographs of trees in high wind. And when the celebrated BBC Radio 4 producer Piers Plowright set out to record 'The Most Beautiful Sound in the World' (BBC, Radio 4, 2000) his first port of call was an English woodland, with the sound of the trees and the birdsong therein. We touch on these studies of trees here rather in the 'culture' section because such are the means by which trees construct place experience.

Body Forms. There are many associations between the human body and the bodies of trees (See Perlman 1994; Rival, 1998a). Moreover, a potent stock of anthropomorphic analogies has been developed which link trees and human bodies. The main trunk of the tree echoes the human torso and main branches are commonly thought of as limbs spreading away from the body of tree. Such human tree body associations operate at different levels of reflexivity and consciousness, although as Rival (1998a: 9) points out, 'the analogy between trees and human bodies is often quite explicit'.

Part of this bodily entanglement between humans and trees is articulated through the vertical axis. Because of our balance, our eye orientation and our verticality, humans are sensitive to a 'vertical dynamism' (Bachelard, 1988). This is why 'verticality has such an immense significance in orientating us in the world' and why 'we connect more fully and sensitively with the vertical relation between sky and earth or between soil and those things that grow upward from it' (Casey, 1993: 80). The very form and stance of trees often resonates with this verticality, and thus impacts disproportionately on humans' visual and sensual appreciations of nature and landscape – it is 'one of the bases of humanness and treeness' (Perlman, 1994: 41).

These various associations between human and tree embodiment are covered in depth elsewhere (e.g. Perlman, 1994; Hutton 1999). It serves our purpose merely to point out that the presence of a tree or trees in particular places is accompanied by inevitable associations, perhaps faintly or perhaps powerfully, sometimes peacefully and sometimes contested. For instance, Harrison (1991) concludes his consideration of the conker tree that stands by his house: 'I defy anyone to share a home with such a prodigal and restless organism and be impervious to its presence' (37). This somehow inevitable association between trees, the body and the filling of human senses as they enclose us is captured by Anita Leslie (1981) in her memoir of growing up in Ireland.

> We returned to the bliss of Monaghan woods. There I could run for hours amidst the huge trees . . . Alone in the woods, I had only to stare up into the leaves to know a sensation of leaving my body. I swept into tree form. Once or twice when autumn had turned our forests to red-gold I came home so exalted by this feeling of transformation, of having roots and waving arms and rustling leaves, that I was unable to speak. (67)

Trees as Representers of Places

These various attributes of trees make them ideal representatives or markers of place. They are objects ready to hand in landscape on which identification and cartography can hang. Most obviously, there is a canon of work which studies place names which are based on tree names in order to recount the history of woodland in the landscape. According to Rackham (1996) 'the most frequent trees in English-place names are thorn and ash, followed closely by willow (including sallow and withy) and oak, then by alder, hazel and elm' (46), and 'Old English settlements that refer to trees e.g., Thornham, Ashton, Sevenoaks, Maplestead, Birch are common throughout England' (1997: 209). Rackham provides a detailed conjectural account of how such namings have evolved and whether they can be used to gauge the distribution of tree–cover and type with any reliability. The point for us, however, is that in this most obvious sense, trees have been and are used to identify place in very practical ways. Indeed we are more concerned with how trees in a place get bound up with the ongoing shifting production of that place, its identity, appreciation and even contestation. Although we illustrate these processes mostly in Part II of the book, we use some different examples here so as to introduce the place characteristics associated with this shifting production.

For example, Mabey (1993: 21) describes how wind-breaks of stunted pine-belts have come to signify the Breckland landscape, embodying a heritage and ecology which has been to some extent lost, but the remainder of which eventually came to be recognized and protected as 'unique and defining' elements of this particular landscape. He also tells how feral fig trees became local symbols in Sheffield and how one local resident claimed that they 'are as much part of Sheffield's history as the old steam-hammers and Bessemer converters' (27).

In another example, David Ley (1995) tells a remarkably rich story which eddies around the felling of two sequoias in a garden of a house in an established upper-middle-class suburb of Vancouver. As Ley puts it, the story is about 'the meeting of the local with the global, the collision of the past with the present, the conjunction of hegemonic blocs with roots in Europe and Asia' (185). He begins his conclusion with an extract from one protest letter which was a small contribution to the '*cause célèbre*' that was prompted by the fate of the trees. In the letter, which is quoted at length, Ley suggests that

> An extraordinary effusion of topophilia, love of place, stands bared. Its point of reference is an English hearth, a repose of caring stability, a narrative of protective custody. In a striking anthropomorphism, the trees become children, a lifeline, a path of succession from a valued past, through a protected present, to a promised future. The trees are an extension of the self, the social self, the confirmation of an identity shared with like-minded others. And so it is a collective neighbourhood loss that is announced in this arboreal obituary. (203)

In other words, these trees, as such potent material presences, soaked up the complex social constructions of this place – for some people – and thus became key place markers. When felled, by others who did not share or care about such associations, it is as if the place itself is being unwoven.

Because trees generally grow slowly (in relation to humans and other beings) and because of their size, nature and form, certain *conditions of a place* can become materially articulated in the form of the tree; thus, they represent places in other ways. The body of the tree both embodies and contains a cartographic record of certain aspects of a place, and represents these in a visible form which contributes to place milieu. For example, the wind-swept trees on parts of west-coast Britain, such as in Cornwall and Pembrokeshire, mark the direction of the prevailing winds, the proximity to the sea and the winter storms, and serve as an embodied reminder of the land's relationship with and orientation to the sea and the prevailing wind and weather (Figure 4.2). In very differing circumstances, the state of ill, neglected or vandalized trees can mark places as unloved, underfunded or having problematic environmental and/or social relations. As Ford Madox Brown noted once of London, 'we may say that London begins where the tree trunks commence to be black' (Ackroyd, 2000: 412).

In addition to marking places, trees are also markers of ways to and from places. Often this was in the obvious sense of being large visual markers for old route ways and this refolds into cultural symbolism and identity. Boyer (1996: 97) tells of how the pilgrim's way to Santiago de Compostela is marked out with trees. Toulson (1989) tells how 'landmark trees' were planted to aid travellers and traders moving about Britain in times before the modern road network with its signposts. Yews were planted on chalk downs to mark drover ways, taller trees marked cross-roads

Figure 4.2 Windswept trees, Pembrokeshire, Wales (Owain Jones)

and other key points. Thus trees mark movement and journeys in the landscape, adding to their practical and symbolic range of 'cultural work'.

Trees and Changing Places

Finally, in this chapter we briefly consider how trees can be bound up with the *changing* nature of places. Such changes can be considered at three levels. First, trees are often deployed to transform landscapes and places (see Chapter 2). Such deployment can range from the construction of country house parkland, through the regeneration of run-down inner-city areas, the landscaping of new development, to the restoration of derelict industrial land. Trees have a very powerful capital in the portfolio of the landowner, the architect, the planner, the landscape architect, and the local authority economic development officer.

In studies of landscape management and of the history of the British Landscape (e.g. Thomas, 1998), trees are recognized to be the medium through which landscapes are created and recreated, even to the extent that existing landscapes are depicted, and then re-depicted as they might look when improved by the manipulation of the trees within them (Thomas, 1998). It is no coincidence that the first ever programme in the BBC Radio 4 *Changing Places* series, featured accounts of how derelict industrial landscapes in England were being transformed by massive tree-planting programmes.

The second way in which trees are responsible for changing places is in the way they can survive, colonize and grow independent of, or even in contest with, human intentions. Trees, by their slow growth to often a large size, can gradually change the nature of a place. In some cases trees can outlive and/or outgrow the reasons for which they were planted, and through their longevity they project themselves into new positions within cultural landscapes. Trees can also colonize many kinds of space if they are left unmanaged. Brown's (1997) story of the 'Greening of the Black Country' shows how wild trees unexpectedly began to grow on heavily polluted and derelict industrial sites in the Midlands and how this led to the transformation of these sites and eventually to the founding of the Urban Forestry Unit.

The third way in which trees change places is in the variability of their qualities on a day-to-day and seasonal basis. We have discussed the streams of sensory stimulation that pour from trees in differing weather and light conditions. These transformations attribute richness and variety to place which contribute significantly to its character and consumption. Many trees, particularly the deciduous trees which are so significant in Britian, change markedly throughout the year. These changes transform landscapes in many ways. A tree-lined square in winter is very different from the square in summer. Autumn and spring are marked by both the idea of, and the spectacle of, the changing nature of trees at these times. The variation within the qualities and habits of trees in this respect adds extra layers of texture which help to construct and orchestrate place. Trees' seasonal habits have been studied by Laidlaw (1960) who presents an analysis of the differing ordering and timings of the changes affecting British hardwood trees. For example the ash tree flowers in early April, comes into leaf in mid-May (one of the last trees to do so), fruits in early September and drops its leaves in late September. By contrast the elder comes into leaf first (as most trees do) in early February (very early), flowers in early June, fruits in early September and drops its leaves in late September.

These detailed tree habits, we suggest, are examples of patterns of ecological time (Macnaghten and Urry, 1998) or to be more precise arbori-cultural time. Any understanding of the contribution of trees to place must take account of their temporality, their speed of growth and the seasonal cycles. John Meehan (cited in Nicholson-Lord, 2000) makes the crucial point that 'trees, and the effect they create, need time'. Trees have the ability to transform places over time. The slowness of tree growth and the scale of change over time mean that in any 'place of trees' there are long-term and powerful reproductions and extrusions of materiality occurring. A new and brash building development, or new landscapes with young trees, will become mature landscapes as the trees mature. A cemetery left unattended becomes an urban wood and, as a consequence, is transformed as a place not only materially, but also politically, economically, ecologically and culturally. We suggest in Part II of the book further examples of the importance of tree-time, which we feel is one of the key ways of understanding how trees make places, along with their formidability, materiality and variegation in both physical and imaginative terms, as we have so far considered.

–5–

Ethics

> Through exclusively social contracts, we have abandoned the bond that connected us to the world . . . What language do the things of the world speak that we might come to an understanding of them contractually? . . . In fact the Earth speaks to us in terms of forces, bonds and interactions . . . each of the partners in symbiosis thus owes . . . life to the other, on pain of death.
>
> (Serres, 1995, cited by Whatmore, 1999: 26)

> This requires an act of considerable moral imagination for those raised in the heart of the monster, the Western dualism of moral insiders and outsiders.
>
> (Cheney, 1999: 144)

> It was a beech, standing somewhat isolated, and still leafless in quite early spring. Suddenly I was aware of its skyward-reaching arms and upturned fingertips, as if some living life force (or electricity) was streaming through them into the spaces of the Heaven, and of its roots plunged in the earth and drawing the same energies from below. The day was quite still and there was no movement in the branches, but in that moment the tree was no longer a separate or separable organism, but a vast being ramifying far into space, sharing and uniting the life of earth and sky, and full of a most amazing activity.
>
> (Carpenter, 1905, cited by Mabey, 1997: 88)

> The sight of a tree in pain is not a pretty one.
>
> (Greer, 2000)

In this chapter we turn to the subject of ethics, and in particular we trace the interconnections between ethics, agency and place as found in the nature of trees. We regard the development of an ethical dimension to arbori-culture to be important in many respects. To a significant degree the exclusion of nature from the 'moral community' of modernity has been based on the view of nature being devoid of meaningful agency. We would argue that the legacies of this 'ethical exclusion' can be seen in the global environmental difficulties faced in the world today, difficulties which are both practical and moral in nature. The connections here are straightforward. If agency is deemed to be restricted to human agency, then a 'moral community' develops in which human concerns are dominant. Any relationships between the human and the non-human are overlain by an assumption of the moral dominance of the human. And as it is humans who presume control over environmental decision-making, the moral community both excludes and impinges upon non-human beings in nature. In Chapter 3 we discussed a view of agency as a relational process, weaving humans and non-humans together in ways which render problematic any exclusion of non-human agency. Such a view disturbs the human-centred moral community, and raises very significant ethical questions about human–non-human interactions.

These questions occur on very different scales. On the one hand they are starkly evident in discussions of what many people regard as a global environmental crisis; on the other, they are just as significant in more localized issues, focusing for example on protecting trees from logging, and from being sacrificed at the altar of new roads or other developments. In these local instances, the fate of trees, individually and collectively, becomes very visible and raises concomitant ethical and emotional issues. The trees often serve to personify deeper and more complex questions about relationships between humans and nature in general, and the beings of nature in particular. Each of the tree-places discussed in Part II of this book illustrates in a different way the visibility of local trees, and the ethical questions which result. These discussions reaffirm that generalized ethical considerations are worked out in the dynamic complexities of particular places. The relationship between place and ethics is therefore a crucial nexus of nature–society relations.

In this chapter, then, we pose some formidable questions. How can shifting ideas of agency change ideas of ethical relations? How can this apply when considering the agency of trees, and trees in place? Trees are, as we have shown, beings of great significance in all manner of relational processes, extending from the local to global processes which co-constitute the world as we know it. Can we afford, therefore, to exclude trees from some form of ethical consideration? In this respect we can widen the question by taking trees to be representative of all 'nature' now excluded from the ethical realm.

These ethical considerations are formidable, and should not be approached lightly or over-ambitiously. Nevertheless, there is now a growing corpus of thought which suggests that a radical expansion of ethical imagination is required in order to take full account of nature-society relations in a more equitable, and less dangerous, manner. Drawing on this body of work, we argue for a higher level of 'ethical mindfulness' as a context against which to understand human-non-human encounters. A generalized form of ethical precautionary principle can be the starting point for more context-specific forms of neo-Aristotelian ethics (Thrift, 1996a) which are able to deal more effectively with particular encounters between embodied beings in specific time-space settings.

In effect then, our argument is about ethical imagination. It is about how an expanded ethical imagination is needed to form the nature–society contract called for by Serres (see at head of this chapter) and to heal the destructive breach between the human and the non-human. It seems clear that there is some form of environmental crisis unfolding on a planetary scale. The recent media focus on issues of global warming, for example, shows that awareness of environmental issues is finally moving beyond 'environmentalists' to the wider domains of public awareness and politics. Trees are, of course, bound into the very centre of this recent debate. The *Observer* newspaper (26 November 2000), in its recent coverage of the environmental crisis, had a picture of some pine trees standing tall against the sky with the accompanying headline 'Can these trees really save the world?' – a reference to the American proposal to offset continuing carbon dioxide emissions by the development of 'carbon sink' tree plantations.

In this chapter, we shall consider how the exclusion of nature from ethical systems is closely bound up with the exclusion of nature from ideas of agency, and we shall discuss the ethical implications of considering non-humans as being capable of at least certain and significant forms of agency. Worldviews which emphasize agency as deeply and irredeemably relational would seem to undermine the drawing of a tight ethical boundary around humanity. Considering trees as vital active beings embedded in creative relational networks seems to reinforce this undermining, and opens out wider questions about other embodied beings in nature.

Clearly, a leap of ethical imagination is required to consider trees as morally relevant. This is why it is necessary to invoke (after Cheney, 1999) 'an ethical mindfulness' in relation to trees and the wider range of beings in nature, so as to establish a form of ethical precautionary principle. This suggestion echoes the notion that nature has 'intrinsic value'; an idea which reverberates through radical environmentalism and which perhaps has been, and is, present in other non-Western traditions of human-nature relations. Attributing intrinsic value to the beings of nature challenges to a significant extent the notion of an ethical hierarchy in which humans are clearly at the top, and some sentient creatures occupy a secondary level, below which an ethical void opens out into which most of 'nature' falls. Relational views of agency challenge this 'ethical cut-off point' within such a hierarchy, pointing instead to a relational ethics which sees all nature–society encounters as bearing an ethical 'freight' (Jones, 2000).

While the establishment of an ethical mindfulness based on broad ethical precautionary principles seems to be an important theoretical advance, there remains an important issue about how to translate these ethical (re)imaginings from abstract arenas into day-to-day operations in the relational world. To address this question we turn to practical ideas from relational ethics and neo-Aristotelian ethics (Thrift, 1996a: 36), in which all encounters and their ethical shadowing have to be grounded in particular space–time contexts. In this context, we return to the notion of dwelling/place as the locus in which encounters are at work and where the 'ethical mindfulness' we call for has to be critically and reflexively operationalized. This then brings us back to place, and fuller consideration both of trees in particular places and of the idea of ethics as process *in* these places.

Environmental Problems

> All radical environmentalists would agree that humanity needs a new self-understanding that will eliminate humanity–nature dualism as well as the kind of anthropocentrism that justifies the heedless exploitation of nature. (Zimmerman, 1993: 264)

The idea of a global environmental crisis is now so familiar that there is almost a condition of environmental passion fatigue at work in the popular consciousness. Although the work of pressure groups such as Greenpeace continues to give environmental issues sporadic high-profile presence in news media, and the place-based resistance of environmental activists offers proof of a sustained environmental politics, much of the world seems to face these issues with a gloomy or even uncaring resignation – it is, as Light and Katz (1996: 1) say, 'a fact of experience'. The continuing environmental crisis is, however, reflected in the big issues of global warming and biodiversity loss, and it is also played out at the local everyday level of the destruction of habitat, landscape, the loss of certain forms of non-human life and the loss of places. Pepper (1986) has shown that initial assumptions that the exposure of environmental problems throughout the 1960s and 1970s would lead to a transformation of society, or at least a concerted effort to address particular issues, have had to be abandoned. At one level, humankind in the West have absorbed the basic message of environmental crisis, and have adjusted to it, often seemingly by ignoring the crisis and hoping that it will go away. At another level, it can be argued that Western humankind have yet to grasp with sufficient urgency the idea that their world is fragile, finite and in serious danger. Most of our collective spiritual, ethical, ideological, cultural, political and economic systems have evolved throughout a history where the planetary nature and 'her' teeming populations have seemed vast, even limitless. Now environmental science and other knowledges tell us that this is not so. However, thus far, collective efforts to address the environmental crisis has been at best fragmented and faltering, and at worst a process of fudge and denial (Doyle and McEachern, 1998; Redclift, 1993).

Despite evidence of growing environmental dysfunction and the pressing efforts of the environmental lobby, Doyle and McEachern (1998: 54) still find it necessary to say that

> so far no government has tried seriously to take environmental concern into the process of policy making . . . mostly whatever has been done has been done to accommodate rising levels of environmental concern and to protect the demands of economic development and economic growth. [This has] varied from the cosmetic to opportunist.

As Naess (1997: 68) suggests, 'extensive free markets and a development towards an "enterprise culture" create conditions favourable to a deepening of ecological unsustainability'. These conditions of exacerbating environmental crisis give rise to profound concern, given the central place of capitalist functions in modern society (see Johnston, 1996). However, the environmental crisis still receives little mainstream political and media focus. The clashes at the World Trade Organization meeting in Seattle in 1999 put down a marker of a potential frontline between environmental sensibilities and the drive of the globalizing industrial logic. But the general sense of collective denial (apart from a dissenting minority) continues within modern industrial society. The questions and challenges which need to be faced are also applicable to the ordinary everyday environments – the places and landscapes which we encounter daily. The environment is not somewhere else, it is what is around us now; the air, the soil, the water, the weather, the trees. There is, therefore, a significant need to translate generalized environmental concern into concern for particular places and particular beings of nature, such as trees.

Material Crisis – Ethical Crisis

The environmental crisis is both material, in terms of 'ecological sustainability', and ethical, in that irrespective of the consequences for humankind, the ongoing destruction of nature inherent in processes of 'development' is somehow wrong. Such a statement is not new, but recognizing the evil has not lead to its eradication. In large measure, this is because nature has been excluded from the moral community on which normative ethical formulations have generally been based. The material crisis cannot be effectively addressed unless the ethical crisis is also addressed; they are inextricably interconnected.

As Buell (1995: 2) puts it,

> If as environmental philosophers contend, western metaphysics and ethics need revision before we can address today's environmental problems, then environmental crisis involves a crisis of the imagination the amelioration of which depends on finding better ways of imagining nature and humanity's relation to it.

In material terms, the focus is on anthropocentric, technocentric environmentalism (Jordan and O'Riordan, 1999) and the key issues relating to ecological and environmental integrity. Are our life-support systems breaking down? If so, then action clearly needs to be taken. And here we emphasize that the fate of trees is deeply bound up in this kind of environmentalism. The clearing of the rainforests has been one of the most persistent issues of global environmental concern. Trees help maintain our atmosphere in a benign state; they conserve fragile soils, prevent flooding, protect against desertification and provide habitat to a vast biodiversity in which many potential benefits to humanity are still hidden.

The ethical crisis, which along with the material crisis is the focus of ecologism (Dobson, 1995; Smith, 1998), is about the right or wrong of what we are doing to others (humans and non-humans), going beyond questions of long-term material sustainability to interrogate the intrinsic value or rights of nature. Trees are also present in this form of environmentalism, but more problematically. Ethical relationships in the context of trees and other non-sentient natural life-forms *are* acknowledged in the philosophical positionings of deep ecology, some ecofeminist positions, and other ecocentric and biocentric thinking. However, the ethical dimensions of the environmental crisis often go unrecognized within popular environmental consciousness. O'Riordan (1989) puts popular support for these kinds of idea at 0–2 per cent of the population. The idea of considering trees ethically soon encounters the conceptual and practical limits of current ethical discourses and practices. As Stone (1972) observes, 'the fact is, that each time there is a movement to confer rights onto some new "entity" the proposal is bound to sound odd or frightening or laughable' (in Smith, 1999: 211). Despite the risk of fright or humour, many radical ecologists feel that only by addressing the ethical crisis will the material crisis be dealt with, and that even if the techno-optimists are correct and the material crisis can be averted this would still not be acceptable. This is a key question in regard to current notions of Sustainable Development. It can be argued that currently dominant formations of Sustainable Development – particularly 'treadmill' and 'weak' forms of sustainability (Baker et al. 1997) – by building on current formations of society without significantly shifting ethical positions, are attempting to work towards creating a position of *sustainable unethical relations*.

Our assumption is that a shift towards ameliorating the ethical crisis is a key element of solving the material crisis, and represents an urgent task in itself. The ethical and material strands are so intricately bound together that they cannot be treated separately. We need new science, new technologies, new social, political, economic and policy formations, but we also need shifts in our basic understandings of humankind and of nature, and shifts in our moral relationships with nature. It is these understandings which will help drag everyday practices of society into new formations. As Regan (1998: 822) states, 'people must change their beliefs before they change their habits', and as Midgley (1996: 2) emphasizes – 'When things go badly . . . We must then somehow readjust our underlying concepts; we must shift the set of assumptions that we are brought up with'.

Ethics and Nature

Having argued that the environmental crisis is at least in part an ethical crisis, we want to proceed by exploring how nature has been excluded from the moral community, and how a more relational form of ethics is required. Before doing so, however, it is important to map out the mutual territories occupied by nature and ethics in order to trace the different interconnections which have occurred. Here, we turn to an excellent summary by Angelika Krebs (1999), who lists a number of different potential answers to the question of who or what belongs to the moral 'universe' or 'community':

1. only myself (egoism)
2. myself, my family, and friends (small group egoism)
3. all people of my class (classism)
4. all citizens of my country (nationalism)
5. all people of my race (racism)
6. all people of my sex (sexism)
7. all living human beings (universalism of the present)
8. all living human beings and those of the past (universalism including the past)
9. all living human beings and those of the future (universalism including the future)
10. all sentient beings (pathocentrism or sentientism)
11. all living beings (biocentrism)
12. all of nature (radical physiocentrism, ecocentrism, radical ecologism, deep ecology, holism). (19–20)

On the basis of this list she poses key questions about the scope for an ethics of nature. Should we be moving from the current norm, that is the universalism of the present (7), to take account of the needs of future generations (9)? Should we include sentient animals, plants or nature more generally (10, 11, and 12) in the moral universe? If so, then a move is required from anthropocentric ethical terrain to a more physiocentric position. Such a move can be conducted in different ways. For example, the human concept of 'moral respect' can be extended to nature. Thus nature or certain parts of nature might be regarded as having a well-being (the pathocentric argument); nature, or parts of nature might be seen as pursuing certain projects or ends, and therefore might be regarded as having an agency good (the teleological argument); or the life-forms of nature might be regarded as having a moral right to life (the reverence for life argument).

Clearly, these extensions of the human moral perspective are likely to take anthropocentric values and then add in different bits and pieces of nature. As Krebs (1999: 22) points out:

> much of nature, stones and mountains for example, does not have a good in the relevant sense. Stones and mountains do not care for health, shelter, emotional contact, autonomy, education and so on. They do not care for anything. They do not have a subjective good. The extensionist strategy will, for certain, not reach them since human moral respect is respect for the subjective good life of all others.

Thus pathocentric arguments can be used to justify moral respect for sentient animals, while teleological arguments seem to justify moral respect for certain higher animals but not for lower animals, plants and the other life-forms, ecosystems and materials of nature. The result of these arguments is that extension of the ethical community is restricted to sentient and teleological animals. An alternative move is to search for values which are not centred on the human value perspective; values which might be absolute (Birnbacher, 1987), impersonal (Frankena, 1979) or detached (Routley and Routley, 1980). Such physiocentric ideas are very difficult to translate from imaginative concepts to practical realities. Moderate physiocentrism is a crucial component of a new ethical terrain for nature. However, epistemologically it is inevitable that ethical perspectives will remain anthropocentric. It is likely therefore that the advance from solely anthropocentric positions will involve some kind of intermediate terrain in which

> the whole range of human attitudes and feelings toward nature, including reverence for the sacredness of nature, the non-instrumental attitude characteristic of the aesthetic contemplation of nature, and the disgust for the maltreatment of animals, can be made sense of and justified. (Krebs, 1999: 137)

We would add that such intermediate ideas might also extend to disgust for the maltreatment of trees.

Using Krebs's framework as a yardstick, it can be argued that relatively little progress has been made in moving away from anthropomorphic universalism. Indeed, much of the debate surrounding the environmental crisis remains at the level of bemoaning the exclusion of 'nature' from moral communities, and arguing for ideas of relational agency to be included in ethical debates. It is to these issues that we now turn.

The Exclusion of Nature from 'the Moral Community'

Rolston (1999: 109) notes that a common assumption persists that 'ethics is for people. People are both the subject and the object of ethics, in the sense that only humans are deliberative moral agents and also that humans have obligations only to other humans'. Plumwood (1999: 69) adds that 'we have tended to assume that ethics and values are exclusively concerned with and derived from the human sphere'. Such pronouncements are common currency in much environmental thinking, and environmental philosophy has been addressing precisely this problem, its causes and possible solutions. Shiva (1988), for example, has emphasized how new forms of knowledge which emerged within 'the scientific revolution in Europe' transformed views of nature and in doing so 'removed all ethical and cognitive constraints against its violation and exploitation' (xv). Moreover, Midgley (1983) – although warning that the history of Enlightenment's relationship with nature is nuanced and complex – agrees that in the end the exclusion of animals (and, we add, nature more generally) from the central contractual forms of morality means that they and others outside of this centre can 'glide unnoticed into the shadows and be forgotten' (47). It is clear that much of ethical orthodoxy treats animals as things, which do not need to be closely interconnected with the instincts and practices of justice, charity or religion (Clark, 1977). Such views are not rare exceptions, but rather the topography of orthodox ethical positioning for animals and 'sub-animal' life forms. Animals and other nature thus become excluded from the ethical sphere because the process of ethical universalization somehow automatically stops at the boundaries of the human community (Singer, 1993).

Although nature has been excluded in this way from the ethical arena, it has in other discursive arenas – particularly that of 'resources' – taken a central position in the human imagination. It is this disjuncture of inclusion and exclusion when grounded through the machinations of developing social, economic and technological systems which has rendered modern human–nature relations so problematic. Ecologism's general acknowledgement and pursuit of the notion of the 'intrinsic value' of nature is an attempt to redefine the moral community so that nature is (once again) included rather than excluded. Such attempts can be founded on an appreciation of the non-human agency of nature (Chapter 3), since the common exclusion of nature from the realm of ethics is closely related to the equally common exclusion of nature from considerations of agency. These two matters are closely bound together. As McPhail and Ward (1988) suggest, '[M]orality implies (without, it seems, any hesitation) a certain conception of agency' (xiii).

Conceptualizations of nature as passive, separate from and subordinate to human society have underpinned the enlightenment and modernity. These concepts resonate in extant formations of ethical and scientific thinking. They were formed at a time of certain distinct understandings of the world, and particularly the human position in that world. Since then developing theories of evolution, ecology, cosmology, genetics, along with a growing awareness of the consciousness and emotional lives of 'higher animals', and of the finitude of nature, have all radically challenged our view of humans, their position in the world, and human–nature relations. There remains a lag, a chronic disjuncture, between these new relational and interconnecting views of the world, and the old ethical and scientific formations which are built on dualistic hierarchical views which predate them. Kropotkin (1992), although thinking in a somewhat different way, presaged this vital point when he stated that Darwin's work in particular heralded a new era in philosophical and ethical thought.

Ethical Imagination

Our argument is that we need to use these new views of the world to help transform ethical imaginations. A critical requirement is that the ethical community be extended from its current narrow anthropocentric basis to a form where nature is somehow incorporated. We need to reconstruct our views of nature and ourselves: there is no easy solution, no 'magic bullet', but seeing the world as active and relational does challenge established ethical formations both in terms of the fixed narrow boundaries of the ethical community and in terms of the extent to which the community should rest on notions of sharply individual autonomous (human) agents.

Any such change will be a long complex process. Rosalind Williams (1992: 2) evocatively suggests that the shift from hunter-gather societies with their 'religions, myths, and *moral conceptions*' to agricultural societies would have taken thousands of years of adjustment. With the current onset of a 'post-natural' era of the world (Braun and Castree, 1998), we may be entering an equally long and traumatic period of 'cultural mourning and upheaval'. The incorporation of non-human nature into new ethical cultures will be one of the greatest challenges during this upheaval. In this context, Marshall (1992) emphasizes Leopold's suggestion that 'it might take 2,000 years to evolve a code of decency for "man-to-land contact"'. Such a time frame represents a source of despair for those radical ecologists who feel that 'time is running out', but as Weston (1999a: 51) points out, the world is too mysterious, undiscovered, dynamic, alive, to ever say it is 'too late'. Ideas have to come first, be they academic, scientific, or new popular practices. The better characteristics of 'advanced' human societies – notions of freedom, democracy, human rights, which are embedded, albeit inadequately and sometimes unthinkingly in everyday human lives – were ideas which had to be imagined and fought for.

What might happen to ethical imaginations in the context of understandings of the world as relational when non-humans are 'given their due', as Thrift (1996a) puts it, in terms of agency? As we discussed in Chapter 3 there is now a range of significant theoretical positions which, for different but related reasons, are concerning themselves with issues of *non-human agency*. Out of these positions are emerging lines of thought which insist that we work toward new forms of ethics which respond to the relationality of the world and which entail radical shifts from current ethical patterns. Conley (1997), drawing on Serres's idea of 'natural contact', argues that these new forms of ethics will entail 'a politics of nature so revolutionary that it would stand to reposition the relation of the human with other organisms' (74). Such a change would 'horizontalize (or democratize, but to a radically different degree than that which is connoted to by the term) the position that 'man' holds in the overall configuration' (74).

Guattari (1989) asks 'how do we deterritorialize and reterritorialize ourselves' into new relational formations? The answer involves a 'rethinking of our values and implies a new ethos, habitus and existential mutation affecting the world at large' (in Conley, 1997: 94). These post-structural views on human environmental relations have in effect led to calls for new ethical formations which are as radical as those made from proponents of deep ecology and other 'deep green' positions. All, in some form, are calling for relational ethics, which moves from a solely human realm to viewing the human in relational formations with creative nature.

Relational Ethics

At present it is quite easy to sketch, very broadly, a pattern of ethical hierarchy in which humanity rests easily at the top. It is clear that our ethical gaze generally cuts off pretty soon after the human level, although the ethical status of certain animals is the bitter front line of animal rights disputes. Below that, ethical status diminishes to nothingness. Accordingly, the manner in which we respond to nature – both individually and institutionally – reflects an ethical hierarchy which is a ghost of 'the great chain of being' (Pepper, 1996) – a medieval cosmology in which God comes first, then the heavenly host, then humans, then large sentient animals, then other animals, then maybe fish, reptiles, insects, and so on down to the plant world and beyond. The ethical shadow of this hierarchy may not be straightforward (spectacular flora such as trees may be more valued than unspectacular fauna) but the relative importance of non-human natures therein is deeply ingrained in the ways in which modern societies work. Changing this hierarchy with its chronic anthropocentric weighting, in some way, is the fundamental goal pursued by radical environmentalists in their ideas of relational ethics.

For example, Whatmore's (1997) assessment of the potential for building a form of *relational ethics* which does extend beyond the human realm, suggests that the relational perspective might

> breach the impasse of individual ethics at a number of key points . . . it releases 'nature' and nonhuman beings from their relegation to the status of objects with no ethical standing in the pursuit of individual self-interest, *without* resorting to the extension of this liberal conception of ethical agency to other animals. (47, original emphasis)

In her analysis, Whatmore turns to the notions of relationality and embodiment in order to establish a canon of relational ethics which extends 'the body politic beyond the human subject', 'displaces the fixed and bounded contours of ethical community' (50) and grounds cognitive processes and rationalities, and ethical communities, within the embodied relational fabrics of the world.

This building of a relational ethic is significant. Ethical formations must correspond to relational formations which perform the world. If the agency which drives this creative outpouring of being is relational, then this agency should interconnect with a corresponding ethical trace. Such interconnections challenge both the tightly drawn anthropocentric ethical community and the notion of ethical hierarchy. They also challenge the notion of an amoral nature which is 'red in tooth and claw'. The complex relationalities of nature, which make life possible, even up to the level of cosmic systems, have to be considered moral/ethical structures. The ecologies and relationalities of nature are creative forces which are implicated in the sustaining of life, and therefore deserve to be considered as a good and a right, replete with appropriate ethical resonance. The relationship between prey and predator is creative in the sense of species evolution, even if, when caught on film, the destruction of one individual by another seems to be an example of cruel amoral nature. This view of nature as a harsh amoral place is bound up with its exclusion from the ethical realm and serves as a justification for its exploitation and subordination to the 'moral' human realm.

'Ethical Mindfulness': Establishing an Ethical Precautionary Principle

Our argument, therefore, is for what might be called 'an ethical precautionary principle'. We suggest that all the encounters between humans and non-humans that are associated with performing the world should be regarded as having an ethical dimension (Jones, 2000). For example, we considered in Chapter 3 how trees as a collective carry out key creative processes in the ongoing relational construction of our world, and how trees as individuals also perform certain forms of agency and purposiveness which challenge any casual dismissal of them in ethical terms. It is therefore essential to deploy an ethical precautionary principle when dealing with trees, as with other life forms in nature. Such a principle cannot be a prescriptive determination of the ethical stance which is appropriate in specific situations. Rather it is an acknowledgement of the ethical resonances of relational agency between humans and non-humans, and a continual reminder that caution and reflection should replace any innate assumption that most non-human life forms do not appear on the ethical map. This means in more practical terms that human society and its ongoing development needs to tread much more cautiously and 'lightly' on the earth.

Common Ground has, in the past, deployed the slogan 'every tree counts', encapsulating the idea that the importance of trees collectively is articulated through the being of actual individuals. Their call is for a careful consideration of every tree, even ordinary trees, in human–tree encounters. One of the base conclusions is that felling should be a last resort in circumstances where trees are in question. Clearly, such a yardstick is not feasible where felling is part of ongoing commercial management cycles. In these instances, the call would be to plant new trees to replace those fallen, in order that the collective presences of trees and the roles they play (e.g. as habitat) be sustained. So this can be a controversial issue as, say, old-growth forest with its ancient trees and biodiversity is replaced by new planting.

Trees which are playing important roles (maybe an ecologically rich woodland or trees which are prominent in a landscape) are given strong individual and collective value and even protected because of these roles, while other trees, which play less conspicuous roles (such as those in new-growth commercial plantations), are valued less as individuals and are considered as fellable so long as they are replaced. Clearly then, an ethical approach to trees does not mean that they should never be cut down, or used in other ways. The relational processes of the world mean that species and beings interact. Such encounters are the fabric of the being of the world, and they cannot be seen as necessarily 'wrong'. Ethical practice cannot revolve simply around the notion 'let beings be' (see Zimmerman, 1993) or partially withdrawing contact from nature (for example in the preservation of 'wilderness') – both of which are still powerful and problematic notions in some environmental thinking (Cronon, 1996).

Instead, trees should be recognized as necessarily embedded in dynamic formations, the relational nature of which has clear ethical resonance. With the position of power assumed by humans in these relational formulations, *the ethical issue revolves around questions of on what basis and in which ways is this powerful participation deployed* (Naess, 1973). Ethical practice, then, is about how we live in particular connection with others against this background of relational ethical resonance. If ethical practice is to be informed, ethical imaginations will need to be expanded. In practice this entails taking more seriously the non-human others (in our discussion, trees) with which we are bound together relationally. This process of 'taking seriously' may be articulated through spirituality, love, compassion, respect, justice or law, but somehow needs to be embedded in everyday encounters and policy and management processes.

It still seems quite difficult to give practical expression to ethical relationships with individual trees, although there are some helpful indicators. Packenham (1997), in his *Meetings with Remarkable Trees* discusses the trees which he considers as individuals 'with a strong personality' (6). Here, and much more deliberately in the work of Kaza (1993), there is a hint of or attempt to create an I/

thou relationship rather an I/it relationship. This formulation of I/thou ethical encounters by Buber (1937) is illustrated in relation to a tree. Buber suggests that a tree can be known in many ways, for example as image, as commodity, as biology. The tree remains an object but

> it can come about, if I have both will and grace, that in considering the tree I become bound up in relation to it. The tree is no longer *It*. The tree is no impression, no play of my imagination, no value depending on my mood; but is bodied over against me as has to do with me, as I with it – only in a different way. Let no attempt be made to sap the strength from the meaning of relation: relation is mutual. The tree will have a consciousness, then similar to our own? Of that I have no experience. I encounter no soul or dryad of the tree, *but the tree itself.* (7–8, our emphasis)

The relationship with a tree described by Buber is a relationship with *a meaningful other in its own terms*. This applies not only to the remarkable beautiful, ancient, huge trees that Packenham – and to a lesser degree, Kaza – considers, but also to all the 'ordinary' trees which are present in all manner of landscapes and situations. For example Merrick's (1997) account of the *Battle of the Trees* (which charts the protests and direct actions against the building of the bypass at Newbury in Britain), and other accounts of tree protests in Britain and in the United States, such as the tree-occupation by Julia Hill (Franklin, 1999), make it clear not only that such protests represent the 'front line' of a battle about institutional destruction of 'nature', the countryside, or local and global deforestation, but also that they relate to particular (often 'ordinary') trees as ethically relevant individual beings, which were forced into the human (ethical) imagination by the threat of their destruction. Such a recognition of trees as an ethical other does have precedent in transcendentalist thinking. Buell (1995: 209) shows how Thoreau 'upbraids himself' for damaging a chestnut tree by throwing rocks at it to dislodge fruit, and a neighbour for 'the felling of his hackberry trees'.

Kaza's attempt to relate to trees as 'Other', and to establish 'human-tree conversations' is an example of Cheney's (1999) notion of 'conversation' between humans and the world, which he argues should be the basis of knowledge (rather than knowledge that emerges from 'a relationship between an active, knowing subject and a passive, known object'). Such conversations allow a form of knowing 'where the earth itself is an active partner' which may help us 'to prepare ourselves ethically and spiritually for the reception of knowledge' (142–3). There is thus a need for 'ethical mindfulness', as Cheney puts it (145), to replace the current ethical void in which human–tree encounters are planned and practised. This suggestion can be seen as analogous to Schweitzer's Christian idea of 'Reverence for life', which recognized the 'will-to-live' in all living things, as well as the Buddhist concept of compassion, or the Hindu principle of Ahimsa (Marshall,

1992). An extreme version of this position would bring an ethical dimension to *all* encounters, even to the non-animate world. As Schweitzer suggests, 'The moral person shatters no ice crystal that sparkles in the sun, tears no leaf from its tree, breaks off no flower, and is careful not to crush any insect as he walks' (Marshall, 1992: 350). Applications of such an ethical mindfulness will inevitably vary, and therein may lie a weakness drawn from relativism, as well as a strength in terms of flexible applications to different situations. Nevertheless, it is possible to envisage some form of ethical mindfulness becoming an integral element in the formation of human–non-human encounters, being part, for example, of the calculation of risk, the application of precautionary principles, or even the formalized process of environmental decision-making systems such as Environmental Impact Assessments.

Grounded Relational Ethics

We also suggest that notions of relational ethics need to be grounded. Flowing networks of agency are usually enacted in the particularities of existence in places (Chapter 2). It must therefore be possible for any general argument about an ethics which reflects relational agency to be grounded in these particularities of place. The nature and role of place-particularities are discussed in Guattari's ideas of 'existential territory'. As Conley (1997: 94) suggests,

> Beings, neither quite autonomous nor endowed with an immutable foundation, assembling for affective reasons on a common *Grund*, an existential territory in movement and transformation, open onto becoming and process. A series of assemblages between humans, animals, plants, cosmos, and machines constitutes an open whole. Assemblages are complex and differential, rather than binary. Territory is a physical *and* mental space that allows for movement between and toward subjects. No moment of sublation or resolution is possible where there prevails an infinity of modes of becoming with moment of intensity, plateaus, thresholds and points of bifurcation. [original emphasis]

We might not concur with the absolute desire for and belief in constant volatility implied here, but the idea of existential territory does convey the rich, swirling, ongoing and particular mixing which performs place in the way we have considered. Here is where ecology can thrive, so here is where ethics has to be articulated.

More specifically, this grounding of relational ethics needs to be effected in (at least) three fundamental ways. First, we need an 'ethical mindfulness' for the particular embodied characteristics of the actants in the relational agencies concerned. For example, it would seem clear that we need a particular form of ethical mindfulness for beings who are sentient, and for those who can feel pain. However, relationships between humans and trees are characterized by an essential otherness of being. Trees live and reproduce in ways different to ours: they are differently embodied, and they die differently to us (Rival, 1998b). Some trees can be cut down to the root and grow again. Indeed, trees which are regularly coppiced in green wood systems can live much longer than their 'natural' counter-parts. We cannot, therefore, simply transpose notions of inter-human relations, or even human–animal relations, to human–tree relations. As a consequence, we need to work out formations of ethical practice which are sensitive to the particular embodiment and practices of trees and the particular relational practices between them and us.

The second grounding is in the particularities of the relational context in which encounters occur. In the ongoing relational processes which sustain and (re)construct the world, the ethical question 'how to act' needs to be constantly asked, and outcomes will depend on the context of the encounter. For example Marshall (1992) reflects Schweitzer's view that it was ethical for a farmer to mow a field of meadow flowers in the process of making hay, but unethical for the same farmer to casually swish the head of one flower with a stick as he walked home. Holmes Rolston III (1999) tells a tree story with a similar (ethical) resonance. The giant sequoia in the Yosemite National Park, which became world famous because it had a road 'tunnel' cut through it in the 1880s, blew down in a winter snowstorm in 1968. When it was suggested that a replacement tunnel be cut in another tree, the rangers refused because there was a 'conviction [that] using trees for serious human needs can be justified; a silly enjoying of prime sequoias cannot. It perverts the trees' (120). In other words one constantly has to judge whether the proposed encounter with trees is justifiable in the contexts of the relational unfolding of the world and its attendant ethical mindfulness. As Whatmore (1997) recognizes, constructing new forms of ethical community will involve an acknowledgement of the specific embodiment and practice of ethical communities. In turn, ethical communities will therefore be founded on the distinction of 'an embodied and practically engaged self . . . from what human beings *do* in the world . . . so as to rediscover the totality of [her/his] practical bonds with others' (43, citing Kruks, 1995).

The search for new ethical communities is part of a broader move away from narrow, universal, abstract ethics toward a position where ethical consideration follows the embodied relational processes of the world. In this way the ethics of encounter is foregrounded rather than lost within broad universalized formulae, and chimes with forms of neo-Aristotelian ethics as propounded by Thrift (1996a), which are 'an active and practical form of ethics founded in an evaluative sensibility arising from the concrete experience of specific situations'. Grange (1997) has identified some of the key characteristics of this form of ethics. In particular, he focuses on a form of 'practical skill', which considers both means and ends. It lays no claim to 'precise formulation' or 'ethical formula'. Ethics is seen more as a process of living in the world – 'a quasi-habitual prudential reaction to the often conflicting demands of life is exactly what the serious person serious about the good life must learn to cultivate'. This process entails 'gaining a training in acquired wisdom [which] comes through experience and practice' (166–7). Thus ethics builds out of being in the world, rather than trying to impose some abstracted ideal upon it.

The third grounding of relational ethics relates to the geographic spaces and places where encounters occur. There are a number of theoretical initiatives which can be seen as in some way working towards some form of placed and materially grounded ethics. One such is Lynn's (1998a/b) deployment of what he terms 'geoethics', which, he argues, is needed because 'all human activity, including moral conflict, occurs at sites embedded in situations, making geographic context a constitutive element of all ethical problems' (1998a: 283). The significance of geoethics is in contradistinction to the rather bland universaliszed 'ideal typologies' of biocentrism and ecocentrism which are 'too rigid to adequately understand our earth' (Lynn, 1998b: 231). Another example is Proctor's (1998) call for an extended engagement between geography and ethics, and in particular environmental ethics, not least through notions of place and space. We broadly concur with these developments and use them as a basis for our focus on notions of place, home, and dwelling. These notions, which resonate very strongly in extant lay and popular knowledges and practices, seem to provide promising and familiar contexts in which to embed and articulate ethical mindfulness.

'The unending task of struggling to live rightly in the world'

Even accepting the necessity for ethical mindfulness, we still must, as Cronon (1996: 90) says, 'get on with the unending task of struggling to live rightly in the world' , and this is why relational notions of ethics have to be grounded in the particularities of encounters. Elsewhere, Jones (2000) has argued that an adapted Levinasian approach can be used to suggest that all human–non-human encounters are ethically charged in some way, and that all the myriad encounters between humans and non-humans that take place in all the differing material/imagined spaces of the world have an ethical freight, even if this is not recognized in a normative ethical gaze. In other words all encounters with trees and nature have an ethical resonance, but the exact formulation of that resonance is always, to an extent, open. Bauman's (1993) 'postmodern ethics' or Rorty's pragmatic 'ethics' demonstrate that there are no certain fixed answers to this openness, but rather that an ongoing open dialogue is needed about how to deal with 'the messiness of the human predicament' and all the 'ambiguity, risk, danger and error' which will be involved with this (Bauman, 1993: 245).

One facet of such a dialogue is the familiarities and belongings associated with 'home' places. Ehrenfeld (1992), for example, describes how he became a conservationist 'gradually, as a result of getting to know a place worth saving' (31). Place, then, reflects one key route towards an environmental sensitivity which challenges the human/nature divide, because as the work of Common Ground shows, it is the unique milieu of cultural and natural presences in a place which is significant. This being so, the 'players' in that unfolding milieu must be given their due, and it is in this notion of place where relational ethics finds a home. This espousal of place as a territory for grounded ethics should, however, be subject to the proviso that notions of place as fixedly bounded and distinct from the global are problematic, and some forms of placed-based environmentalism can therefore be questionable.

In further support for the grounded nature of places Adams (1996) turns to notions of place in his quest for effective nature conservation in Britain, arguing that 'knowing nature in its turn demands a particular commitment to *place*' (154, original emphasis). In this context, he reprises Berg and Dasmann's (1978) argument of 'reinhabitation':

> Becoming native to a place through becoming aware of the particular ecological relations that operate within and around it . . . means understanding activities and evolving social behaviour that will enrich the life of that place, restore its life-support systems, and establish an ecologically and socially sustainable pattern of existence within it. (Adams, 1996: 155)

In one sense, there is a problematic bio-regionalist ring to these ideas, which is resonant in some American environmental literature. The notion of place in these perspectives is too fixed and Euclidean, and the notions of nature and community equally so. But Adams recognizes that in 'reinhabitation', the aim of harnessing people's ideas of and feelings for place to the environmental cause is worthwhile. 'People do recognise place, and the challenge of "living in place" is of considerable relevance' (155). Equally Buell (1995) explores the possibilities of place for moving toward more ecocentric forms of human–nature relations. He points out that place *has* been a central theme, particularly in much American environmental writing by the likes of Thoreau, Lopez, Snyder, Wilson and Berry, and that this sense of place does not necessarily mean benign environmental attitudes. Nevertheless, place might hold out more hope in this respect than 'atopia or diaspora' (235).

We feel it is important to develop this idea within a fluid multi-scaled idea of place. Our home, our locality, our region, our country, our continent, our planet, even our cosmos are all places where we live. Each of these scales requires appropriate attention and care which will in some ways bind them together. For example, in terms of dwelling and place, the earth can be seen as 'a global dwelling' in which trees play a key role which has to be acknowledged and nurtured. The formation of British cultural identities can be seen as national/regional dwellings where trees again play a key role. English identity is palpably tied up with notions of trees, woodland, forest and the countryside (Cloke et al., 1996a; Schama, 1995). Yet tree cover in Britain has been reduced to around 7 per cent, the lowest in Europe. In reaction to this and other factors, there are various reforesting initiatives such as the National Forest and the Community Forests, and a whole plethora of NGOs dedicated in part or in whole to tree issues. If trees are so active – biologically, ecologically and culturally, generally bringing a whole range of creative capacities to a spectrum of relational constructions in our multi-scaled home places – how can they be disregarded as creative beings and discounted morally? The loss of tree presence on global and national scales points to some rupture where our understanding of trees and their multifaceted significances is not translated into (ethical) relations with them as embodied individuals.

While these larger-scale dwellings are extremely significant, there is also a need also to recognize the importance of the local scale, with particular places and landscapes with trees, because it is here where more *fine-grained* contextual, relational processes are at work, and where, perhaps, much of the hard work has to be done. Accordingly, Wendell Berry (1990) feels that the environmental question

> is not how to care for the planet, but how to care for each of the planet's millions of human and natural neighbourhoods, each of its millions of small pieces and parcels of land, each one of which is in some precious way different from all the others. (cited by Weston, 1999b: 194)

This is in essence a plea for a dwelling perspective; a plea for a recognition of the relational processes which sustain and (re)construct the world, and the need to embed our (environmental) ethics in those processes. We would add that the notion of dwelling itself needs to be adapted to a more multi-dimensional fluid and deep perspective which can take into account different interpenetrating scales of place and the networks which weave through and between them (see Cloke and Jones, 2001).

Ethics as Process in Place

So, we have arrived at the conclusion that ethics can be viewed as a process of trying to live rightly in the world. This process carries a cargo of ethical mindfulness which enshrines more general ethical aspirations and values, which themselves also reflect a process in that they are constantly reviewed because of the shifting nature of things and our knowledge of them. These ethics as process are always 'in place' in one way or another, with places varying from the global to the local.

Our position chimes with some pragmatist views of ethics which also advocate a view of ethics as process. This sees philosophical ethics 'as an *ongoing* attempt to determine what is good, and what actions are right' (Parker, 1996: 30). Environmental ethics is 'one of several new disciplines that have emerged, first to *extend* and then *transform* settled ways of thinking about value. From the pragmatic perspective, this emerging ethic of relationships appears to be ontologically more sound than traditional ethical theories' (Parker, 1996: 31). Parker here is drawing on Weston's (1996) writing about pragmatist environmental ethics, in which ideas of ethics as process are espoused. Thinking about ethics, then, involves 'simply opening some questions, unsettling some assumptions, and prying the window open just far enough to lead, in time, to much wilder and certainly more diverse suggestions of "criteria" (151). This procedure entails 'a long period of experimentation and uncertainty' which is 'expected and even welcome' (148).

Weston and Parker's contention also confirms that place will play an important part in this process, as the focus where experimentation and new forms of ethical practice can occur:

> Neither the wilderness nor the city as we know it are in 'the real world' . . . We might take as the most 'real' places the places where humans and other creatures, honoured in their wildness and potential reciprocity, can come together, perhaps warily, but at least openly. (Weston, 1996: 153)

Considering the animal rights and ethics of 'creatures' such as dolphins and primates does, in one vital sense, extend the boundaries of our ethical community. In another sense, however, it does not. Such creatures are often thought of as much more like humans than had been previously allowed. They are part of 'our privileged family', but have been mistakenly excluded from the ethical community. To bring other forms of nature into the ethical community – others who are palpably not like us, in this instance trees – *is* a challenge and would mark a much more radical extension of the ethical community.

So we have suggested that one component of such a move may come through the acknowledgement that all manner of non-human actants do possess significant forms of agency. This cannot be deployed only in defending their rights as significant beings in themselves, but also through a view of the relational nature of agency. We also have suggested that ethical communities somehow have to shadow the relations which make up the world. Established modern ethical formations which engender anthropomorphic privilege cause a dangerous schism which has had deleterious effects on our relationships with the environment. These modern ethical structures were established under conceptualizations of the world and the human position within it which have been, if not swept away, then sharply challenged by new views of the world. As Weston (1999) so cogently argues,

> western cultures [are] systematically denying and obscuring the human dependence upon and immersion in nature. The results are vast blind spots in our vision of ourselves and the world, through which modern forms of domination have been able to move, and indeed to seem perfectly natural. (178)

It seems that in some indigenous cultures relational views of the world have engendered a relational form of ethics (see for example Callicott, 1994). But the modern world has created a whole new range of relational processes. Can we build ethical formations which respond to these processes? We suggest that an 'ethical mindfulness' is a first step, and the development of languages and systems which can apply such a mindfulness in the complex situations of the myriad emplaced encounters represents a long hard battle which will have to be fought and refought, for all sakes.

Part II
Trees in their Place

Preamble

> To what extent is there consensus about the value of nature in any particular place?
>
> (Burgess, 2000: 276)

> One of the basic premises of woodland ecology [is] that woods are more than just collections of trees. They are *places*, landmarks and communities.
>
> (Mabey, 1980: 63, original emphasis)

> More trees are valuable to local communities, wildlife and the environment. But there is a cultural and spiritual dimension which is just as important.
>
> (Evans, 2000)

We now turn to considering trees in particular places. We have argued strongly throughout the book that place is the arena where arbori-culture comes into action. Here, place is not being used as a shorthand for a few very significant and specific locations where trees have particular importance. Rather, place is being used to represent a wide variety of different locations where trees are present. In each of these places, trees contribute to a unique milieu, taking their part in the distinct formations of networks and dwellings which are acted out as those places unfold in time and space. If arbori-culture in general is rich and complex, the consideration of arbori-culture in any particular milieu presents a further dimension of complexity and richness. In the chapters that follow we tell the stories of four particular places with trees, and through these we trace out the themes explored in the first half of the book – culture, agency, place and ethics – alongside *other themes* that the sites and the trees themselves seem to insist on having articulated.

These chapters are based on detailed research into four sites which were selected according to a number of criteria. We sought out sites which somehow tapped into wider frameworks of arbori-culture in multiple ways. Thus, for example, we were particularly keen to research an orchard in order to tie in with the work of Common Ground on trees and orchards; we were keen to consider sites in urban areas to connect with discourses about contexts of nature. We were keen to select sites in which the trees' roles were folded in complex ways into other narratives and ensembles. We were also keen to choose sites where the risk of redevelopment and status of conservation was varied, so that the implications of 'threat' and risk could be evaluated. On a more practical level, we selected places where access to the site and to the key actors was feasible, and places which offered some possibility of studying a historical perspective, through access to records and/or oral accounts of their past. These various criteria were fulfilled by studies of an orchard (Chapter 6), an urban cemetery (Chapter 7), a conserved woodland area located on the spoil heap of a disused coal mine (Chapter 8), and a tree-lined urban square (Chapter 9). It should be reiterated, however, that although each site yields fascinating individual narratives about the roles of trees, the sites more generally can be taken as examples of places where trees are co-constitutive actants. In this light, the specific locations serve only to demonstrate the kinds of place-making, agency, cultural construction and ethical consideration which might arise in any tree-place.

In the last chapter, we revisit our opening themes in the light of the case studies set out. We pay particular attention to ethics, for here a discussion of how 'general principles' apply to the specific characteristics of the different sites demonstrates the complexity and the potential of new ethical approaches: these ethical considerations interconnect with issues of time, notably the need to take full account of the ecological time of trees.

–6–

Orchard

> Paradise is often equated with the Garden of Eden, a lost garden of innocence – an orchard of fruit-bearing trees.
>
> (Franklin, 1999: from caption to 'Orchard' plates)

> They are orchards which refresh the soul.
>
> (Miles, 1999: 149)

West Bradley is a 65-acre orchard in the Glastonbury area of the county of Somerset in south-west England. In this chapter, we briefly introduce it as a place before going on to weave some of our previous theoretical preoccupations, particularly agency and dwelling, through our account of it.

West Bradley is privately owned. The owner lives in a house on the edge of the orchard and takes an active role in the strategic management and development of the orchard in conjunction with a manager who also oversees day-to-day operations and a small, flexible workforce. The orchard is 'drawn' or marked as a place in multiple ways. For example, it has an overall perimeter hedge which physically demarks it; it is mapped on legal deeds of ownership; identified as orchard on Ordnance Survey maps; has signs proclaiming itself, and is classified as orchard in local authority surveys of agricultural land-use and orchard-cover. It is well known locally in a number of ways: for its farm shop, as a source of seasonal casual work, as a place to visit for PYO apples, as a place of spectacle in blossom and fruiting times, as a place that keeps up the local and regional traditions of orchards, and as a place of orchard practice for other local producers (there are local producer associations).

The orchard produces a range of predominately apple 'products', although it also includes a small number of pear trees, and recently a few walnut trees have been planted for future harvesting. The apples which are grown are routed into three main production/consumption streams: retail, cider and processing, each of which is associated with a range of products and outlets. Thus the orchard produces dessert and culinary apples which are sold on site at a small farm shop and via seasonal PYO (pick your own) weekends, supplied to local shops, and passed on into larger cooperative wholesale systems which supply major food retail chains. The cider apples grown in the orchard are sold both to local concerns and to further-flung markets for cider production. The orchard's process apples are shipped to specific companies to be used for making juice and baby food products.

To achieve these outputs, a complex mix of people, organic entities, technologies, and knowledges are present in the orchard, at the centre of which stand the trees. The production practices range from 'traditional', long-standing orchard practices (e.g. hand-picking and -pruning) to modern commercially developed practices (such as the use of pesticides and modern fruit varieties). This complex collectif is maintained by a stream of inputs into the site such as new root stock, fertilizers/pesticides, and information from commercial research bodies, human labour, hardware, and fuel for machinery.

The orchard is divided into a number of areas – named The Bees, The Park, The Wilderness – dedicated to the various production streams and defined by hedges, ditches and tracks. A combination of tree varieties and attendant forms is spread throughout these areas, and different management regimes work with them. For example, the old cider orchard comprises well established standard ('full-size') trees and is hedged, and has cattle running in it at certain times of year. The pick-your-own section and the trees which produce many of the dessert and culinary apples are mainly half-standard ('half full-size') trees, while some newer varieties for the cider and culinary market, and for the more recent process apple market, are in the form of bush (small) trees. The variety of apple and tree types grown is designed to not only feed different apple qualities into the various markets supplied but also to do so at different times of the season. Figure 6.1 below gives some indication of the details of this precise production–consumption gearing.

The creativity which enables such precise product is a relational achievement from the orchard collectif, with the apple tree varieties playing a key role *as agents*. The density and texture of all this at work *in place* makes the orchard a *place*. So the orchard can be understood as being contemporaneously both an achievement woven by a complex set of networks and a place marked by different imaginative and material articulations. In this chapter, we shall discuss how the orchard can be considered as a dwelling place, and as being woven into wider ideas of place, and we shall show that this orchard identity is connected with all manner of cultural resonances which fold into the place milieu in fluid multidimensional performative ways. We shall also show how obviously, yet fundamentally, the presence of the trees and their creative abilities are at the heart of this whole achievement.

The Orchard as Dwelling

In our research at West Bradley, we became fascinated by its potential as a grounded example of the concept of dwelling (Chapter 4). As we argued there, dwelling suggests a rich, intimate and ongoing togetherness of beings and

Cider apples 20.6 acres comprising of

- standard trees planted about 1974, 10.4 acres
- half standard trees (two blocks) planted 1978/80, 5.8 acres
- young bush trees (two blocks) planted 1990/92, 5.8 acres, and one block planted May 1999, 1.4 acres. The cider varieties have been Dabinet and Michelin. Only bush trees have been planted since 1990.

Processing apples 9.1 acres

- all planted to Jonagold in 1998/9

Dessert and culinary apples (and pears), total area 35.0 acres

- old trees planted around 1974, 5.0 acres
- and 15 varieties of trees planted 1987–1999, 30 acres

These include

Discovery, an early fruiter
Worcester Pearmain and Merton Worcester, mid-season fruiters
Charles Ross a large handsome apple suitable for eating and cooking, September to November
Blenheim Orange found at Woodstock near Blenheim in about 1740. The oldest variety grown as West Bradley (a cooker and eater best from October through until Christmas) **Kidd's Orange Red**, a late delicious apple which is popular nearer Christmas and which stores well until March
Cox's Orange Pippin, the premium English apple; picked in mid-September, its full flavour emerges by the end of the month and lasts through February/March
Egremont Russet, an autumn apple with a unique nutty flavour, perfect with Cheddar cheese from October to December
Jonagold, new variety proving most popular – a large apple which is an also an excellent sweet cooking apple. Stores well until March
Fiesta, the new English-bred variety, somewhat like Cox, keeps its firmness and flavour until March or April.

Figure 6.1 The Different Apple Trees at West Bradley (taken from information leaflets produced by the orchard (1999)) materials which constitute and reconstitute landscapes and places. These conceptual togethernesses seemed to come alive at West Bradley orchard. Our account of the orchard as a tree-place, then, focuses on issues relating to the interconnections between trees, place, landscape and dwelling. It draws on ideas recently made popular by Tim Ingold (Macnaghten and Urry, 1998), but it also talks back to these ideas, raising concerns about how dwelling is presently articulated.

In West Bradley's 1999 publicity leaflet, there is more than a hint of the notion of dwelling in the description of the orchard's situation in the landscape:

> Our orchards are situated three miles due east of Glastonbury, at the edge of the Somerset moors and tucked under the shelter of Pennard Hill. The combination of this shelter, soil type, and the gentle climate of south-west England, gives us a flavour which cannot be easily matched.

There is an implicit assertion here of nature and culture coming together harmoniously, and of an authenticity and rightness which resonates of dwelling as it has been articulated from Heidegger onwards. But as we shall show West Bradley cannot be seen simply as a traditional, authentic orchard landscape, ideas seemingly so significant in ideas of dwelling. It has adopted 'modern' practices such as modern fruit types and pesticide systems which, being elements of globalized industrial fruit-growing practice, could be said to be anti locally embedded 'dwelling'. We shall argue that dwelling is a more fluid notion than this which can incorporate 'modern' practice and ideas of networks within dynamic notions of place, and that the orchard illustrates this well.

A closer look at the orchard reveals a deep hybridity of people, nature, and technology – new and old – which is embedded in a complex array of networks, but which also has a time-thickened, place-forming dimension, and the trees are at the creative centre of all this. Just as Ingold (1993) places the pear tree in Bruegel's painting at the heart of his account of the dwelling that is depicted in the picture (see Chapter 4), so the fruit trees at West Bradley are at *its* heart as a place, as a network mode, or however else it is constructed. Like Bruegel's pear tree they offer multiple, specific, dense, performed relational materiality/agency which actualizes dwelling.

In the orchard the human 'actants' engage with the non-cider trees with great intimacy, pruning (Figure 6.2); painting (covering the pruning cuts to prevent infection), thinning (reducing clusters of young growing apples to two so the remaining apples will grow bigger and have more space to develop), and picking. This intimate relationship in not just networking it is also the stuff of dwelling. (And this is not to say that this work might often be regarded as boring, a grind, low-paid, insecure.) This is because it is about temporal materiality expressed through repeated rounds of doing. There is science, abstract 'objective knowledge' (of nature) here with regard to how and where the branches of the tree are cut, at what time of year, and with what objective in mind, and there is 'art' too. Those pruning the trees assured us that it was an 'art form' and every tree had to be approached as 'an individual'. Each tree presents a unique pattern of branches, through its own disposition for growth and previous rounds of pruning, which in turn 'the art of pruning' engages with year on year. It might even be suggested that each tree is an individual taskscape developed over time. These kinds of intimate skill and relationship are part of the idea of dwelling and, in the more conventional senses, account for the cultural attraction of orchards and similar manifestations of intimate fine-grained material relationality. Indeed Macnaghten and Urry (1998) call upon Common Ground's accounts of traditional orchard loss to discuss dwelling and its destruction. Although Common Ground campaigns for the overall continuation and regeneration of orchards in Britain, they are 'particularly worried about the fate of traditional tall tree orchards. These are special places' (Coward, 2000) which are understood to be extraordinarily rich in cultural/ ecological terms.

At West Bradley this attraction is indeed particularly articulated through the larger older trees. The owner, manager, and workers all admitted to some sadness when these were grubbed out and replaced with new bush trees. These older trees were seen as 'unique characters'. Their form, created by rounds of pruning and

Figure 6.2 Pruning half-standard apple trees, West Bradley orchard (Owain Jones)

growth, is an example of the materialization of place narrative which we considered in Chapter 4. These older trees then contribute to the unfolding of the place (as well as the network) in this way and also others. There is concern when they have to be replaced, and a determination to keep at least some of the standard and half-standard trees in place to preserve the image of the orchard, and in fact local council landscape grants are dedicated to supporting the areas of older cider trees. These larger trees are closely connected to traditional orchard culture of the region and the continued practice of local ceremonial customs. Being taller than people, these trees make the spaces of the orchard enclosed and intimate, and give the rows and paths a maze-like quality. The new bush trees, being about the same height as a human adult, do not produce this effect to the same extent, and are not so visually prominent in the landscape.

Surrounding these intimate processes of human–tree interaction and their cultural accretions, there are all manner of other components to the orchard taskscape. To aid pollination, beehives are kept and crab apple trees dispersed throughout the orchard. To protect the trees and crop, rabbit guards are placed around the trees, fences maintained (against deer), kite bird-scarers are flown, and various chemical insect pest- and disease-control systems are employed. There is a paraphernalia of technology such as tractors, mowers, ladders, sprayers, stakes, crates, and an infrastructure of packing sheds, grading tables and cold stores. These are all deployed in different combinations within the three different areas of production.

The preceding account is by no means intended as a comprehensive depiction of the orchard and its processes which represent very complex and detailed hybrid networks (see Williams, undated). Rather, our aim is to give *an impression* of the intimate mix of nature, humans, and technology which make up the taskscape therein and the network elements which thread through it. These relational agencies can be seen in terms of actants and networks, and such a perspective could easily be enhanced by tracing more precisely the particular interconnections which constitute particular chains relating to production and consumption. However, to do so would be to stray from the place-related togetherness of the orchard. Our analysis of West Bradley, therefore, is as a dwelling place of contextualized lived practices, a taskscape which articulates practices of dwelling.

The important characteristic of local embeddedness for the notion of dwelling is echoed in understandings of (traditional) 'orchard culture'. Coward (2000) identifies more than 6,000 varieties of English apple, and suggests that most of these are 'extremely localised, only growing in certain areas [and] in certain conditions'. This 'incredible variety is the result of a long history of natural and human interaction . . . Natural biodiversity spread out to fill the niches but local expertise and tradition preserved and developed the best adaptations'.

It is the weaving together across the nature–culture divide represented in this history which produces the incredibly rich cultural/natural ecology which Common Ground among others have been so keen to preserve. As Cronon (1996) and others have argued, to see nature as a pure realm which can only be depleted through interaction with the human realm is to completely misread the nature–society relationship. The ecological/cultural diversity exemplified by this example is the outcome of non-human/human relational agency at work in particular formations. This is how the idea of dwelling should develop, as a way of seeing the intimacy of these interconnections as they perform the diverse world, but it needs to avoid certain static views of the local, of landscape and place as we shall set out below.

The Trees as Creative Agents

We want to emphasis that a dwelling perspective can make room for the *creative* presence, the non-human agency of 'things', in its accounts. At West Bradley orchard, from an ANT perspective, the trees are enrolled by human actors, and all manner of other actants are deployed in performing the production of fruit. However, we emphasize that the trees bring to this process the unique creativity of being able to produce fruit in the first place (Figure 6. 3). We have noted Whatmore's (1999) concern for the *creative* presence of organic beings, and we argue that the creativity of fruit trees is obviously essential to the networks and place-characteristics of West Bradley. Furthermore the different types of tree produce different kinds of fruit which stream off into the three main markets supplied by the orchard. Thus there is both a general creativity of producing apples and a more specific creativity of producing particular types of apple with particular properties, which is at the heart of this relational achievement. *It is precisely this unique creative ability of fruit trees which is mourned, and considered a potential economic and scientific loss, when particular rare varieties of fruit are lost.* Thus there are 'rare-breed collections' working to preserve such creative wellsprings. At present, at least, this is a creativity which humans cannot re-create, a fact which suggests that there is a form of agency at work here which is beyond that of humans.

Moreover, it is not just this key creative ability that can be termed as non-human agency in a relational achievement. Many of the different management and production techniques which are deployed to sustain and nurture this creativity are also relational achievements. A good example of this is the pruning of the trees which is carried out to maximize, specialize and control the growth, shape and fruiting habits of the trees. This may seem to be merely a form of human control over, and imposition on, the trees. But acquiring of pruning techniques and knowledges is a relational achievement developed over time. The nature of the

Figure 6.3 The heart of the orchard and the creativity of the trees (Owain Jones)

trees – how and when they grow, form branches, fruit and leaves – *has shaped pruning as a practice*. It works with and within the active capacities of the trees. In other words the trees have 'shaped' the art of pruning (and the forms of pruning equipment), just as pruning shapes the trees.

In the remainder of the chapter, we want to use this intimate mix of nature, humans and technology which make up the taskscape of the orchard to develop three important questions relating to the notion of dwelling which we have touched upon already: these refer to issues of authenticity, spatial proximity, and the framing of the landscape.

Orchard Dwelling as Authenticity

Many commentators (notably Macnaghten and Urry, 1998) have suggested that modernism in its many forms is destructive to the practice of dwelling. Still considering Ingold's archetypal illustration of dwelling – Bruegel's painting *The Harvesters* – and applying it to many other imaginations of traditional landscapes, it would be a forceful illustration to say that the construction of a new motorway across the scene might interrupt, if not eradicate, the sedimented layers of meaning and practice which are interpreted within. Indeed, new practices would immediately result which are not sedimented into the temporality of the landscape. As Macnaghten and Urry point out, new roads are the antithesis of dwelling and of taskscapes that have sedimented into a landscape over time. Such an argument assumes a relationship between authenticity and dwelling which poses important questions about nature and landscape under contemporary conditions which we will explore in the context of the orchard.

In Heidegger, authenticity is a critical element, not only in his notion of dwelling but in the wider notion of *Dasein* (the fact and possibility of being-in-the-world – Guignon, 1993b) and seems near impossible under the conditions of modernity. As Vycinas (1969: 268) states, 'When we rule things, as the modern man does, we are homeless; we are homeless even if we have a place to live'. The obvious concern is that from this perspective, dwelling has been obliterated by alienating modernity and becomes an impossibility. Harvey (1996) worries about this, asking 'what might the conditions of "dwelling" be in a highly industrialised, modernist, and capitalist world?' (301), and Bender (1998: 37) asks 'what happens to those not rooted, not dwelling. Perhaps not "authentic"?' So should the notion of dwelling be abandoned as a useful conceptual view of the world and of landscape because of this problem of a lack of authenticity in the terms described above? As Harvey (1996) points out, a number of writers show that the notion of authenticity is itself a modern construction. As soon as authenticity is prescribed, or preserved, or even re-created within modernity, we can begin to stray into the world of simulacra.

The view of authenticity of being as some original (natural) form, some blessed state, can certainly be found in writings on orchards. For example Massingham (1988a: 167) asserts that 'apples are never really at their best unless they are grown in their own local soil'. Once local varieties are moved from 'their home' and 'industrial practices' take over, we are apparently on the steady downward slope towards the modern inauthentic apple, 'hung in a motorway service station shop . . . protected within its moulded case of plastic, shiny and unblemished . . . Perfect in every cosmetic way, but fatally flawed' (Koziell, 2000: 44).

Taken to their extreme, these arguments lead to a view of true nature, or authentic landscapes, or communities, as consisting of diminishing pockets of harmonious authentic dwelling in an ever encroaching sea of alienation. This seems a deeply flawed view and one which would make the deployment of dwelling as a view of landscape, place and nature redundant. As a consequence Macnaghten and Urry (1998) argue that even Ingold's vision, which is also of authentic relationship between community and landscape, will have to be adapted to the modern condition of landscape and nature.

Any notion of the 'authenticity' of West Bradley orchard is problematic. Here, traditional practices (such as pruning and the keeping of bees to aid pollination) merge with, and are interspersed by, more modern forms and practices such as the use of mechanical harvesters and state-of-the-art chemical fungicides and pesticides. But of course those traditional methods would themselves have been innovations in the development of orchard practice. Miles (1999: 146) points out that traditions of orchard cultivation stretch back to ancient Roman and Greek civilizations and beyond. This time-depth which challenges notions of simple authenticity is seen in the types of apple grown at West Bradley. Of the fifteen or so types of culinary and eating apple grown at the orchard, the oldest type – Blenheim Orange – dates from 1740, while Fiesta and Jonagold are modern apples types developed by commercial plant suppliers. Some areas of the orchard are of traditional standard trees, while since 1990 only small-bush trees have been planted. Does this, and the use of tractors and other technologies, mark the orchard as compromised in terms of an authentic landscape? Our view is that such simple concepts of authenticity do not sit well with the notion of dwelling wherein landscape can be seen as being temporally complex, with the past being co-present with the future through both material and imaginative processes. At West Bradley we do not uncover a sterilized museum of past landscape and dwelling, somehow untouched by change or even current technologies and practices. Instead we see a series of practices which have evolved over time, and changes which are constantly informed by shifting economic, technical and cultural formations, and a place that is not conducive to fixed-point notions of authenticity.

West Bradley was bought in 1858 by the grandfather of the last-but-one owner. Through the later part of the nineteenth century it was not an orchard at all but a small dairy farm in the Somerset tradition. The farm was planted as an orchard at the turn of the century because the son who took over from his ill father was allergic to cows, so he immediately sold the cows and started planting apple trees. So this switch in land use was pragmatic, but was clearly guided by the fact that 'the countryside around Glastonbury is still renowned as one of the best cider apple growing areas in the country' (Legg and Binding, 1998: 7).

Cider apples were at first the only crop. A cider-making business was soon built up; a small-scale enterprise selling 4.5-gallon barrels made to particular requirements of customers, such as sweet or dry, clear or dark. In later years the production set-up was quite advanced, but continued to supply small private customers rather than supplying the retail trade as the larger cider companies did. As the dynamics of cider production shifted, other markets were pursued. The orchard was one of the earliest to plant and grow Bramley (cooking) apples on a commercial basis, sending apples in barrels to wholesalers in Leeds by train. These developments were all bound up with innovative modern commercial and technological practice (such as the cold storage of the crop), but throughout these changes, we suggest, the authenticity of the orchard *as an orchard* has been maintained in two ways.

First, over time, in this and other orchards, series of innovations and changes (such as the use of modern fruit types, and agrichemicals) constantly weave together with some older threads (such as old apple varieties, pruning, the keeping of bees) creating new *hybrid forms and practices* which are neither authentic nor inauthentic. It does, though, remain distinctive because, secondly, the new technologies which have been brought in to 'modernize' production cannot be seen purely as abstracted, undifferentiated modernity being imposed upon and obliterating 'traditional' practice. The new technologies adopted carry the marks of orchardness. For example the tractor, imported from France, is of a special narrow design for moving up and down in between the rows of trees (Figure. 6.4).

In contrast to the 'eaters' which are still traditionally (and laboriously) picked from the tree by hand, cider apples are picked up from the ground after being knocked off the trees (with long poles – an old practice), by modern machinery hand-guided around and under the trees. The mechanized cider-apple harvester also has appleness and orchardness embedded in its materiality through the way it is designed to pick up apples and move through the orchard. This may seem an obvious point, but it is crucial in that the new techniques and equipment are bound into, even enrolled into, the continuation of a form of orchard identity. Orchardness

Figure 6.4 The modern technology used in the orchard can bear the mark of 'orchardness' such as the special tractor designed to move between the rows of trees (Owain Jones)

may shift over time, but it retains some form of dynamic identity as it migrates though economic, technological and cultural space. The authenticity of dwelling, then, should be seen as a form of dynamism, of ongoing freshness, rather than anything static, but which at the same time retains an identity.

The individual trees at West Bradley are routinely grubbed out and replaced, either with new trees of the same type, or often with new types of trees for new markets, or with better yields, or lower related production costs. The cider trees are left longest, but no 'working' trees have lived through the lifespan of the orchard. It is the orchard itself, an ongoing presence of trees, which is the ongoing taskscape. The ongoing rich mixture of nature, technology and humans retains a form of oneness which is bound together in some form of cohesion, which perhaps can be seen as 'authentic', but only in a dynamic time-embedded sense, rather than in comparison to any fixed time-point referencing. This view of 'authenticity', that it is the ongoing orchardness of the orchard which gives an authentic form, could perhaps be re-located in Heidegger's notion of authenticity of Dasein 'which is characterised by a distinct temporal structure' where

> an authentic life is lived as a unified flow characterised by cumulativeness and direction. It involves taking over the possibilities made accessible by the past and acting in the present in order to accomplish something for the future. (Guignon, 1993b: 229–30)

We need first to re-emphasize here, as we discussed in chapter 4, that there is no *necessary* equation of dwelling with goodness, morality or aesthetic benefit (as there seems to be in Heidegger). Secondly, it is also important to note that the 'authenticity' relayed by West Bradley is not confined to its spatial boundaries, but rather is projected on different scales, and this adds a layer of complexity to understanding the orchard as landscape or place.

Placing West Bradley

One of the key cultural markings of the county of Somerset is that of 'a rural landscape with orchards'. For example, the website of Somerset County Council depicts a series of 'images of Somerset', designed to get across the 'spirit' and 'flavour' of the county, and to attract inward investment through it being seen as an attractive location to visit or even relocate to. The first image in the series has a basket of cider apples in the foreground with an orchard behind. The presence of orchards in the landscape is a *relatively* unique aspect of the Somerset countryside (a few other English counties are famous for orchards), and therefore one that is valued and emphasized in efforts to establish/preserve a separate, distinctive, positive identity. As Legg and Binding (1998: 63) write:

> Orchards are one of the most distinctive features of the traditional Somerset countryside, helping create a small-scale, enclosed seasonal landscape where the pink and white blossoms of spring are followed by the deep rich green of foliage in the summer and turning to a range of green, reds, and yellows in autumn as the fruit matures and ripens.

The County Council also insist that orchards are one of the most distinctive visual features of the Somerset countryside, and that they are a distinctive feature in the cultural ecology of the county:

> Orchards are central to Somerset's history: the cider once being a staple drink for farm labourers and forming part of the weekly payment made by the farm owner to his men. In many parts of the county each village and farmstead was once fringed with orchards and the growing and picking of apples together with cider making and drinking, was an integral part of the rural scene. (Stone, 1994: 1)

Once again there are strong hints of dwelling in these depictions. The technologies, landscapes, and customs which surround the production and consumption of apples (and pears) are collected, recorded, and in some instances still practised in more or less reflexively 'traditionalist' ways. Photographs of 'orchard culture', published in books (e.g. Legg and Binding, 1998; Common Ground, 1989a; Sutherland and Nicholson, 1986) and as photographic cards (Common Ground, orchard postcard series), depict this relationship of orchard to community, as well as the traditional methods, and the characters who employed them. This unique richness of place, and the central role of orchards and orchard products is eloquently described by Sutherland and Nicholson (1986: 88) who write,

> The local quality of cider is precious, it is – or now perhaps was – the lubricant of tight communities . . . It may have been a necessary narcotic but it was also part of a system in which there was a short and obvious journey between production and consumption, between the life of the people . . . and the materials and tools with which they made that life work . . . The virtue of it . . . was the inter-reliance of the physics, the biology and psychology of the place . . . It was the links that mattered, that made *the extraordinary wholesomeness . . . and created its dominant air of congruity, of being fitted to itself.* (our emphasis)

It is also important to note that, as hinted at in the above extract, the dwelling vested in Somerset's orchardness is made more crucial and more valuable, because it is constantly portrayed as being under threat. For example,

> Surveys indicate that over two-thirds of Somerset's orchards have been lost this century. Despite more recognition in recent years the traditional orchard is still being lost. Many of the trees are becoming old, unstable and vulnerable to winter gales. Other agricultural

uses are tempting. The location of orchards at the edge of villages makes them potential sites for housing developments. (Stone, 1994: 1)

In Britain in general there has been a marked decline in orchards. Koziell (2000: 45) states that 'over 60% of UK apple orchards have been lost since 1970'. This is particularly so of less productive 'traditional orchards' and this is reflected in Common Ground's 'Save our Orchards' campaign. This campaign not only highlights the local distinctiveness of different local orchard traditions, it highlights England as a place of locally distinct orchard traditions, as in the Common Ground 'Apple Map' poster (a map of England showing local apple varieties, cultures and technologies). The romantic notion of the traditional English orchard, with all its imagined resonances of dwelling, clearly inspires Miles (1999: 149) as he tries to evoke these spaces:

> The orchard has been much more than a field in which fruit trees grow. It is the ancient piece of rough pasture behind the old moss-covered farmhouse where the sweet and juicy eaters were gathered by the farmer's freckled faced daughters; it is the clump of sturdy well-pruned trees which proffer their huge green globes to the flour-dusted, sleeves-rolled-up wife who seeks her pie filling. It is the avenue of the sharp and bitter-sweet promises shaken, carted, crushed and pressed into bright golden nectar by fellows who can barely wait to sip their prize. It is the greensward where Old Spot pigs scoop up the fallen and fast-fermenting fruit. It is pale pink, bee-drowsy draught of honey, offering sweet repose to the turtle dove and the swooping woodpecker deep within their rugged home. They are orchards which refresh the soul.

This dwelling that is the imagined 'traditional' orchard is seen to be threatened, even snuffed out, not just by the loss of orchards, but also by modern orchard practice. As Sinden (1989: 5) states 'modern orchards make a sharp break with this tradition. They are hardly worthy of the name, with their close-packed ranks of bush trees, permanently staked, heavily pruned, disturbingly premature and growing in bare, herbicide scorched earth'.

To understand West Bradley as a place, all these wider contexts and flows of meanings need to be grappled with. It is an orchard in Somerset, it is also an orchard in England and bound up with developing cultural and commercial articulations of the orchardness of England. The authenticity of West Bradley is in some ways challenged by the introduction of modern methods, but in other ways it is buttressed by the growing local and national sensitivity to the presences of orchards within our landscapes. Thus West Bradley becomes a place in an imaginative symbolic network a well as a node in more material networks of commerce and technology. This complex overlapping and interpenetrating of layers and networks of practice and meaning opens up yet another problem with the dwelling perspective which needs to be carefully thought through if the notion of dwelling is to be able to address modern landscapes. This question concerns the 'localness' of dwelling.

Dwelling and Spatial Boundedness

The degree to which the togetherness of dwelling relies on (harmonious) spatial boundedness is obscure and problematic. Casey's (1998) close reading of Heidegger's philosophical journey leading to the notion of dwelling shows how there is a move from a gathering (of things) to nearness, to dwelling, which is always 'dwelling in nearness'. 'To be in a place is to be near to whatever else is in that place, and pre-eminently the things that are co-located there' (281). In his vision of the farmhouse in the landscape of the Black Forest, Heidegger depicts a place where the material and design of the house, and the topography of the land (the house is placed in the lee of the hill for shelter), permit divinities and mortals and things to enter a 'simple oneness'. But simply being in the same place does not necessarily create dwelling. To illustrate this, Ingold (1995) uses the example of a house being merely a building or a building that becomes a home, a lived place. It is the latter which is a dwelling house, which will bear the mark of past and present living. Similarly, in Ingold's account of the Bruegel landscape the emphasis is on those who have made this landscape, who work it, who are dwelling there, and it is this connection, this oneness which in his view creates such dwelling. Oneness implies rootedness where people and landscape become joined. In this kind of oneness and being rooted in the landscapes that Heidegger and Ingold discuss, there is a correspondence between community, landscape and place. There is a fixedness of the space in terms of a bounded local space. This is the kind of idyll that Bakhtin (1981) considers, where communities and their corresponding landscapes are closed, and have a pointed temporal dimension in terms of the purity of the space being projected in the future. Eisenberg (1998: 143) considers most forms of idyll are ways of 'denying or declawing change' and this may be because, as Sibley (1999: 115) suggests 'familiarity and predictability are important for many people. There is a common desire to live in a place which is stable and orderly'. Closed intimate spatial boundedness is a key way in which such stable familiar idylls or dwellings are imagined to be formed.

This kind of oneness and rootedness, then, like authenticity to which it is closely linked, has a powerful appeal and intuitively seems best delivered within intimate, stable local sets of relations. Like authenticity, these characteristics are seen 'to be destroyed by the spread of technology, rationalism, mass production, and mass values' (Harvey, 1996: 302). To be rooted is to have a localness; to be rooted in a local space that is distinct. Thus Common Ground in their defence of place emphasize '*Local Distinctiveness*' (Clifford and King, 1993). This is, in effect, the local taskscape: the particular dynamic of dwelling formed of rich, dense local relations between people and environment.

As with the concept of authenticity, such a view of dwelling as a local spatially bound distinctiveness of nearness is highly problematic (see Harvey, 1996; Thrift, 1999). In part, such problems stem from the sinister (nationalist) rustic romanticism which pervades Heidegger's ideas. Ingold's pursuit of dwelling also has a certain romanticism (albeit in a more innocent form – Bender, 1998). If dwelling is to be a serviceable concept for contemporary landscapes, it needs to shed this reliance on local boundedness and instead reflect a view of space and place which is dynamic, overlapping and interpenetrating.

In the case of West Bradley, as for most modern places and landscapes, this idea of oneness and simple rootedness is a redundant vision. The owner, those who work at West Bradley, those who visit it, and those who encounter it in other ways all live spatially complex lives which take them through all manner of spaces both practically and imaginatively. Through these people and those who know West Bradley through other means – such as the County Council Tree Officer (who takes particular interest in orchards), the members of the local cider apple growers' association, the commercial suppliers, and those who are supplied by the orchard – West Bradley is clearly being engaged with sporadically, partially, and through widely differing socio-cultural constructions. The meanings of West Bradley as an orchard cannot in any way be seen as confined to the space itself. As we have outlined, meanings and materials flow in and out of its space in complex ways.

One major flow is the concern for the loss of orchards in Somerset and in Britain, set within wider concerns about environmental decline and the destruction of the countryside more generally. Another major flow is the notion of Somerset as a place of orchards. The material and cultural environment in which West Bradley is immediately set is marked with constant reminders of the orchardness of Somerset. Local cider is advertised and sold in shops. The local radio station is 'Orchard FM'. Pubs bear names and images of traditional orchard culture. The local media constantly use apples as visual icons and cover local orchard stories. Such cultural discourses are more or less consciously, and differently, carried into West Bradley. For example, some of those engaging in the PYO weekends were clearly doing so in part as a ceremonial partaking in the regional apple culture.

Moreover, there is also an awareness of Englishness at work. Apples produced by the orchard are marketed as 'English apples'. Many of those who come to the orchard to buy the produce from the farm shop, and particularly those who come to pick-your-own, are also more or less reflexively aware of larger scales of landscape and production dynamics. Many are concerned to support local orchards and concerned to support the English landscape in the context of competition with and hostility toward France and the EU in particular, it seemed.

Bender (1998: 37) sees in Ingold's discussion of dwelling a 'determination to think of landscape as something created out of people's activities rather than through their representations'. Her observation is significant in a number of different ways. First, representations as well as practices are important here. Representations will actively render any spatially bounded notion of dwelling permeable to the cultural flows of ideas, meanings, significations and symbols operating on different scales. Secondly, practices themselves are multiple, suggesting multiple taskscapes associated with any one dwelling. To return to the example of the taskscape depicted in Bruegel's painting, is it reasonable to consider it as a single taskscape? The paths are described as being worn by countless journeys of the community, but those journeys are likely to have been markedly different in their nature. The labourers, the owners, the priest, the village officials, the women, the men, the children, the sad, the lonely, the happy, the poor, the wealthy, will have walked those paths doing different tasks in different ways and constructing the landscape differently. As Bender herself points out, the focus on activities alone may well lead to a loss of any sense of historical particularity which an acknowledgement of representations could provide. We want to argue therefore that dwelling's oneness is formed of a complex multiplicity of practice *and* representation. Further, in the context of both practice and representation, spatial proximity alone cannot map the boundedness of dwelling encountered at West Bradley orchard.

At West Bradley the experiences and constructions of the owner, the manager, the casual labourers do have differing, often contested, representations of the place. The present-day labour relation of this landscape and wider labour relations of agriculture are part of the elements contained here and should not be glossed over by some organic harmonious vision. Yet they remain bound together in a complex material and imaginative taskscape by all manner of forces, which range from the material boundedness of the place itself to common cultural constructions, and to the disciplines of the networks which flow to and from the place.

Dwelling and the Framing of Landscape

A final concern about the perspective of dwelling as recently articulated relates to a continuing tendency toward framing landscapes as the vista from a fixed point. Seeing the landscape in this way, in a closed frame or as a fixed view, has the effect of putting the viewer at a fixed point – outside, or on the edge of the landscape, with a single static orientation, frozen in time. Often, for fairly obvious reasons, landscapes afford a view in which a large tract of land is visible and readable in some sense or other. A view from a hill or some other advantageous perspective makes a landscape. The gaze is static, or perhaps pans across a vista, but is taken from a static point. This is emphasized by Ingold's use of *a landscape painting* to illustrate the notion of dwelling (and by Macnaghten and Urry's enthusiastic redeployment of it). In Bruegel's *The Harvesters* the vantage of the hill gives the painting the perspective which shows the valley, the distant village and church, and the path that leads up to the place of work in the foreground. The selection of the *vantage point,* as in countless other landscape paintings, photographs, and acts of viewing, is done precisely *because* the chosen (fixed) point of viewing gives *a view*, creates *a landscape*. But seeing landscapes and the derived notion of dwelling from this perspective causes a number of potential problems.

Dwelling suggests a perspective which is about *being in the landscape*, about moving through it, in all the (perhaps) repeating yet various circumstances of everyday life. Being in and moving through landscape is different from gazing upon it from a point which always seemingly puts you at the edge of it, or even outside of it. The landscape surrounds you, it will often be unreadable from any one given position, and your orientation may be constantly or frequently, even habitually, shifting. It is about fleeting intimate details that your senses can pick up from being *in* a landscape, not viewing it – like the way a thin branch of a paloverde bush gives and springs as a black-throated sparrow lands on it (Barry Lopez, cited by Harris 1998: 262). Ingold (2000: 429) does raise this point and returns to the work of Lowenthal (1978) who remarked on such differences between a portrayed landscape and landscape as 'being in'. It is the latter which is resonant of dwelling and this may be seen as the antithesis of 'viewing' which has had such a powerful position in approaches to landscapes.

West Bradley, being a 64-acre orchard laid out on flat land, is not readable as a landscape as a framed view at all. It presents itself in many, many ways. It is trees showing over the lane as you drive or walk past; trees which may be in flower, or in full leaf, or in fruit, or in winter bareness. It is glimpses through gateways and into rows of trees. It is being on the main paths, looking along, where the end of each row going off at right angles is marked by the end tree. It is looking up one of the rows of trees. In many positions trees may blank out any depth of view at all, their foliage filling your field of vision. Or in the area of old standard cider trees, in summer, you are in a wondrous space under the canopy (Figure. 6.5). Where the small bush trees are planted you can see over them and into the surrounding landscape. All these views change significantly through the seasons. Sounds and smells emphasize your being in the landscape, and as you walk your orientation changes, and your head and eyes move about. It is an embodied embeddedness.

You may (or may not) be carrying, and be more or less consciously engaging with in your mind, imaginative constructions of trees, orchards, Somerset, England, countryside, freshness, supermarkets, militant French farmers, EU bureaucrats, pesticide residues, bullfinches, and so on. Images of the orchard at

Figure 6.5 Under the canopy of the standard cider trees (Owain Jones)

differing times of the year may flash into your mind as seasonal comparisons and preferences. In other words, dwelling is an embodied and an imaginative embeddedness in landscape. These combine to create complex sensory and imaginative, dynamic collages of being-in-this place. The view is never the same twice, even for any one person, yet the place can and/or does remain deeply familiar. The orchard may be framed imaginatively as a whole, for example as somewhere owned, as somewhere where there are so many apples to be picked before the weather turns, as a source of casual labour, as an element of the orchard landscape of Somerset, as an example of a working orchard with certain working practices, as a place to go and see in blossom, or to go and pick your own fruit. These are imaginative dwellings, which interact with the dynamic spatial/temporal process of viewing it as described above. Dwelling cannot be happily represented or understood in terms of a fixed gaze upon a framed landscape. Rather it should suggest an embodied, practised, contextualized mélange of experience within that landscape. This view of dwelling has much more chance of doing justice to the rich experience of being in place than does the fixed view. To return to the example of the path in the painting, if it is countless journeys which have made that path, the fixed view of the path itself is merely the husk of dwelling – the kernel is the multi-embodied multi-practised business of moving along the path. And in our orchard it is the practices of, say, pruning – leaning, bending the branch with one hand, sawing with a pruning saw with the other – which is an element of dwelling, rather than the postcard view the researcher takes in the quest for 'a portrait of the orchard as landscape'.

In many ways, we are aware that our interpretation of West Bradley orchard still chimes rather too neatly with the romantic overtones which beset the illustrations offered by Heidegger and Ingold. Orchards, after all, seem to be deeply appealing landscapes as Browning (1998: 6) testifies. We have asked ourselves whether the concept, and the equally romanticized notion of taskscape, would be as applicable in harsher conditions where everyday practices involved more industrialized or socially or ethnically regulated procedures. Would dwelling prove to be as appealing a concept among the huge industrialized orchards of the American state of Washington, or as an aid to understanding of the taskscapes of Black labour in Apartheid (or even post-Apartheid) South African agriculture or viticulture?

The conceptual appeal of dwelling is not necessarily negated by such questions. In our view, it offers an important acknowledgement of how human actants are embedded in landscapes, how nature and culture are bound together, and how landscape invariably has time-depth which relates the present to past futures and future pasts. That these acknowledgements may in some cases reflect the conditions of an anti-idyll, the taskscapes of repression, or the unromantic oneness of pragmatic industrialized labour relations is merely to problematize any unidirectional expectations of the senses and experiences of dwelling, rather than dwelling itself. Landscapes of conflict clearly can be just as rich, intimate and hybrid, even if all the qualities are terrible in form. We see dwelling as concerned with this rich intimate mixing, which are all in one way parts of networks at work, but which also fold and hold space into particular forms and characters that can become places of some kind or other.

However, it is clear that the conceptualization of dwelling requires a new and more complex imagination in order to lift interpretative horizons beyond limited local and fixed-point expectations. Dwelling can only be a useful concept if it can adapt to a world where views of authenticity as some form of idealized past original stable state are clearly unhelpful; to the complex interpenetration of places with other places, and to the flows of ideas, people and materials which co-constitute and co-construct those places; and to the need for dynamic rather than fixed ways of understanding embodied engagements with landscapes.

To return to themes raised in Part I, we note that the trees at West Bradley, and the other places we now consider, and like other trees in other places and other networks, have (active, creative) materiality and symbolic presences which can make them key players of places and dwellers in place.

–7–

Cemetery

> Gazing across a concrete jungle, many of us city-dwellers perceive, because scarce to our view and necessary for oxygen, that trees are a vital ingredient in a beautiful landscape.
>
> (Franklin, 1999: 1)

> One of modern man's [*sic*] problems is that he misses one sense, that of the interdependence between people and other animals, interdependence that extends . . . to plants as well.
>
> (Brosse, 1998: 302)

This chapter explores the historical development of a Victorian cemetery in Bristol – Arnos Vale – in order to discuss how the non-human agency of trees has been enrolled into particular networks of environmental change and conservation. We argue that trees have both acted as socialized actors in the narrative of the changing nature of Arnos Vale and contributed significantly to the relational agencies involved. Trees have thereby been implicated in processes of resistance at the site, particularly through their incorporation in practices of monitoring and surveillance. The changing tree presence at Arnos Vale has served to recontextualize and resignify the site, and the monitoring of trees has made this bricolage known, prompting the construction of a significant site of resistance, where the privatization of public space has been contested.

Here in particular we explore some of the complexities, uncertainties and dynamics which permeate the essential interdependence between people, trees and places. The roots of our exploration here are twofold. First, we contend that place characteristics are often wrapped up in the dynamic presences and absences of the living being of what is commonly constructed as nature. Our second point, and one which underlines the first, is once again the desire to take non-human agency seriously, but we show it here doing different kinds of work to that in the previous chapter. As we have already considered in Chapter 3, interest in non-human agency is commonly expressed in abstract terms, but there is a need to go beyond the realm of the general and abstract, and encounter non-human agency in particular things in particular contexts.

The Story of Arnos Vale

Arnos Vale cemetery is a 42-acre Victorian cemetery situated in central Bristol and is a prominent example of the Victorian metropolitan cemetery movement. It was initially laid out in 1837 and, unusually, has remained privately owned to the present day. Its history, particularly since around 1970, has been one of steep decline, dereliction, development threats and considerable controversy. Through this history a very striking landscape has developed. This consists of spectacular grave monuments, ornate chapels, thousands of more plain graves, a network of main paths, a labyrinth of minor paths, a rich variety of mature trees (planted and 'wild') all laid out on both flat and steep terrain and all, now, gradually disappearing beneath the spread of young wild tree saplings and undergrowth which is habitat for a rich flora and fauna. It has remained a place of burial and remembrance but has also become a place for walking and recreation (e.g. bird-watching and 'tree gazing') and also for vandalism and even black magic ritual.

After it very earliest years, funded by a sale of shares, the cemetery was laid out in the manner of Louden, an influential Victorian landscape architect who came to dominate the style of Victorian cemeteries, through his 1843 book (Louden, 1843). In from the grand but now neglected gates and gate lodges there is a large flat area wherein are situated key graves, a Garden of Rest (for the scattering of ashes), two chapels and a crematorium, all linked by a circular main drive. Beyond this area the land rises, steeply on one side and less so on the other, to upper areas of newer burials and a secondary entrance gate. A main roadway links the two entrances; other main paths run up the extensive slopes, which are dissected by further paths making areas which have long been filled out with graves of various types and ages. This layout, which was adopted as the cemetery developed, follows in style and logic the ideal layout for a cemetery on hilly ground as set out by Louden (Figure 7. 1).

From the very outset trees played a central role in this landscape. Louden's cemetery strategy was centred on path layout, burial technology and practice, and also a very detailed advocation of the planting of certain types of tree. Details of the tree-planting are visible in Figure 7.1. Louden (1843: 95–8) lists 44 types of tree which he considered to be 'cemetery trees par excellence', and 127 further tree types for further variation in larger cemeteries. The 44 best recommendations of tree types were all evergreen, and selected not only for colour, foliage, shape and size but also for being hardy and for having the ability to grow in low-maintenance regimes. These 44 species were then broken down into 9 types, grouped by shape, size, and branch configuration. For example the first group of 6 are 'evergreen trees, with needle leaves, and the branches fastigiate and vertical', and the second group of 6 'evergreen trees with needle leaves, of narrow conical forms, the branches horizontal'. The last group of 4 is described as 'evergreen trees

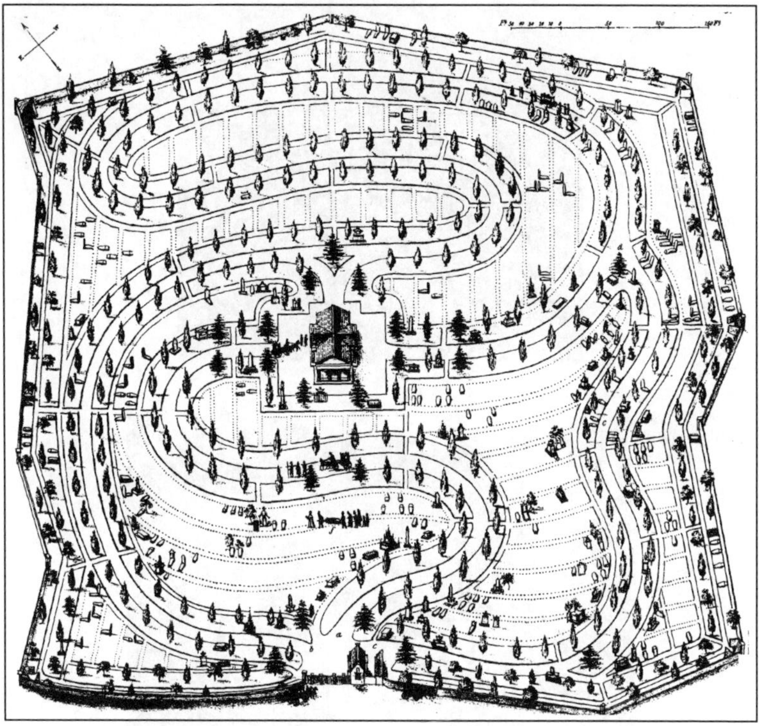

FIG. XLI. DESIGN FOR LAYING OUT AND PLANTING A CEMETERY ON HILLY GROUND.

Figure 7.1 Louden's ideal layout for a cemetery on hilly ground. The perimeter is marked with a double row of trees. The main winding paths are lined with trees with key trees at junctions. The minor paths mark the grid in which grave plots are made and smaller trees are planted among the tombs. Arnos Vale came to follow this style closely.

with needle leaves and pendant branches, peculiarly well adapted for being used in cemeteries so as they droop over monuments'. So Louden not only specified types of tree, he was also concerned with their size, shape, nature of foliage, and so forth, using their precise materiality to very specific symbolic and practical ends. Early photos and newspaper reports show that Arnos Vale was planted in this way (Figure 7.2). In contrast, and to illustrate the subsequent discussion, Figure 7.2 also shows the cemetery as it is today.

Louden's specification of predominantly evergreen coniferous trees, particularly cypress, juniper and yew, should be understood in a number of contexts. He was aware that certain evergreen trees, particularly the cypress and yew, had ancient associations with sites of burial. Furthermore their dark, sombre colour suited the Victorian 'cult' of death and burial, and their lack of leaf litter and prim forms suited the desire for symbolic and practical order. This was also the great

Figure 7.2 Arnos Vale in 1855 (top) showing developing 'Loudenesque' landscape, and in 1999, showing the extent of tree cover which is formed of both the planted evergreen trees and self-seeded 'wild' trees (Owain Jones)

period of Victorian plant-collecting which included a great enthusiasm for 'pinetea' from north-west America and other locations and this provided many new exotic variations of evergreen trees to choose from.

The new metropolitan cemeteries of the 1820s and 1830s were in part prompted by the crisis in older urban burial grounds which were overfull, and often considered to be health hazards. Such scenes are portrayed by Charles Dickens in *Bleak House*, where a London churchyard was 'a scene of horror' where there were piles of bones and burials which could be uncovered merely by sweeping away a thin layer of dirt. By the mid-nineteenth century many of these older churchyards were closed, boosting the fortunes of the new cemeteries. In addition, the seeking out of new styles of worship and ceremony by nonconformist denominations reinforced this momentum towards the establishment of cemeteries. Dunk and Rugg (1994: 11) suggest that many of the cemetery companies which proliferated from the 1820s onwards 'were founded by Dissentors wanting access to larger tracts of burial lands'. From the outset, Arnos Vale was planned to have two chapels, one for the Established Church, and another for the use of Dissenters. These wider trends ensured that for the latter half of the nineteenth century Arnos Vale was very successful, with the cemetery slowly being aggrandized with flamboyant monuments and tombs of the great and the good of Bristol, and filled by more modest graves of other citizens. The cemetery was by now a notable 'Arcadian' landscape undergoing continuous improvement and expansion, wherein the role of trees remained paramount. A local newspaper, the *Bristol Mirror*, reported how a nursery (Garraways) had been engaged to plant trees and extend and improve the path network. It records (29 March 1845) that 'the directors have ordered various walks, paths and terraces to be immediately formed, and nearly 2000 trees and shrubs viz cyprus, red cedar, juniper, yew, laurestinus, laurel, common and variegated hollies, Austrian pines, arbutus etc. are to be planted this season'. These trees of 'Loudenesque' specification were added to the trees already planted which were growing in stature, and the mature deciduous trees which were 'inherited' from the previous country park land use.

The burial grounds within the city of Bristol, with a few exceptions, were ordered to be closed in January 1854 under the Health in Towns Act. This boosted the 'trade' of the new cemetery considerably, and for fifty years Arnos Vale was the city's principal place of burial. The monuments in the older parts of the cemetery are witness to the growing political and industrial importance of Bristol. Thus was created a sedate, sombre, yet also grand landscape consisting of well-kept grounds, with winding main paths and with grids of smaller paths and graves running between them, all this vertically punctuated with the large grave monuments and the dispersed pattern of the individual trees with their distinct forms.

But by 1900 'the golden years of Arnos Vale had passed' (Owen, undated). This came about through shifting legislative patterns and cultural attitudes towards burial, and the growth of Bristol as a city. Arnos Vale faced competition from three other cemeteries taken over or established by the City Council, and the application of commercial logic to burial was questioned. In addition to these external pressures, the cemetery had become increasingly full of graves. By 1906 there had been some 90,000 interments, which meant increased management and maintenance demands and diminishing areas free for new burials. But at this time contemporary press reports still told how the cemetery was 'a beautiful spot, *very carefully conserved and admirably managed.*' (Owen: undated).

The twentieth century saw a continuing slow decline in the fortunes of the cemetery in the face of the pressures outlined above. In addition to these pressures, cremation became a growing trend, taking 'trade' away form the cemetery. This decline was significantly manifested in the retreat of management from older areas of the cemetery and a downturn in the overall intensity of management, apart from that of the most prominent areas near the entrance and chapels where many key monuments stood. As management retreated, some areas began to become overgrown, trees began to self-seed and planted trees grew too large for the location in relation to the grave monuments. Over time, these changes allowed the cemetery to become of considerable ecological importance and a valued green space in what was now a densely built-up inner-city area.

Prompted by financial problems, ownership changed hands on two occasions, on the latter occasion due to the insolvency of the cemetery company. By the 1980s, in the contexts of the property boom and political-economic deregulation, persistent rumours of prospective development on various parts of the cemetery caused great concern for those with relatives buried in the cemetery or who owned family plots, and for those who saw it as a treasured ecological/recreational green space. This 'threat' and the decline in the management and condition of the cemetery was a persistent story-line in the main Bristol newspapers.

In response to this, in 1987 the Association for the Preservation of Arnos Vale Cemetery (APAC) was formed. The society's aims were to resist any form of redeployment of the site, to conserve and enhance it as a place of burial and remembrance and to conserve and enhance it as a site of ecological and cultural heritage. These aims broadly reflected the concerns of two main factions associated with the cemetery: those who were concerned about its fate and condition as a place of burial, and those who saw it as site of ecological value. Initially there was considerable conflict between these factions over the desired extent of clearance of trees and undergrowth in order to protect graves and provide clear access to them, and to a degree this tension remains. But under the threat of ongoing dereliction, closure and possible redevelopment these groups have increasingly adopted a strategy of collectivizing their aims. Under the auspices of the preservation lobby, a series of very heated public meetings was held where the owners and, on occasions, the council faced much anger – again attracting substantial media coverage.

Certain trees had by now colonized the site vigorously, developing the ecological (to an extent – see below) and recreational value of the site. These 'wild trees' were either seeded from the original ornamental planting, or seeded through processes of colonization. In particular many ash saplings appeared (some from two originally planted ornamental ash), and also many sycamore saplings (some seeded from one spectacular 'mother' tree which was one of the trees present at the outset of the cemetery). These new trees 'used' the cover of the tombs and graves to get established. Any form of mechanized management such as mowing/strimming (by the now depleted cemetery staff) which would have kept them in check was impossible around the tightly packed graves. The gravel beds and joints within the masonry of the grave monuments provided safe havens for seed germination.

Various short-term publicly financed job-creation programmes in the 1980s were deployed to 'clean up' parts of the cemetery, and some of the young saplings and spreading undergrowth was cleared. But this only served to boost the progress of the trees' occupation of the site. The cleared trees were in effect being coppiced and grew back with renewed vigour, while undergrowth such as bramble, which might have overwhelmed the saplings, was cleared. Despite these tree problems, with the original planting and consequent growth of other trees the site had become rich in arboreal terms. A unique list of the tree species now in place at Arnos Vale has been compiled by Mr Tony Titchen who conducts 'Tree Gazing' walks around this and other 'tree places'.

• female monkey puzzle • Lawson cypress • golden form of Lawson cypress • yellow form of Lawson cypress • south European cypress • Sawara cypress • Nookta cypress • black Austrian pine • western red cedar • cherry laurel • yew • Irish yew • holm oak • purple cherry plum • double Japanese flowering cherry • holly • field maple • English elm • Japanese spindle • sycamore • false acacia • English hawthorn • horse chestnut • double midland hawthorn • Himalayan cedar • English oak • laburnum • cherry • rowan • weeping ash • lilac • Aucuba laurel • variegated English holly • Lebanon cedar • elder • European larch • bird cherry • Norway spruce • apple

These trees bring a wide variety of place-related agency to the cemetery site (see Chapter 4). They bring different texture, colour, shape, sound, life and seasonal cycles, different abilities to colonize and so forth. For example, one frequent visitor to the cemetery pointed out that one particularly large and prominent horse chestnut acts as a form of 'sentinel to the seasons', because it is the first of the deciduous trees to come into leaf in spring and the first to turn to autumn colours when all the others still remain green. This is recognition of the subtleties and rhythms of ecological time which are embedded in particular ways in which different trees can become bound up with the intimate reading of place.

However, the intention of the owners to develop some or all of the cemetery became increasingly public despite no planning permission actually being sought. One of the founding members of APAC told us that the owners 'had left a big plan clearly visible through the window of the lodge (gate house) showing the place developed, terraced; the main bowl of the cemetery terraced with houses – a sports centre on the top flat ... [it] was a hell of a shock. And that's why APAC was formed really'. The owning company was renamed 'Arnos Vale Village' and the local newspaper continued to run frequent high-profile stories focusing on the problems of the cemetery now coupled to the threat of redevelopment. But for the owners there were many impediments to potential development. Prominent among these were the remaining active status of the cemetery with a significant number of recent burials, the 'live' ownership of many of the plots, the sheer number of graves, and the fact that many of them were of great historical, architectural, and sentimental interest, with a number being listed monuments. The historical Arcadian landscape and planting was also of conservation interest, and the site was noted for its ecological richness and for its new status as, in effect, an urban woodland.

Although some of the graves have been maintained throughout this turbulent time, thousands of graves have been and are still being destroyed by the spreading, growing trees. This has made the site dangerous in many places, with the tomb structures being gradually toppled and destabilized by roots and expanding trunks, particularly on the sloping areas. More generally the site as a landscape of historic interest has slowly been submerged and degraded by the spread of these wild trees along with areas of brambles and other plants.

In addition to this, and somewhat paradoxically, the spread of the wild trees has also begun to diminish the ecological value of the site. In its extensively/semi-managed mid to late twentieth-century state, it became a significant grassland site with a notable bio-diversity of flora and fauna (particularly butterflies). The now unchecked spread of the trees has diminished this value. Accordingly, the site for

Figure 7.3 The destruction of graves by trees. In many areas each grave seems to have a 'companion' tree which has taken root in its masonry. The trees here show that they have previously been cut back and are now growing in coppiced form (Owain Jones)

some has also become 'more spooky, because it is so completely overgrown; some parts of it are very sinister' (interview with female adult visitor).

The local media and pressure groups on a number of occasions have accused the owners of adopting a policy of deliberate neglect in anticipation of the cemetery eventually losing its historic value and amenity capacity through these processes, thus lessening resistance to development. But, conversely, the growing presence of trees on the site has secured its reputation as a green space in the city, which has attracted the attention of individuals, pressure groups and the City Council. The site remains ecologically rich and pressure groups and individuals have gone to great lengths to chart this richness and to bring it to the attention of the council and the public. For example the Bristol branch of the Green Party has information about the ongoing fate of Arnos Vale on its website. In 1999 a local naturalist, Peter Brain, compiled a list of 320 flora and fauna species for submission to the Botanical Society. The council have also designated the cemetery as a city landscape feature, the trees, standing on a steep hillside, being seen from many parts of the city. This decline in the business fortunes of the cemetery and its consequent 'wilding' needs also to be seen in the wider contexts of growing public sensitivity to environmental issues (often articulated in tree-protest sagas as at the Newbury bypass actions), and concern for 'urban green space' where again trees serve as a key icon (as in the Community Forests initiatives and the work of the Urban Forestry Unit).

The cemetery was closed by the owners in April 1998, with the last staff being laid off, and the gates being left permanently open (before, they were shut each night). By this time APAC had renamed itself 'Friends of Arnos Vale Cemetery' (FAVC). They saw the conditions of closure as a further threat to the cemetery because the lack of surveillance and open access at night would provide opportunities for vandalism and other crime. The degree and kinds of threat posed to the cemetery if left open and without monitoring was exemplified when three people pleaded guilty in Bristol Crown Court to taking a corpse from a vault that had been broken into (*Bristol Evening Post*, 18/11/2000). Although FAVC regarded direct action as an unsuitable practice for their purposes, individuals joined together to form the so-called 'Arnos Vale Army', and since then they have co-ordinated a daily presence at the main gate, locked the gates each night, and carried out a small amount of work on monument maintenance (in particular cutting back new trees growing in the joints of key monuments) and keeping some paths clear. But this action is controversial and the owners have taken various volunteers to court for trespass and attempted to have them evicted from the site. The overall legal position is very complex, with grave owners having rights to access and to clear around and maintain their plots, but with any other work being prohibited. The main local newspaper – the *Bristol Evening Post* – has continued to run a high-profile 'save our cemetery' campaign and has closely associated itself with the protestors. The city council, after a long, intermittent, and much criticized involvement with 'the Arnos Vale cemetery question', has taken action to prevent further damage to the main buildings, which are listed, and has commissioned a report to consider possible future ownership, funding and management strategies for the site. A major part of these future plans focuses on the extent to which the cemetery is 'restored' and the extent to which areas are left 'wild' as they now are.

The agency of trees in Arnos Vale has clearly been an active co-constituent in the changing nature and contested cultures of the place. Trees have made 'wild' the very place where they were deployed to contribute to order, and the dwelling presence of some of them has complexly transformed from being 'in-place' to being 'out-of-place'. These changes have been enrolled by different parties in different ways. The owners of the site claim that the trees have overrun the cemetery, and effectively usurped its character, thus clearing the way for redevelopment. For others, however, the agency of trees has been co-constitutive of a remaking of place, specifically into a 'green space' and a 'wildlife haven'. Intriguingly, trees have also been implicated in attempts to monitor changes at the site from different perspectives.

We want to argue not only that trees act as socialized actors in the narrative of the changing nature of Arnos Vale, but also that they contribute significantly to the relational agencies involved. To assert that trees can perform some kind of intentional agency would be both essentialist and naturalist. However, to argue that a form of *purposive agency* is detectable, whereby trees reproduce, colonize, and eventually change the nature of a place, may be a significant contribution to the understanding of what is involved in relational agency (see Chapter 3). It is on this basis that the non-human agency of trees has been inextricably bound up in processes of resistance, monitoring and surveillance of Arnos Vale cemetery.

Resistance and the (Re)construction of the Nature of Nature

The assertion that the non-human agency of trees has been implicated in *processes of resistance* at Arnos Vale requires some further elaboration. We agree with Mitchell (2000) that resistance can usefully be understood as an infinite variety of processes and practices by which people engage with and redefine places as the materials for the construction of their everyday lives. At the individual level de Certeau (1984) has conceptualized the ways in which the everyday practices of city-dwellers are foreign, different and resistant to the geometric and panoptic constructions of city spaces by planning and policing agencies. For instance, the practice of walking can be viewed as an appropriation of the topographical system, an action which is out of its rightful spatial place. Walking in the city, then, can create shadows and ambiguities within spatial organizations thus representing acts of resistance to those institutions seeking to order both space and lives. In de

Certeau's terms, the *strategy* of powerful forces is thus opposed by the *tactics* of everyday practices which by their very lived-out nature can subvert the official narratives of a particular space.

These individual resistances present multiple pathways of practice, the intersections of which can translate individual resistance into social movements, in which protest becomes public and a cultural politics emerges which serves to contest the meanings and boundaries by which we make sense of the world (see Jackson, 1989). At this point, intentional enrolment of actants can be used to develop more formal networks of resistance. The intersections of practices of resistance can also lead to the enrolment of particular places – and a wide range of human and non-human actants in these places – as sites of resistance in the city. Such practices of resistance are vividly illustrated by the growth of skateboarding in the city. Here the city becomes redefined by non-human objects – slopes, ramps, rails, edges – the presence of which permits the production of skateboarding places which in turn become sites of resistance against the architectural city, and its orthodox behaviours (see Borden, 1998).

One typical site of contestation and resistance is the public park. Zukin (1996) has shown how public spaces have progressively been privatized, being transformed from collective spaces reflecting the civic achievements of their nineteenth-century roots to areas of decline often characterized by a lack of local government investment and increasing levels of an everyday fear of crime (see also Barker, 2000). This has been the fate of many cemeteries similar to Arnos Vale but which were set up or taken over by civic authorities. A very recent Government report into the conditions of graveyards and cemeteries, published by a House of Commons environment sub-committee, stated 'we were taken aback by the sheer magnitude of the problems facing our cemeteries' which are 'unsafe, littered, vandalised and unkempt' and which 'shame all society' (Guardian, 31 March 2001). Some have been cleared, others remain in a parlous state, while others are now subject to conservation and regeneration.

Meanwhile the public sphere is recolonized into privately-owned spaces often managed and policed privately. Privatization of space is alienable in nature. A control over land and property gives owners the right to control the nature therein – for example by deciding which trees are permitted and which are not, or by letting trees 'go wild'. The policing of the nature of nature in cities is thus increasingly turned over to the private sector. Arnos Vale, being privately owned, has been in some ways an example of this, but its definition as private or public is intensely ambiguous; it is used as a park for walking, is open in the day, locked at night, and has thousands of privately owned plots which en masse make it almost publicly owned. While the owners first manipulated, then battled with, then abandoned the roles of nature and in particular of the trees, other groups have enrolled the trees on the site into complex tactics of resistance.

Discussions of resistance in the context of youth culture have recognized a process of *bricolage* in which objects are re-ordered and re-contextualized in order to communicate fresh meanings (see for example Clarke, 1976; Hebdige, 1979). In this way, objects which previously carried sedimented symbolic meanings are seen to be resignified in a new context in relation to other artefacts. Resistance, then, as Hall (1996) explains, is constituted by repertoires whose meanings are specific to particular times, places and social relationships. We want to argue that non-human agents such as trees can be integrally co-constitutive of sites of resistance such as public open spaces, and will therefore be implicated in shifts in public culture such as that which Zukin describes. It can often be the case that trees themselves become symbolic of the nature-value of a place and thereby become the focus of individual and social resistance based around a particular place. Non-human agents are therefore subject to forms of bricolage, implicated in processes of re-contextualization, and resignified accordingly, taking their place in new repertoires of meaning and relational agency. In some ways, this is what happened at Arnos Vale cemetery. However, it might also be argued that non-human agents such as trees are partly responsible for some processes of bricolage, in that a transformation of the nature and extent of tree presence at a site is itself capable of recontextualizing and resignifying that place, prompting different kinds of relational agencies therein.

Monitoring the Nature of Nature

We further argue, from our research at Arnos Vale, that the non-human agency of trees is also implicated in how the nature of a place is monitored. Here we focus on how the changing nature of places is made known, and incorporated both into a planned (re)structuring and (re)ordering of place, and into resistance to these overarching spatialities. Processes of monitoring and surveillance can occur in both the public and the private sectors, but will often be directed to particular elements or artefacts of nature, charting their presence, extent, vitality, viability and so on.

It is interesting at the start to recognize the subtle but significant discursive slants embedded in the terms *monitoring* and *surveillance*. In lay discourses at least, monitoring suggests a supposedly neutral, often scientific 'keeping an eye on' a place, process or situation. Surveillance on the other hand, reflects a similar process of 'keeping watch', but there are overtones of power and morality. Surveillance is undertaken for a purpose, often because negative or criminal consequences are suspected. To be 'under surveillance' seems more threatening than to be 'monitored'. We argue here that in fact, both monitoring and surveillance are embedded in more general processes by which discourses of nature and environment are generated, empowered and resisted; processes which are replete with issues of empowerment and moral judgementalism. We want, therefore, to discuss three interrelated sets of processes by which monitoring and surveillance have impacted upon *both* the place-characteristics of Arnos Vale cemetery, *and* the ensuing intentions and actions of power and resistance relating to the site.

'Monitoring and surveillance as processes by which discursive knowledges about nature are generated, accumulated and circulated' (Luke, 1999)

The deployment of scientific techniques and knowledges will often be assumed to be above or outside of any manipulative practices of discursive framing, but as Macnaghten and Urry (1998) insist, 'this assumption that environmental problems exist in nature waiting to be "read" by evolving scientific knowledge and techniques has been subject to critique' (95). Not only is the relationship between science and policy itself subject to significant negotiation but also there are important cultural assumptions inherent in how the changing nature of, and threat to, nature are defined and materialized within scientific knowledge-making (see for example Shackley and Wynne, 1995a; 1995b).

There are therefore likely to be multiple discursive framings taking place around any particular controversy over nature-places. Macnaghten and Urry further argue that 'such variable framings have far-reaching implications for how environmental messages and risks come to be understood and consumed by the wider public' (1998: 99).

It is our contention that these implications also apply at the local level, where various framings of a particular place, and the attendant messages about the risks to the present character of that place from proposed future uses, are often articulated in terms of processes of monitoring and surveillance. Not only will discursive knowledges about nature be generated in this way, but also the resultant discourses will then be subject to what has been called discursive 'slippage'. Competing discourses will be porous to one another, and debates over a particular site will involve shifting between different discursive modes: shifts which, as Harvey (1996: 89) argues, 'imply all sorts of slippages, ambiguities and incoherences'.

Monitoring and surveillance as processes by which particular human agents are empowered to interpret nature

As implied above, scientific monitoring and surveillance are often deployed by key actors in order to extend their power over particular places or practices. Put simply, the power of the owners of a site, for example, is often expressed by their ability to present accounts of what happens therein – accounts which themselves are imbued with the 'results' of monitoring and surveillance practices. State regulators of that site will also depend to some extent on monitoring and surveillance as the basis of potential intervention. As Harvey (1999) suggests, state intervention will typically only occur when there is clear evidence (preferably strong scientific evidence) that market failure has led to serious damage. Other powerful agencies such as media organizations will also make use of monitoring and surveillance techniques to empower their voice(s) on the issues concerned.

Much of the conceptual attention to empowerment over nature relates to large-scale issues of environmental damage and pollution. We argue, however, that these concerns are replicated at the more local level. Differing discourses and contestations of meanings relating to nature can clearly arise when particular localities become entangled in the hierarchical relations of powerful external forces (Mauzé, 1998). However, some such issues of empowered discursive control also occur over localized place-sites, where smaller-scale issues of the place of nature can also be contested using the tools of monitoring and surveillance.

Monitoring and surveillance as processes by which hegemonic discourses and interpretations can be actively resisted

As well as being practices of the powerful, aspects of monitoring and surveillance – as we have shown – can also be viewed as tools of resistance, to be employed by those wishing to defend nature's places from change and thereby implicate scientific discourses in campaigns of political and moral justice. This case is put lucidly by Torgerson (1999):

> How is a place to be defended? In a context where prevailing power relations, closed policy deliberations, and narrowly constructed discourse are amenable to the advance of industrialisation, the clear answer would appear to be more politics. The need for a cultural politics in defence of place seems obvious and inescapable. (190)

Such cultural politics will sometimes employ scientific monitoring as a counter to that used to (re)produce hegemonic discourses. At a local level, however, it is often not feasible for place-defenders to exercise monitoring and surveillance of the environment to the same extent as landowners and state regulators. Issues of access, resources and legitimacy often stand in the way of 'parallel' monitoring. Moreover, such resistance can turn to alternative means of expression and communication – what Iris Marion Young (1992; see also 1990) has called the heterogeneous publics of passion, play and aesthetic interest. She indicates here the possibilities for 'guerrilla theatre' and 'chants, music, song and dancing' to make political points (129). However, we would add that the specific case of tree-places seems to induce other forms of passion, play and aesthetics. Rival (1998b), for example, has suggested that

> Trees are meaningful not only for what they represent but also in themselves, as sources of actual and sensual involvement with the world. Performance, the ritualisation of theatrical symbolic actions . . . [are] key to political actions that address the materiality of the world and take life as a primary issue for political intervention'. (17)

Our research at Arnos Vale cemetery suggests a series of low-key but significant public theatres of performance and aesthetic actions of resistance. Participation in 'tree-gazing' walks, meticulous cataloguing of tree types, and posting a 'guard' at the gates: all represent means by which practices of monitoring and surveillance become bound up with public displays of passion and resistance, in which performance and aesthetic passion are integral to the political point being made.

Monitoring and Surveillance at Arnos Vale

A number of different strands of monitoring and surveillance are evident in the unfolding narrative of Arnos Vale. These are important for a number of reasons, not least because they represent attempts to construct knowledges of the ongoing flows of relational agency, and to chart the character of these flows, in order to enrol agency in steering the fate of the cemetery in particular directions. Discussion of monitoring and surveillance also highlights different appreciations of the same site, and contesting attempts to enrol and translate the agencies at work in the cemetery.

From its inception, the cemetery represented a space which was specifically designed with surveillance in mind. First, place-making was connected to the general surveillance of burial practices. Louden's designs were specifically aimed at the ordered disposal of bodies in ordered cemeteries. The cemetery was a good place to be seen dead in! The trees which were planted were thought to be those which were suited to this order, through a combination of colour, form of growth, size when fully grown, lack of leaf litter and the ability to grow without intense management. Trees complemented the large ornate tombs, and in sum Arnos Vale was designed as an ordered Arcadian landscape in which the burials and the visiting of the cemetery could be done with due dignity and order. For example Arnos Vale, like the new cemetery layouts advocated by Louden, was designed with circular main paths with one-way traffic flows so incoming carriages would not have to pass those leaving from previous funerals.

With its decline from this heyday, the link between surveillance and order began to slip significantly. Facing competition from municipal cemeteries, Arnos Vale became less economic, and the ability of the owners to manage the entire cemetery began to diminish. Monitoring and maintenance was thus withdrawn to the key central area with the most important tombs, to areas recently used and still being used for new burials, and the main paths and building. The agency of nature became significant as it 'encroached' into these now unmonitored unmaintained areas. The trees which each year shed their seeds now 'saw' those seeds getting established rather than being checked by mowing or other management practices. The order of the cemetery declined markedly, and visitors could not help but monitor the blocked paths, the toppling gravestones and the ensuing vandalism which was hidden from surveillance by the encroachment of trees on the site and the depletion of staffing levels.

At some point, a *lack* of surveillance became an advantage to the owners. With the site being uneconomic as a cemetery, it was in their interests to permit overgrowth and despoliation which further emphasized the site's lack of utility as a graveyard. The agency of the trees was effectively enrolled into arguments for the end of the old land use, and therefore the inevitability of a new more economic use as a prime residential site. Initial surveys were carried out for the purpose of designing potential layouts for new housing. Scientific monitoring of the land was reinvested, this time for a very different, though similarly ordered, purpose. The owners were content that others should monitor the dilapidation of the site in order to produce discursive knowledges about its decrepit nature that would in turn be enrolled into the desire to build houses there. In this case, then, the empowering of the owners came through offering powers of monitoring and surveillance to other interests, in the expectation that the owners' interpretation of the nature of the site would be adopted.

Other regimes of monitoring and surveillance were also woven through the site. The Commonwealth War Graves Commission, which has responsibility for the upkeep of graves of Commonwealth service personnel who died in the First and Second World Wars, paid regular visits to the site to monitor the condition of the numerous war graves in the cemetery. Thus it was possible to encounter single small graves in the middle of the most overgrown areas of the cemetery, where the encroaching undergrowth and trees had been cleared away. Various local naturalists were listing the flora and fauna of the site. In 1982–83, a leading figure in this group – Peter Brain – conducted a tree survey of the site, with 1353 trees being closely mapped and identified (Figure 7.4). These kinds of observation contributed to the data held on Arnos Vale by the Bristol Environmental Record Centre, which serves to provide 'baseline' data of bio-diversity for ongoing environmental monitoring and land-use decision-making. The site is now listed to host approximately 350 species of plants (including the 40 or more species of

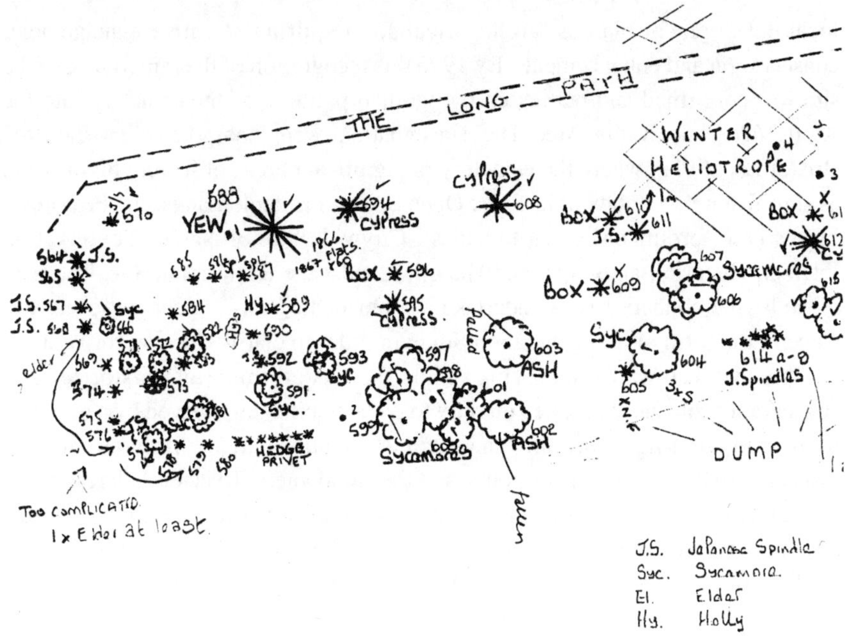

Figure 7.4 Extract from Peter Brain's tree survey, 1983. Each tree was mapped in relation to the cemetery paths, then given a number and recorded in a log, giving size, type, and other information. Later, Peter Brain was one of the co-authors of the Draft Management Plan drawn up by APAC, and used in negotiations with the owners and the City Council.

trees), 35 species of breeding birds, 25 species of butterflies, plus bats, amphibians and slow-worms.

During this history of Arnos Vale, there are two key intersections between the monitoring of the site by its owners and that of the regulatory body concerned – Bristol City Council. The first came from the 1890s onwards when the newly created local authorities were empowered to develop municipal cemeteries. The private-sector graveyards were still viewed as insufficiently regulated, and so state-sector surveillance of burial practices was introduced. This change contributed directly to the decline of Arnos Vale as a cemetery. The second intersection occurred sporadically through the period following the Second World War. The city council was given new planning powers under the 1947 Town and Country Planning Act, and intermittently became concerned at the despoliation of the historic importance of Arnos Vale. This surveillance of the site was, however, relatively weak given that the council regularly reported on its inability to intervene in the site because it was privately owned. Only later, with the onset of other forms of public monitoring and surveillance of the site, did the city council act more decisively. In the early 1990s the council designated the site of the cemetery in its local development plan as 'an historical site requiring sensitive management, conservation and enhancement'. By 1996 this recognition of the importance of the site was confirmed and buttressed by the incorporation of the cemetery into the Arnos Vale Conservation Area. These designations were incorporated into the 1997 Bristol Local Plan where the cemetery or significant areas of it were highlighted as significant in 5 policy objectives: Open Space; Principle Landscape Features – in this case 'prominent green hillsides'; Citywide Site of Nature Conservation Interest; Historic Landscape; and Historic Landscape Restoration Site. The next move by the council was to undertake a sophisticated form of scientific surveillance in the form of a Regeneration Study in order to clarify the way forward.

The switch towards surveying Arnos Vale as an important historical and conservation site can be related directly to the council being swayed by a different form of monitoring of the site, and the interpretations arising from an inherent resistance to the hegemonic discourses of the landowners. To label such resistance as 'public opinion' is significantly to under-represent particular strands of user-discourse which emerged during this time, and between which much entangled 'sliding' of discourses has occurred. These strands may be identified as

- people who have friends/relatives buried in the cemetery
- people cherishing the ecological value of the site
- people using the site as a local amenity space
- the local newspaper – the *Bristol Evening Post*.

The first group have constantly submitted reports to the owners on the poor state of Arnos Vale. They were co-founders of APAC in 1987, but before that time they had actively sought to enrol the local newspaper so as to make public the state of the cemetery. One prominent member of this group – Les Owen – has undertaken to identify and record all the graves of interest (in terms of design, local history, and national history), thereby adding heritage factors to discursive interpretations associated with remembrance and personal attachment to the site.

The other founders of APAC were groups or individuals who had recognized the increasing importance of the site as a nature reserve. Individuals and groups regularly came to the site to look at different species of trees and butterflies, and bird- and badger-watching were also important. After extensive survey work, APAC drew up a comprehensive draft management plan, which has been used as a lever in negotiations with the owners and the council. This detailed monitoring added scientific credence to the arguments of the group, charting as it did both the continued existence of key Loudenesque trees and the rapid incursion of self-seeding trees. More recently Arnos Vale has been the location of regular tree-gazing walks (Figure 7.5) run by a local expert under the auspices of the council, and further contributing to the surveillance of the site.

Figure 7.5 Tree-gazing walk in Arnos Vale cemetery conducted by Tony Titchen (Owain Jones)

APAC formed in the face of rumours that the owners were to develop the site for housing. These rumours were circulated via the *Bristol Evening Post*, which had been publishing stories about the cemetery since at least the late 1970s. By the late 1980s the newspaper joined with FAVC (formally APAC) to campaign for a clean-up programme for the site. Here, the tensions between those who were interested in conserving the graves, and those who were primarily concerned with nature conservation themselves were producing contesting surveillance reports. Equally, others were content to use the existing site for local recreation, both as an interesting place for a walk among trees and graves or, in the case of children, building dens and tree-houses – a place in which to 'get lost' and escape the 'surveillance' of the city.

As we have reported, the internal divisions in APAC were largely negotiated away on recognition of the collective strength of combined interpretations of the site. However, when the owners tried to close the site in 1998, the informal group calling themselves the Arnos Vale Army intervened without the permission of the owners to open the cemetery on a daily basis and kept a caravan at the gates as a base for their 'watch' to ensure that the cemetery was kept open but that vandalism was restricted. They also organized a well-attended and noisy march from the cemetery to the Council House when a council committee were debating Arnos Vale. Here they occupied the public gallery, and threatened to occupy the council chamber itself, all under the gaze of press and TV cameras.

Arnos Vale is by no means typical of the ways in which environmental monitoring impacts on nature-places in this surveillance society. After its well planned and ordered inception, most of the subsequent monitoring has been undertaken by enthusiasts who have been seeking to use their surveys to resist the non-decision-making of both owners and local authority. These surveys were labours of love by skilled individuals who were placed outside of formal decision-making networks, but who ultimately, and particularly by enrolling the power of the local media, were able to resist the wishes of the landowners.

It had been the hope of landowners that the site would be recognized as being so overgrown as to be spoilt for its original purpose, and therefore ripe for profitable redevelopment. However, once local resistance had gained momentum, the landowners were faced with monitoring and surveillance that they could not afford to counteract. The unprofitable nature of the site rendered counter-monitoring and even counter-surveillance as too expensive. Thereby their seemingly hegemonic position as generators and circulators of discursive knowledges about the site was undermined.

The power of monitoring and surveillance as tools of resistance is, however, amply demonstrated at Arnos Vale. In this case, interests of resistance were (unusually) more able to operationalize practices of monitoring and surveillance. Moreover, they matched pseudo-scientific discourses with alternative expressions of passion, performance and aesthetics. Bringing interested individuals to the site for 'tree-gazing' walks appealed to what Rival (1998b: 17) describes as the 'sources of actual and sensual involvement with the world' offered by trees. The caravan at the gate, checking entrances and exits while publicizing 'campaigns', collecting signatures and generally acting as 'pseudo-owners' of the site was pure theatre: a showpiece of ritualized symbolic action. The march to the council house by the Arnos Vale 'Army' was accompanied by the kind of singing and chanting which Young (1992) refers to. All were forms of surveillance, but bound up with public displays of passion and resistance, in which a telling political point was being made.

Posters and information sheets issued by the protesters often used the image of the trees and wooded landscape to depict the quality of the place. In these kinds of ways, the trees at Arnos Vale were very much implicated in the policing of the nature of nature at that site. Control over property is usually thought to ensure the right to control nature in that place, but in this case the monitoring process served to socialize and democratize the monitoring which took place. Surveys by local activists and enthusiasts were initially carried out for their own sake, but became enrolled as an essential part of a more planned social resistance. The changing tree presence at Arnos Vale induced a form of bricolage, serving to recontextualize and resignify the site. Monitoring of trees made this bricolage known, and prompted the individual pathways of practice to be translated into key intersections of social movements of resistance, and in turn to the construction of a significant site of resistance, at which the privatization of public space could be contested.

This resistance has to date been successful. Plans to redevelop Arnos Vale for housing have been averted, and the local authority has been persuaded to regulate in favour of a future for the site which combines its status as cemetery and conservation area. The current situation is that the city council has fully taken up the cause of the cemetery. In November 1999, a report commissioned by the council on the potential regeneration of Arnos Vale concluded that the cemetery is not 'viable as a working burial ground' and it 'or any part of it, has little development value'. Therefore, for the future,

> The cemetery's unique character, landscape, historic interest and environment will . . . allow its role in the City's life to be extended beyond that of a burial ground to provide an amenity accessible to the public, a major urban green space, a reserve for urban wildlife, an amenity recreational and leisure resource and an educational resource for the City. This can be achieved without prejudice to its historic integrity. (Niall Phillips Architects, 1999)

To achieve these ends, the council is continuing to negotiate with the owners, and it has taken the decision to prepare the way for the implementation of a Compulsory Purchase Order for the site if these negotiations are unsatisfactory. It is hoped that this lengthy process can be avoided, as it would prevent any major preventative work getting under way. The historic records of the funerals and burials at the cemetery remain in one of the abandoned buildings which is in poor condition, and there is great concern over the fate of these unique records. And all the while the 'wild trees' are continuing to spread and grow. In the meantime the Council is setting up a Charitable Trust which will take control of the site and begin the process of regeneration, and is investigating possible sources of funding support from such programmes as the Lottery Heritage Fund.

The fate of Arnos Vale mirrors a wider concern for the future of other Victorian cemeteries and burial grounds across Britain. Some have been cleared, some remain in states of semi-dereliction, while others, most notably Highgate in London, are being managed in new ways and for new purposes, similar to those now envisaged for Arnos Vale. A host of contingent factors determine the particular narratives of these different places. At Arnos Vale the shifting and growing presence of the trees has been an influential thread to this unfolding story, this unfolding place.

Many questions remain, however, about the future maintenance of the site, and specifically about who plans for the 'shaping' of trees at Arnos Vale, and who pays for that shaping. The success of resistance has only been the first step to securing an environmentally and democratically acceptable future for the site. In particular the transformation of the site from an ordered, relatively stable functioning cemetery and Arcadian landscape to a site with a significant more unruly and dynamic ecology, presents delicate problems of planning the co-existence of these two key elements of this place. How the 'lay knowledges and expertise' of the campaigning groups (such as the tree survey and management plan) is incorporated into the new institutional shaping of the cemetery will also be a vital question.

Here again we have tried to show how trees have been bound up in the ongoing folding and refolding of this place in symbolic and material terms. Their place-transforming capacities are evident through both their insistent material dynamism and the shifting imaginative attentions they attract. We have shown that trees have both acted as socialized actors in the narrative of the changing nature of Arnos Vale and contributed significantly to the relational agencies involved. Trees have thereby been implicated in processes of resistance at the site, particularly through their incorporation in practices of monitoring and surveillance. The changing tree presence at Arnos Vale has served to recontextualize and resignify the site, and the monitoring of trees has made this bricolage known, prompting the construction of a significant site of resistance, where the privatzation of public space has been contested.

–8–

Heritage Trail

> The xenophobia non-native trees often inspire was then tackled . . . conifers were seen as alien imports, 'plainly lacking the cultural credentials of the native broadleaf . . . [L]ike other immigrants, these fir trees "all look the same" to the affronted native eye'.
>
> (Tsouvalis, 2000: 308, citing Wright, 1992)

> I know they may say that they are not native, but the conifers were very dramatic. (Camerton resident and protester against tree felling)

Camerton is a village in the county of Bath and North-East Somerset, in south-west England, some 20 miles from the city of Bristol. It is sited on the old Somerset coalfield, and indeed one of the 70 or so collieries of the coalfield was located in the village. Camerton's interest as a tree-place is wrapped up in this industrial history. We particularly want to draw attention to part of the old coalfield site which was a bare spoil heap at the end of the last century, and was planted with conifers soon after. These conifers were gradually joined by other self-seeded trees as the use of the site for coal mining declined and, after nationalization in 1947, was finally closed in 1950 and left dormant. More than once, the site has been threatened with clearance, as the legacy of the coal-mining years has faded away. However, with a growing concern for the environment, and with helpful shifts in forestry policy in the 1980s, the site was acquired for the local community as an open space in 1987, and was subsequently developed and managed as a mining and natural heritage site. It has since then been managed as a woodland site and in 1997 was designated as a local nature reserve. Embedded in this bare narrative are a number of often controversial twists and turns in the development of a place, in which the trees have played a central role. Here we find a local folding of national discourses of arbori-culture, and the pressing materiality and agency of trees in place over time.

One of our aims in this chapter is to link discussions of Camerton to the practical concerns of those responsible for the management of sites which have a tree presence within them, be they parks, woodlands, forests, orchards, or other places where trees are major contributors to the place milieu. In particular we suggest that the story of the Camerton site highlights the complexities and difficulties associated with processes of 'stakeholder involvement' which now abound in the culture of governance (see Rhodes, 1997). Multiple agent partnerships involving the state, private-sector concerns, voluntary organizations and 'the community' are now a key structural component of contemporary governance. These partnerships are often involved in vital fund-raising activities, notably bidding for competitive 'challenge' funding, which in part configure the governance of a range of different public functions, including environmental management. The seemingly virtuous nature of these configuring processes serves to conceal a plethora of important questions relating to equity, access to funding and the relative priority given to different needs – questions which have come under critical scrutiny (see for example Peck and Tickell, 1994), not least in the context of local rural state functions (Cloke et al., 2000; Goodwin, 1998; Murdoch and Abram, 1998).

The notion of 'stakeholder involvement' represents an important context for understanding environmental management systems in general, and woodland systems in particular. Stakeholders will bring particular local knowledges (both historic and contemporary), values, power relations and constructions of community identity to processes of negotiation and contestation. Moreover, it is clear that the contingent componency of a particular place – cultural, ecological, political, economic and so on – often generates a unique chemistry which can be equally influential on the outcome of negotiations and on the nature of any contestation. Indeed, more recent approaches to environmental management such as Local Environmental Agency Plans (see Burgess, 2000) provide explicit acknowledgement of such a chemistry.

At Camerton, the presence of coniferous trees planted on the colliery spoil tip early in the twentieth century, and of the other trees which have self-seeded and grown on the site, have established this as a *woodland* place. It has been argued over, managed and funded in terms of its woodland nature, and in terms of its aesthetic, experiential and bureaucratic categorization as woodland. In what follows we consider the unfolding 'socio-ecological' construction of this site through the conceptual lenses of stakeholding and partnership. We suggest that all tree-places will be formed in part through such processes, and that the approach we take offers the opportunity to understand both the specificity of emplaced nature, and the processes by which such places are constructed culturally and naturally. We also chart how national 'tree discourses' are folded and even inverted in this local scenario, and we stress – pressing the key themes of the book – the place-making creativity of the trees present.

The Production of the Local Landscape

Camerton was one of the 70 or so collieries which comprised the Somerset Coalfield in south-west England. The coalfield is now defunct, with the last colliery having closed in 1973. Although there was evidence of mining in medieval times and before, mining in the area burgeoned in relation to the industrial revolution. Down and Warrington (1971) suggest 1790 as marking the beginning of this modern period of coal extraction which continued until a decline began at the beginning of the twentieth century. The Camerton colliery, named as such for its location in the village and parish of Camerton, consisted of two pits. The 'old pit' was sunk in the 1780s, and the 'new pit' was operational by 1800. The old pit was closed for coal winding in 1898, but the shaft was kept open for ventilation and access for the new pit. When the new pit was connected underground to a neighbouring pit (*c.* 1930) the old pit was closed and dismantled. The new pit continued to produce coal until closure in 1950. Thus both pits were producing coal and, significantly, colliery spoil for a century or more, and as was regularly the case, the spoil was tipped close to the pithead. In this way the huge spoil heaps ('batches' being the local name) characteristic of coal-mining areas were gradually formed.

Figure 8.1 shows a map of the Camerton colliery in 1883 with the spoil heaps spreading out from the pitheads of both old and new pits. At this time the spoil was moved using horse- or human-drawn wagons running on rails. The tips were slowly built up with the track being extended as the tip expanded. If topography allowed, the spoil would be tipped below the level of the pithead, thus avoiding having to drag the spoil upwards. At Camerton the ridge of the old tip which marks the route of the extending track rises gradually, thus gaining height which increases the capacity of the tip site. As the ridge of the tip gradually rises, and the ground below drops away, the sides of the tip become increasingly high and steep. This new artificial topography, made entirely as a by-product of production, in the future was to provided a distinctive landscape form which adapts and is adapted by the subsequent use of the site.

In the case of Camerton 'new batch' (the waste from the new pit) as Figure 8.2 shows, mechanical spoil-moving devices which were capable of moving the spoil up steeper inclines were introduced around the turn of the century. In this way, more spoil could be deposited in the same area, and the more modern conical spoil heap was formed (see 1910 inset, Figure 8.1). The new batch thus consists of an early section of old-style tipping with the later-style conical spoil heap superimposed on it. This again has created forms which influence future uses of the site. The scale of the tips in relation to what is now a small community located in an intimate steep valley typical of the area ensures that 'the batches' are dominant landscape features.

This is so for the other 'batches' in the area also. Interestingly, in the Somerset coalfield, more than in many other mining areas (for example the South Wales coalfield), these coal tips have remained relatively undisturbed in terms of clearance or alteration. The reasons for this retention, and the implications for

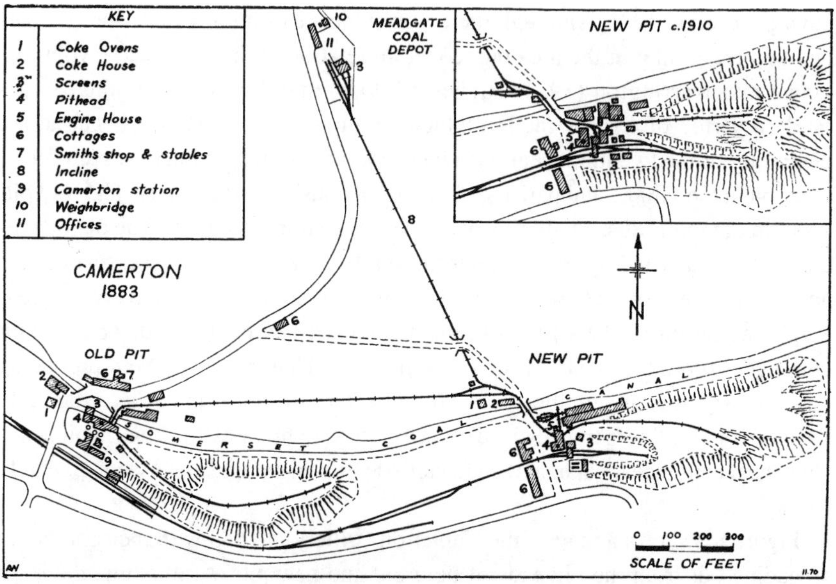

Figure 8.1 Map of the Camerton Colliery 1883, with insert of new pit 1910, showing spoil heaps

Figure 8.2 Photograph of the new pit batch, possibly 1930s, showing a Mclean Tipper, the steeper tip form, and the bare condition of the tips when working

landscape and heritage, have received very little study, although they suggest a fascinating prospective series of case studies of ecological regeneration. As in other coalfields the abandoned tips became prominent features of the local landscape and were seen, by some at least, in negative terms. Little (1969), in his portrait of Somerset, wrote that Camerton was 'still a little gaunt with the relics of its colliery, and with the great pyramid of spoil which blotches the hillside' (23). The survival of the tips may in part be due to their size (they are smaller, for example, than the vast scale of the tips which dominated the industrial landscapes of South Wales) and in part because they are placed in what generally is imagined as a rural landscape. To some extent the tips had gradually become reabsorbed aesthetically into the local, rural, hilly landscape. As Buchanan and Cossons (1969) noted, since the closure of the mines 'the process of reversion to rural countryside has gone on apace' and the large spoil heaps at Camerton were 'now becoming overgrown' (96, 97).

However, the story of the Camerton batches as with other local batches is not as straightforward as this suggests. First, a significant number of batches were planted with conifers in the early part of the twentieth century, and these plantations remain a distinguishing feature of the local landscape. Amid the green hills and valleys of this rural landscape the domes and peaks of the darker dusty green of the conifers stand out on the skyline, often alongside many of the bigger villages and towns which grew with the collieries. These conifered 'hills' have become a distinguishing feature of the area. Secondly, the natural recolonization which has taken place on all the batches has added significantly to the range and diversity of habitats in the area, and given the general decline in the biodiversity of the agricultural landscape the batches now stand in, they have become places of considerable ecological significance (Cam Valley Wildlife Group, 1998). Thirdly, the batches have become important sites of local industrial archaeology and community history. Other physical reminders of the mining era, such as the pitheads and the networks of canals and railways which served the collieries, have been gradually cleared away. The lingering presence of the spoil heaps serves to provide the last visible manifestations of local community histories and memories of the mining era. For example, a larger, more prominent tip at the nearby town of Midsomer Norton has now been designated as a feature of industrial archaeology, to avert the threat of it being cleared.

The Trees and the Reconstruction of Place Identity

Of the 35 or so batches in the Cam Valley area, half or so have areas of conifers on them, with a few being totally covered (Preddy, 1999). Camerton 'old batch' was one of those planted with conifers. The local County Council Woodland Officer who assessed the site in the 1980s when purchase by the local community first became a possibility, and who drew up the initial management plans for the site, recorded the conifers as a mix of Douglas fir, with some Corsican pine, Scots pine and European larch. He added that 'nobody knows exactly when they were planted, but my impression was that it was at the turn of the nineteenth century . . . certainly no later than the First World War'. This planting seems to have been a practice distinct to parts of the Somerset Coalfield at that time, and information about the exact timing and reasons for planting is difficult to come by. Local knowledge, including that of those who have charted the history of the Camerton Colliery and who have become involved in the running of the batch as a Heritage Site, suggests that the conifers were planted in order to stabilize the batches and to provide a crop of timber to be used in the working of the mine in future years. This explanation has logical appeal. First, the stability of larger, steeper spoils heaps has long been a concern in the mining industry (NCB, 1970). Secondly, Williams (1976), in his history of another nearby Somerset colliery, describes in detail how round section timber, as would come from conifers, was the key means of constructing of roadways and working faces in the mines, with wooden 'arms', 'collars' and 'lagging' forming a frame which secured the 'rippings' (73). He adds that the timber was usually 'home grown', on local farms and estates, and that in difficult workings (as many of these mines were) 'the cost of the timber was sometimes as much as the selling price of the coal' (ibid.). So the incentive for the collieries to grow their own timber would have been strong. So the trees' introduction to these site may well as been as 'working trees' fulfilling roles and producing timber directly geared to the mining process.

However, two other historians of the Somerset coalfield have suggested that the conifers would not have been planted for the future production of pit props (Dr C. Chillcott, and Mr J. Cornwall, 1999, personal communication). Chillcott, for example, draws on local oral history accounts to suggest that the conifers were planted around 1920 as an 'enlightened act' of the then colliery owner, in an effort to landscape the numerous bare spoil heaps of the time: in other words, the trees may have been planted more in an amenity or even therapeutic role. More generally, the planting of conifers would conform to the practices of the newly formed Forestry Commission (1919) which was beginning to establish conifer plantations in order to ameliorate the deforestation caused by the needs of the First World War. (See Tsouvalis-Gerber, 1998; Condry, 1974). Tsouvalis-Gerber (1998: 222) charts how coniferous species were favoured because of their quick growth and their suitability to grow on 'poor' ground. Thus the trees may well have been planted in a multi-role sense, following wider forestry trends.

The Somerset collieries at this time were privately owned by landowners such as the Duchy of Cornwall and the Waldegrave Estate who had sought to capitalize on the boom of coal production driven by industrialization. Camerton was owned by a local landowning family, the Jarrets, until 1911 when it was sold to Sir Frank Beauchamp (Down and Warrington, 1971). According to Macmillen (1990: 31) Beauchamp had purchased other local collieries with the intention to 'amalgamate the collieries into a more economical system of working in order to compete with the more favoured mining districts elsewhere'.

Whichever of these accounts as to why and when the trees were planted is more accurate, the circumstances of the mines swiftly changed for the worse, due to the evolving economic and technical characteristics of the coal-mining industry, in relation to the conditions in the local Somerset pits where the easily accessible coal was of poor quality and the working costs were relatively high (Macmillen, 1990). In the first decades of the twentieth century, many of the collieries were in serious decline. Camerton was taken into state ownership, along with the rest of the remaining Somerset Coalfield, when the industry was nationalized in 1947. Working continued for a few years but 'the last coal was wound on the 14 April, 1950' (Macmillen, 1990: 34), and after a brief period of salvage work the colliery was closed. The pithead structures were dismantled and the shafts capped off, and the branch railway became disused.

In the meantime the batches themselves were left relatively undisturbed. While the mine had been working, older completed areas of the tip were left undisturbed while tipping continued alongside them. In this space, and other redundant spaces of the site, 'nature' would have already been finding its way back in. For example, now prominent on one part of the site, and featured in the site interpretation literature, are two spectacular beech trees which seeded in abandoned areas of the railway sidings which ran along the south side of the old batch. Then the conifers were planted, and began to grow in the last working years of the pit. On the closure of the mine, these tree actants – the planted and the wild – and other flora and fauna were left undisturbed. The dormant economic nature of the site created favourable spaces and conditions for the continued growth, reseeding and expansion of the tree populations on the batches. We note here the special qualities of trees to act in these ways. Their slowness of growth, but their eventual size and consequent visual and habitat-forming impacts means that their presence was likely to have much more impact than if the site were colonized by other forms of nature such as brambles and grasses. These too can create habitat and green space, but thy don't have the material and cultural presence which trees can, and in this case did, bring to the site. These trees were to become significant players when questions of the use and fate of the site we raised some thirty years after closure.

A sense of the gradual but powerful transformation created by the growth of the planted trees can be gathered from the accounts by local residents of their memories of playing on the site as children. One resident told us,

> I should think [the conifers] they were planted about I should say 70, 80 years ago because when I was a kiddy – those trees on that batch – well I can remember some of them being planted, but some were about 2 feet high so they had been in probably three or four year by then . . . Oh we always played on there, it was our only means of playing . . . Well the trees then were about 6 feet high [and by the time the mine closed] oh they were good trees then . . . very strong trees.

Another, younger resident told us of her post-war childhood memories of the batch,

> all I can remember is tall conifers and where everything was so dense there was hardly any undergrowth there and there were lots of tracks because us kids used to play there in gangs.

These memories also illustrate how this site of 'industrial wasteland' was now being appropriated by the local community as a recreational space, and how the trees provided a fabric and cover for this process.

In terms of the 'creative' active capacities of trees we considered in Chapter 3, the sheer ability of the trees to grow in such a location is significant. The photograph in Figure 8.2 shows what the working batches and the freshly tipped spoil were like; a bare, lifeless and apparently 'unnatural' land form. Moffat and Buckley (1995) chart the problems and importance of understanding soil conditions when planting trees on disturbed ground, paying particular attention at one point to colliery spoil. Such soil, they suggest, may well present a number of adverse factors to tree-planting and -growing, and they summarize the results of trials in which different tree species were planted on spoil heaps. In the case of Camerton, it is unlikely that such information was readily available at the time, and there was probably more of a de facto recognition that if planted, certain trees might well grow. The abilities of the trees to adapt to the 'soil' conditions are crucial forms of creativity in the story of this site. Today this capacity is still deployed in the transformation of other colliery-waste landscapes which, as an achievement, can only be see as relational between people and trees. For example, Arnot (1999) describes a typical use of planting on such landscapes:

> Graham Howe, head of coalfield regeneration for English Partnerships . . . pointed across the road to where saplings were poking through the sparsely grassed surface of the former spoil tip. 'We're putting in about 100,000 fir trees to make it look presentable and hoping to attract foreign inward investors'.

In instances such as these, it *is* of course the human actors who are the enrollers, in ANT terms, of the processes of transformation. However, without the capacity of the trees to 'tolerate' such 'unnatural' conditions and then, through growth, to recreate this landscape through their burgeoning materiality and symbolism, these processes would be unworkable. Clearly, then, even 'planted' trees do contribute meaningfully to what is termed *relational agency*, just as the apple trees bring their creative capacities to the orchard we have considered. The other, 'wild', trees which were continuing to self-seed onto the Camerton site, and which come to play an important role later in its development, can be viewed as bringing a more independent creative agency to the (re)production of this place. Self-seeding trees can become enrolling actors in networks. It can be imagined that the trees have enrolled the human actors who eventually helped keep this site from clearance and thus helped maintain the trees' presence. Trees' actions, and the implications of tree spread for the changing nature of place, can often be instrumental in attracting the attention of human agents to new possibilities for landscape. This ability to enrol is clearly shown in Brown's (1997) account of the formation of the Black Country Urban Forest Project, which we have already discussed in Chapter 3. In these instances, and many others, the agency of trees in transforming decrepit industrial landscapes prompts management strategies geared to reproduce that precise outcome via schemes of planned planting.

Eventually, the nature of the disused batches at Camerton moved beyond the initial stage of trees which were merely tolerating or more actively colonizing the site. The more the trees grew and spread, the further the site was (re)produced beyond the intentions and circumstances of those who had planted some of them. In this way the trees became detached from their initial culturally constructed identity and role and, through their continued independent presence and growth, they projected themselves into new cultural constructions which came to form around them. In Actor Network terms, the planted trees remain an active remnant of a previous network through which power has ceased to flow. In Thrift's (1996a: 24) account, the numerous fragments of failed or abandoned networks which litter the world are 'the equivalent of the faded silk flowers in the attic'. In other words they are static, lifeless. However, trees and other elements of nature, which may be remnants of failed or defunct networks, are neither dead nor static. Indeed they retain a life of their own and may be involved with the initiation of or interconnection with new networks. In this way, trees may be viewed as rhizomatic in terms of agency, sprouting from a break or tear, and growing from the middle, or from a fragment of an old or damaged network.

These processes are, we suggest, a common feature of tree agency. Trees continue to grow and develop in the 'vacuums' which sometimes appear between the breakdown of one formation of a culturally constructed landscape and the forming of a subsequent landscape configuration. As with the old oaks of Sherwood Forest (Watkins, 1998a/b), the trees 'outlive' the social constructions in which they are initially bound up and become embroiled in new associations. Given the longevity of trees and how their agency is expressed in a time-frame slower than that of human agency, they push their developing presence through subsequent 'depositions' of identity constructions of places and landscapes. In Camerton, the trees had a presence associated with the working mine, the closed mine, and the 'dormant' site. These phases spanned a period from the first decades of the twentieth century well into the latter half of the century, by which time attitudes to landscape, nature conservation, the environment, public access to open space and forestry and woodland management had transformed dramatically, not least because of a growing awareness of environmental and nature conservation issues at the global, national and local scale (see Barrow, 1999).

Other local developments also occurred during this time. The village of Camerton had shrunk back in population size from a mining community of 2,386 at its peak to a much smaller population of around 530 by the 1950s. The industrial phase had brought with it a related set of social constructions of community. The journal of one Revd Skinner (1971) presents a locally famous and colourful account of his time as rector of Camerton (1803–1834) during which he was often apparently engaged in open warfare with the mining community and their lawless 'godless' habits. With the decline and cessation of the mining industry, a rather different social formation gradually (re)formed, with Camerton taking on the mantle of pastoral rural idyll. In time, residents felt it necessary to display this new-found character by entering the 'Best Kept Village' competition – a move which highlighted a strong contrast between the faded industrial and the rural. In particular the residents considered that the old pithead site, inconveniently positioned opposite the then village post office, was detrimental to their 'Best Kept Village' cause, being as it was overgrown with brambles. So in the early 1980s the Parish Council opened negotiations with the Coal Board with the aim of acquiring the pithead site, or access to it, as a public space for the village, thus gaining an amenity and tidying up a problematic site. Initially, owning and managing the batch was not part of their intentions, because the site, as an area of mature trees to which there was some 'unofficial access', was not seen as problematic to re-ruralizing and tidying the village.

However, at this time, the practice of clearing coal tips within the major coalfields of Britain was seen as a priority in terms of economic restructuring, and still retained a momentum from the aftermath of the Aberfan disaster. Specialist companies had sprung up focusing on the business of recycling spoil heaps. Any coal recovered was used in coal-fired power stations, and aggregates could also be put to use in the construction industry. The land so recovered then became available for redevelopment. One company which had been involved in clearing tips in South Wales proposed to clear the Camerton batches and began discussions with the Coal Board. The current Chair of the Camerton Heritage Committee (which was formed by the Parish Council in 1989 in order to manage the site once it was eventually acquired) told us that at this point a public meeting was held about the batches and 'that's when all hell was let loose'. Another resident recalls that 'there was quite an uproar . . . the batch as such had to remain, locals didn't want it disturbed or anything like that, no way'. Not only was there a strong sentimental affection for the batches, but also there was also considerable concern in the village about the disruption which would result from the massive physical undertaking of removing the spoil heaps. Negotiations between the community, the Coal Board and the local council developed momentum in the face of this threat of clearance of the site including its trees.

Discussions with the Coal Board were slowed by the 1984 miners' strike, when according to the Chair of the Heritage Committee 'everything stopped whilst the lawyers considered the strike'. But eventually the Coal Board agreed that the site should be made available for acquisition by the 'community'. However, as the Chair recalls, 'when we eventually got around to buying it [for a nominal sum] they said, well, we will let you have it provided you take responsibility for the whole of the 5-acre site and not just the pithead'. At this point, the local authority stepped in, recognizing that the purchase of the site was a positive step but also a mammoth task for the small Parish Council. The local authority undertook to conduct the legal transactions with the proviso that the Parish Council took full responsibility for the site thereafter. Transfer negotiations were protracted and the site was finally transferred to the ownership of the Parish Council in 1987.

It should be emphasized that, in the efforts to protect the batch from clearance and development, the trees had become central foci: not only had they helped to create a particular place, but they became central to efforts to secure its conservation. One of the major weapons used by local activists was to persuade the local authority to issue Tree Preservation Orders for significant trees on both batches. With such orders in place, the clearance of the batches was impossible to carry out legally, since clearance would involve felling the preserved trees. In the meantime other actors had also become interested in the site, prompted by nature conservation considerations. In 1985, ACCES (The then county council's community works programme) conducted a comprehensive ecological survey of the site and drew up a proposed management plan for the batch. This report established that the site was 'a particularly interesting woodland as an example of what can develop on a sterile coal tip, given time and lack of harmful interference. Part of its function, indeed, could be a demonstration of such reclamation' (3). The report also stated that local knowledge placed the planting of the conifers in the 1890s, and recorded the presence of various self-seeded trees and shrubs. These included

> beech saplings dotted under the coniferous canopy and one dense thicket of ash saplings on the north slope, and examples of English oak, turkey oak, holm oak, wild cherry, silver birch, English elm, wych elm, Norway maple, sycamore, yew, rowan, holly, hawthorn, blackthorn, pussy-willow, elder, hazel, privet, gelder-rose and wayfaring trees. (2)

Such variety added weight to the recommendation of the report that the site '*be maintained and enhanced as a developing woodland*', and 'to create certain features (paths, glades, etc.) which encourage the public to appreciate it as such, but which do not detract from its wildness' (4). The local authority, in the form of its Woodland Officer, was also drawn into discussion about the conservation potential of the site and became involved in the negotiations over its fate. It was this kind of often tree-based pressure to protect the batch and obtain the pithead that eventually encouraged the Coal Board to transfer the whole site to the community.

So pressure to construct the site as woodland which was best used for nature conservation and public access was finally successful. Having taken ownership of the site, the Parish Council organized a clearance of the bramble on the old pithead, and set up a Heritage Committee to deal with the overall management of the site which included the adjacent batch, by now mostly covered with mature conifers, and the other trees which had self-seeded and grown where space was available. Figure 8.3 shows the batches as they are today. Prompted by the pre-purchase reports, from the outset the Committee took the decision to treat the whole site as an opportunity for public access, as a site of commemoration of the mining industry which had produced the batch and which was still a powerful symbol of local identity, and to enhance the ecological status of the site as a woodland. The presence of the trees presented both opportunities and difficulties in these respects and the trees continued to be central political figures in the story.

Figure 8.3 The Camerton Batches, viewed from the south-west (Owain Jones)

The opportunities open to the Committee reflected the possibility of attracting funding in the form of woodland grants, and grants from other sources which supported nature conservation and public access to open space. The problems were that, according to the then Local Authority Tree Officer the trees made for a 'fairly user unfriendly site which was very dark'. The conifers had been planted in quite a dense pattern and had 'not been managed as a forest for some generations – if ever – which has meant the original planted trees have grown very closely, very tall, with restrictive girth' (ACCES, 1985: 3) (Figure 8.4). The trees were thought to be 'nearing 100 years of age and subsequently at the end of their natural life span' (Camerton Heritage Committee Report, 1993: 1). In response to this position,

> a scheme devised by the County Council Woodland Officer was drawn up to replace the old conifer trees on the batch with broadleaf species over a ten year plus period under the funding from the Forestry Commission, with the idea that sales of timber from the old trees would help offset the cost of redeveloping the site into an Industrial Heritage and Public Open Space/Amenity area ensuring that the area would be retained for the benefit of local residents. (Camerton Heritage Committee Report, 1993: 1)

This scheme had derived some of its information and rationale from the earlier ACCES report. Work got under way when a local forestry contracting company agreed to carry it out, taking felled timber as payment.

Figure 8.4 An example of the conifers on the old batch (Owain Jones)

'Little Switzerland'

As discussed in Chapter 2, conifers – particularly as deployed in what became the notorious afforestation policies of the Forestry Commission – have generally had an extremely bad press, as exemplified by Massingham's (1988b) analysis of 'The Curse of the Conifer', Condry's (1974) comparison of walking in an oak wood and that in a coniferous forest, and Wright's (1992) analogy between such coniferous woodlands and totalitarian political regimes. Many other examples of such sentiments abound. So, at a national level, the cultural construction of trees and woodlands has generally conferred on conifers some severely negative connotations, particularly when compared with 'native' broadleaf woodland.

These negativities in turn became articulated in institutional policy when the Forestry Commission instigated its 'Broadleaves Policy' in 1985 (see Tsouvalis-Gerber, 1998; Forestry Commission, 1985) in an attempt to reconfigure state forestry functions and public opinion of them. So by the time the management of the Camerton batch as a woodland, and the application for grants to do so, was under way, the Forestry Commission was giving particular, even exclusive, funding emphasis to the (re)planting of broadleaf woodlands.

Thus the scheme to clear fell the conifers on the site in three stages and to replace them with broadleaf trees was driven by a number of considerations. First, the scheme developed partly in response to the conditions of the site and the old age and 'poor' form of the trees. It is noticeable that on similar sites only a few miles from Camerton the tall thin conifers have now started to lean and fall as they reach the end of their life expectancy. Secondly, the scheme served as a response to concerns about protecting, enhancing and recreating, wherever possible, sites of native ecology and biodiversity. Thirdly, the scheme was driven by a shift in cultural attitudes toward tree species where planning decisions were taken in the 'anti-conifer' culture of the period. Relatedly and fourthly, the scheme was driven by the conditions of the Forestry Commission funding. As the Chair of the Heritage Committee summed up – 'we clear felled [the first area of conifers] and replaced with broadleaf because *that's the Forestry Commission's edict*'.

However, once the felling of the conifers got under way, there was an extreme adverse reaction to the scheme within the village. One of the contractors told us that 'the moment we actually started work on the site we were accused of being the "massacrers" – the butchers'. The couple living in and running the then Post Office opposite the entrance to the site apparently gave the contractors 'an earful' every time they went into the shop, although they 'tried and tried and tried' to explain the logic of the felling and management plans being followed. Local opinion has it that this couple became so upset at what was happening that 'they sold up and moved away'. Another public meeting was held, in which the Local Authority Tree Officer was asked by the Heritage Committee to explain what was happening and he recalls that 'people's opinions were very strong, and their emotions were running very high . . . Their main objection seemed to be the fact that we were – their perception was that we were cutting down all the conifers and replacing with dominantly hardwoods'. The Chair added that 'it caused a tremendous amount of feeling [with] the Parish Council who were the saviours [having saved the batch from clearance] being the demons'. 'Everyone nearly lynched the Parish Council Chairman'.

This seeming reversal of opinion is fascinating. The approved conservation scheme for the site reflects existing wisdoms about how certain types of trees 'fitted' the landscape. The configurations of partnership-style governance had adopted these wisdoms both as knowledge frameworks for action, and as emphases for competitive funding arrangements. These pointers reflect a broad-scale disapproval of conifers and their impact on the nature of local landscapes. At Camerton, however, the batches – including the conifers that helped to make them so distinctive – had become a local landmark and were nicknamed 'little Switzerland' because of the steep terrain covered in conifers. The objections to the clearing centred around the threat to this landscape identity, the threat to the trees as a perceived habitat, the threat to the trees as 'representatives' of nature, and the threat to the trees as a 'memorial' for the mining days. One of the most vociferous objectors told how it was the threatened loss of this loved landscape feature which motivated her:

> I know they may say that they are not native, but the conifers were very dramatic . . . I used to have to struggle up there early in the morning to wait for the bus [to a point which has a view of the two batches from the other side of the Cam Valley] and sometimes it was misty and, you know [like] those lovely old Japanese . . . prints, and you see these little pointed things with the mist rolling around – [it was] quite like that sometimes in the mornings.

Another who objected in the meetings, and on the site, said that she had done so on the grounds of nature conservation, saying,

> I was one of them what protested . . . because there was so much wildlife along there and there's so many different sorts of plants along there and deer and buzzards. It's a haven for wildlife. You get so many different species of butterflies along there because the buddleia's took over the bottom.

The trees were also serving as markers of the industrial past that characterized the older community, and were thus still valued in terms of identity and memory. We were told that the opposition to felling the trees had come mainly 'from the older generation'. The cutting of the conifers was a felling of memories, even though there was the promise of new trees on the site. As one of the contractors said, 'I would call it almost like a memorial garden, because those conifers there represented the flowers on a grave of something that is no longer [there]'. The links between the conifers and the past, and their ongoing presence in the landscape meant that it was these *particular trees* which became the talisman of memory. The trees became the bearers of powerful local symbolic freights which bestowed on them a value that was not easily assessed by those whose views were being formed by broader cultural, management or even ecological perspectives. In general, the felling of trees does have a strong and negative visual impact and this further added to the adverse reactions from local people in Camerton. The site after felling and extraction of the timber looked to some people like 'an eyesore because it sort of looked like it had been ploughed through, it looked like a hurricane had hit it' (see Figure 8.5). Tree growth and tree management are embedded in long slow time frames. Clearly a plan to 'replace' Camerton's batch conifers with what might be constructed as trees of a more suitable deciduous nature fitted this ecological time frame but transgressed the need among residents to avoid short-term devastation as well as longer-term removal of iconic markers of heritage.

The subsequent management of the site was clearly impacted by this strong and unanticipated outburst of feeling. The assumed partnership of forestry expertise, local governance and rural 'community', previously enrolled together in financially and environmentally driven networks, became transformed. Local people used their stakeholder status to resist the outcomes of the network. Given that the

Figure 8.5 A view of the old batch soon after felling on the middle section (Alistair Rankine)

network depended on discourses of community – level stakeholding, as well as more centralized finance – the disrupted partnership had to be recovered via rapid changes to the planned management strategy. The plans to clear fell the remaining conifers in two further stages were abandoned. This change according to one of the contractors, 'was a victory for the people of Camerton who have been resistant to taking down the trees' and has put the Committee 'in a very difficult position'. This because there was now a tension between community expectations and the conditions embedded in funding agreements. Other management objectives were also deflected. In the original management plan, the regeneration of the woodland using broadleaved trees was to be achieved through natural regeneration. This strategy was favoured as a means of producing woodland because it would achieve local ecological integration and because, through processes of natural selection, the trees most suited to the site are more likely to flourish. Indeed, as one of the contractors put it after the clearance of the conifers, the natural regeneration 'was phenomenal, trees just springing up everywhere'.

However, after the local protests this planned natural regeneration was augmented by additional planting of new broadleaf trees. According to the Local Authority Tree Officer this was 'in many ways like a PR exercise because it made people see that we were actually replacing [the trees]'. The local school was involved in the new planting scheme as a means of making fresh connections with the community. Those responsible for the management of the site now recognized that these local-level expressions of partnership, involving intergenerational community 'ownership' of the scheme, have represented a beneficial process by which to achieve the necessary replanting: far more beneficial for example than shipping in outside contractors to perform the change on behalf of local stakeholders. These factors of local involvement cross-cut the debate about whether woodland should be regenerated naturally, or by specific planting schemes. As Harmer and Kerr (1995) emphasize, the choice of whether to plant, or to encourage 'nature' regeneration is crucial in economic, ecological and aesthetic terms, not least in relation to the potential for offsetting the higher cost of planting against 'the earlier visual impact it can achieve' (125). Another issue is the composition of any new planting. The Local Authority Tree Officer at Camerton suggested: 'I didn't want it at the end of the day to look like an arboretum', but rather as 'natural as possible in the landscape'. In retrospect, however, he felt that the planted trees (which included oak, ash and beech) did not quite fulfil this aim.

Local resistance to the management plan for the Camerton batches, and especially to the loss of key conifer trees and the impact of tree-felling in general on the site, led to some considerable frustration among the forestry professionals involved. Here there was a clear divergence in the ways in which particular actors in the network were imagining and acting upon particular and different discursive terrains. Professional discourse was responding to prompts relating to tree management and broad-scale cultural constructs of 'appropriate' forestry practices. Local residents were deploying a rather different discursive cartography, placing specific ethical and heritage-related value to particular trees, and finding themselves unwilling to bear the destructive consequences of clear felling on a cherished local landmark site. These divergences led to uneasy compromises. As one forestry professional related to us: 'The site is kind of a hybrid monster as far as I can tell – that's my own feeling about it – the hybrid monster which people seem happy to visit and [there is a] let sleeping dogs lie attitude about it now'. He added 'Camerton is more of a slog with the added hassle of the local opposition'. The Local Authority Tree Officer who initiated the management scheme told us 'I would dearly love it to happen, but have never been able to pull it off . . . people's reaction has always been horror. During National Tree Week you have a whole area of trees cut down'. For forestry professionals, tree felling is an acceptable, even 'natural' element in the life cycle of tree-places. The history of woodland management is told in terms of long-term cycles of growth, clearing, felling and regeneration (Mabey, 1980). Such discursive frameworks are very difficult to communicate to local non-professionals who are expressing horror at the short-term impacts of felling of *their* trees in *their* place and time. Equally, the local cherishing of trees and tree-places is difficult to communicate to professionals who 'know how trees work'. The discursive divergence is not due to lack of education, or even lack of communication; it is more that the discursive terrains which accompany enrolled actors in a network will often slide past each other, causing discursive disjunction often triggered by a seemingly agreed action, the consequences of which highlight underlying differences in the imaginative cartographies being deployed.

The Camerton batches therefore became 'hybrid' tree-places. The site now has a circular path built on it. It starts from the site of the old pithead where there is a large statue of a miner and an information point with leaflets and a map. The path then follows along the top of the tip (the old tipping route) to the far end where it descends the tip face by means of a long set of steep twisting and turning steps. The path then runs through a flat area at the foot of the tipping now being managed as a picnic/open space area, with some of the trees and undergrowth having been cleared. It then climbs up another flight of steep steps to rejoin itself on the top of the batch and retrace its steps back to the beginning. A series of information points are marked around the walk, corresponding with information provided on the educational leaflet which highlights with text and drawings some of the historical and ecological features of the site. Thus is the gaze of the visitor directed to ecological and heritage characteristics of the place. In October 1997 the site was designated as a Nature Reserve under the 1949 National Parks and Access to the Countryside Act, adding an important conservation component to the political and cultural complexity of the site. One resulting issue is that one of the main practices which defines the site, that of local residents walking their dogs, has been reconfigured. Dogs now should be kept on leads. Humans (and their pets) have become part of the ecology of the site just as much as the trees (and wider nature) are part of the culture of the site.

Other funding and support has been attracted to facilitate the development of the site, ranging from input from the British Trust for Conservation Volunteers and the Rural Action Trust to grants from the Local Authority. There remains, however, some uncertainty and unease about the future of the site. In the eyes of professionals engaged in the planning and practice of site management, uncertainties lie both in the difficulties of squaring ecological and arboreal management requirements with the expectations and feelings of the local community, and in the fate of the site once the present extremely dedicated and pioneering members of the Heritage Committee retire from their positions. Some members of the local community also experience other uncertainties, reflected in the poignant observation made by one of the objectors to the initial felling: 'Any time I hear any [chain] sawing now I wonder what's going on'. This seems to suggest a lack of trust within local partnership networks, as well as some continuing contestation of management strategy. Such fears are invariably linked to the necessity to capture a confining stream of competitive funding in order to support development and maintenance costs. Often, funding comes with strings attached, and the fears of local people are that the implications of funding will divert the course of managing their tree-place.

Partnership and Heritage

The Camerton Heritage site can in many ways be presented as a success story of environmental management. For example, the Open Spaces Society (Lutley, 1992) cite Camerton as a 'best-practice' example of how to create new open space from derelict land and thereby derive access-related and ecological benefits. It is evident from the foregoing account that this area of woodland – this tree-place – has 'evolved' through a complicated and contingent coming-together of different ecological, technological and cultural elements over time. These elements have changed and faded in and out of the picture as they combine and recombine over time. Within these changes, however, the trees have been a creative material presence, folded and refolded into all manner of symbolic formations. Thus at the Camerton site, as in other tree-places, the trees are players in the socio-ecological processes which sustain and perform a recognizable and characteristic place.

The simple notion of an environmental success story, however, belies the complexities which surface in the ongoing narrative of the Camerton batches. One insight into these complexities can be gained from an understanding of the governance which has underlain local management and planning decisions. A recognition of the importance of governance involves a re-evaluation of the old distinctions between market, state and civil society so as to recognize new dependencies and relationships. Recent conceptualization of governance (see for example Goodwin and Painter, 1996; Rhodes, 1996, 1997; Stoker, 1996, 1997) suggests a new interdependence of governmental and non-governmental agencies, and a new collectivity of action moving away from expectations that the central or local state will be the prime mover of political activity. It emphasizes how a wide range of actors and agencies are now required to contribute resources and skills to a tangled web of policy-making, and how in so doing the very meaning of government action is being altered. Governance has thus become characterized by the development of localized policy networks which are rooted in resource exchange. As Rhodes (1997) suggests,

> The distribution of resources between actors in a specific network remains central to any explanation of the distribution of power in that network. Equally, the different pattern both of resources, and their distribution between several actors in networks, explains, in part, the differences between networks. (37)

The generation of complex policy networks is also often characterized by the valorization of partnership. As Cloke et al. (2000) argue:

> Lurking close to the surface of partnership discourses is the vague promise of citizen self-government – an opportunity to participate in these new forms of governance and an opportunity to raise the profile of issues, interests or client groups by entering into partnerships. For some, the new partnerships of governance offer an opportunity for revitalised systems of bargaining, negotiation and collaboration in the fragmented post-Fordist context . . . however, only those citizens and voluntary groups with the pre-requisite resources and skills are likely to be able to discharge the responsibilities that partnership entails. (113)

In the context of Camerton, some aspects of the partnerships which have come together over the heritage trail reflect these expectations. The gearing of management schemes to reflect the parameters required for competitive funding, the primacy of professional knowledges directed from within the local state, and the contribution by local people of time, skill and enthusiasms have all characterized the localized policy network. Where Camerton offers a different perspective on partnership and governance is in relation to the importance of place, and of the trees which in this case characterize place. In some ways, then, we want to argue that non-human actors, such as trees, need to be recognized as 'silent' partners in local environmental policy networks. The imaginary and discursive tensions which arose in the management partnership in Camerton were due, at least in part, to conflicting constrictions of place and the cultures that are embedded therein.

Human actors tend to want to fix place, to form attachments. That is why, as we have discussed through comments by Eisenberg (1998) and Sibley (1999), notions of stability and familiarity are important in the formation of community and place identity. The presence of things (such as trees) can clearly play a role in this. As Buell (1995: 257) notes, 'thus the sight of virtually every landmark, no matter how insignificant to the foreign visitor . . . [can] bring deep emotional satisfaction'. Disruptions to such people, place, place-marker relationships can be problematic, and again Camerton shows that this can be particularly so in relation to trees given their material prominence and endurance over time.

At Camerton the mutually understood gestures included a familiarity with and a valuing of the stability brought to the local landscape by particular trees. The nature of places is, then, a somewhat paradoxical and double-edged phenomenon because, while people try to fix them in their identity and familiarity, places are in the end dynamic fluid entities. This can lead to uneasy situations for those managing tree-places such as Camerton, as such places are in part the result of the unruly dynamic forces of the developing patterns of tree life, and of the cultural associations grafted onto them. Such tensions can go relatively unnoticed, but when they are formative of the geographical imaginaries which underpin the discursive participation in local partnerships, the forces and tensions can build up enough to cause a rupture, like a shift along a fault line causing an earthquake, and disruption and disquiet may occur.

At Camerton the original trees (the conifers planted on the batch all those years ago), the trees which seeded themselves, and those now subsequently planted are all critical in the formation of and, in this case, disputes over place identity and consequent environmental management. Trees have material (size, form, longevity) and symbolic qualities which mean that they are likely to be powerful players in the formation of place identity, and they carry – as Mabey (1980) and others suggest – a significant baggage for the management of tree-places.

At Camerton the trees have performed multiple interrelating roles. They have been product (pit props perhaps), landscaping agents, habitat, symbols of a past (industrial) heritage and bearers of community remembering, construction of native or 'alien', and a local landscape feature and icon of distinctiveness. As such the trees themselves have not been merely the passive recipients of contesting social constructions. Their seeding and growing abilities, their materiality and their longevity have played an active role on the complex constructions and reconstructions of this particular place, and therefore in the partnerships that have formed in relation to the changing nature of that place.

Jacquie Burgess (2000), in her account of the implementation of the New Forest Local Environment Agency Plan, lists the members of the group drawn from the public, voluntary and private sectors, and maps out the stakeholders drawn into the process. She describes how the process involved, which 'combined systematic appraisal with group deliberation', aimed to make 'explicit, and to value, the differing knowledges stakeholders possessed. This was done by facilitating dialogue between scientific and economic knowledge, *and other kinds of knowledges that are embedded in local places and communities*' (297, our emphasis). Here we recognize an example of where the partnership process has been able to draw in local understandings and valuing of particular sites or places. As trees can be such prominent features of landscapes, and can attract so much particular local emotional and symbolic freight, this would seem to be a particularly important requirement for decisions about tree-places and related landscapes.

One further insight into the complexities which surface in the narrative of the Camerton batches relates to interconnections between landscape and heritage. As Muir (1999) points out:

> The association between landscape and history converts landscape into heritage and introduces a new dimension of significance into any debate concerning the uses and function of countryside. (42)

Much of this debate has traced the interconnections between landscape and heritage at a national level, showing how particular landscape types become iconic of national identity and vice versa, and how grand themes of landscape such as wilderness in the United States or prolonged occupation in Britain weave heritage through landscape. Our concern here is with a much smaller scale of landscape heritage which is nonetheless powerful and serves to trace and retrace the issues and impacts of larger-scale representations of heritage in and of landscape, thereby acting as place-markers. Notions of heritage will often be wrapped up in such place-marking. Landscapes not only exist as historical texts, but also represent arenas where history, aesthetics and local place characteristics are conjoined in various comings-together as heritage. At the local scale, such comings-together can help to imbue communities with their characteristic identity. In Camerton, for example, the national-level aversion for conifers in heritage landscapes has been inverted to the extent that the clearing of conifers to be replaced by oak and ash and other native species was bitterly contested due to the local heritage of the Camerton landscape.

Lowenthal (1985) has insisted that an awareness of the past is critical to the identity of individuals and communities. The dwelt nature of place will involve the coming together of the past (through memory and heritage) and future (through imagination and expectation) as co-present constituents of the here and now. Even though the 'present' of dwelling is continually shifting, past significances and values will linger into new configurations of the present, even if past places and landscapes are marked by pain, as in many coal-mining communities. In Camerton the trees and the spoil heaps themselves are the material presences that link present to past, and because trees are long-lived and can survive outside human intention and management they may be, more than many other artefacts, messengers of the past. As Lowenthal (1979: 42) argues, 'we perceive the past through artefacts, physical traces, and objects in the landscape'. The trees thus become ghostly messengers: pivotal bearers and receivers of fixed and floating signifiers which contribute significantly to the comings-together that are place.

It is often the case that heritage landscapes are commodified into theme parks, museums and 'visitor attractions'. Such commodification is rampant both in post-productionist rural landscapes and in urban landscapes which are restructuring from industrial to service landscapes as the Fordist industries that made the landscape fade or rust away. Jackson (1989: 183) shows how there have been problematic readings of local or even regional culture from 'certain arbitrary aspects of a region's rural or industrial "heritage"'. In some ways, the worse the past industrial conditions were, the more successful the corresponding heritage interpretation may be (Urry, 1988). Interestingly, Camerton does not easily fit into this kind of analysis, important though it is. Access to the site is free and unrestricted, and it has been a project generated by the local community, for the local community, at least initially. Furthermore, the site is now being 'connected' to a wider amenity audience through its status as a nature reserve and links to a regional footpath network. In some ways, then, Camerton represents a geography of local popular memory rather than part of the voracious societal drive towards heritage commodification. As such, it might be seen as chiming with the ideas expressed by Samuel (1995) in which the issue of community discourse is local conservation, village newsletters, local meetings and local group activities. Camerton is, in this light, a place which 'makes memories cohere in complex ways' (Hayden, 1995: 43). In other ways, Camerton might be viewed as conforming with wider practices and productions of commodified heritage. For example, some residents who have lived in the village only more recently, and who therefore do not remember the coalfield days personally, have nevertheless energetically embraced the cause of heritage with regard to the Camerton batches. For many in-migrant rural dwellers, there does seem to be a buying into the particular history or heritage of place, and this 'buying-in' can itself be read as a form of heritage commodification.

Jackson (1989: 183) suggests that in analysis of regional identity and the heritage of iconic landscapes which may 'embody' that identity, 'much larger questions are involved concerning the relationship between local and national cultures, urban and rural environments, concepts of work and leisure, ideas about the past and prospects for the future'. These themes, and others, are evident at Camerton. The Camerton Heritage Trail is now a place of leisure where people are encouraged to think of the (hard) work of past lives, all framed in the (perhaps) soothing balm of a tree space. The trees play multiple roles in other ways too. Not only do they mark and help protect the heritage of this site, they also bring in all the other symbolic discourses of nature conservation, access to the countryside, and urban-rural comparisons. Many residents of Camerton as well as other visitors to the site will experience urban landscapes on a daily basis (through work) and value Camerton as an 'antidote' to that lifestyle. It would seem that ready access to a tree-place of your own (whether owned or borrowed) may be an important part not only of community identity and participation in partnership, but also in unlocking for individuals the diverse mysteries of dwelling in a rural place.

–9–

Square

City parks and planted squares are small pauses in the breathless narrative of traffic and work. We need those pauses.

(Winterson, 2000)

A forest [or wood] is like a thing so changeful of its nature that change clings to it as a quality, apparent even during the glance of a moment . . . It is one of those things which a man [*sic*] cannot fully receive, and which he cannot fully re-express to other men.

(Hilaire Belloc, cited by Thomas, 1998: 91)

We had a lovely ash tree on the corner that was blown down in those gales, . . . and that was terrible for those of us who lived here, and the person next door actually sat up watching it, watching it . . . and she sat there and cried and cried while they cut it up.

(interview with local resident)

Victoria Square (Figure 9.1) is a small urban square in the parish of Clifton in the City of Bristol, England. As a space to visit, walk through, and view, it is now dominated by a mixed population of trees. This presence of trees has developed since the square was set out as private gardens for fashionable speculative housing developments undertaken in the middle of the nineteenth century. As with our other tree-sites it has changed markedly in nature over the last century or so. Thus Victoria Square has been transformed from a private space to a public amenity, and from an intensively maintained garden to small-scale parkland dominated by trees but also offering grassy areas for relaxation and leisure. These transformations have not occurred via 'natural' or 'organic' land-use change; rather they have been the subject of periodically intense and controversial contestation, exposing deep-felt valuation and ethical attachment to aspects of the nature of the square. At the heart of both transformations and nature–society relations has been the developing presence of trees in the square. It is the established presence of these trees in relation with other relevant actors which has stabilized the identity of the site in its current form.

The outside of the square is surrounded by roads, and imposing terraces of 11, 13 and 14 houses respectively face onto the square over these roads on three sides.

Figure 9.1 View of Victoria Square, winter (Owain Jones)

A row of 5 large detached villas forms the fourth side. Many of the houses have been converted into flats, and the villas into business premises. The square is divided across one diagonal axis by a paved path which is a busy thoroughfare for pedestrians going to and from work, shopping and recreation venues. The path thus divides the square into two triangular grassed areas, and the trees are interspersed in and around these areas. They line the perimeter of the square, which is defined by a low stone wall which still bears the marks of a substantial set of railings that were removed during the Second World War. The dissecting footpath was also walled (and railed) in the same way. Among the trees there are open areas of grass, a few benches, a few remnants of ornamental statues, and a number of small patches of shrubbery. In all there are approximately 90 trees present in the square representing forty or so tree types. Some of the trees are large, mature and spectacular, others have been planted quite recently, and there are others of various ages in between. As in Chapter 7, where Mr Tony Titchen provided a list of trees found at Arnos Vale, here he provides a list of the tree types present in Victoria Square. The wide variety of tree types brings their multiple textures, colours, sounds, forms and rhythms to the rich experiential quality of the place.

Bhutan pine • purple crab • English lime • Lawson Cypress • purple beech • Lebanon cedar • purple cherry plum • Fulham oak (now fallen and cleared) • Irish yew • black mulberry • holly • female variegated holly • female non-serrated holly • female golden variegated holly • Aucuba laurel • narrow-leaved Aucuba laurel • cherry laurel • double pink Japanese flowering cherry • English yew • wych elm • sycamore • honey locust • bay laurel • fern-leaved hornbeam • lilac • upright hornbeam • Japanese spindle • ash • beech • horse chestnut • red horse chestnut • common alder • tree of heaven • tulip tree • plum-leaved hawthorn • hybrid Chinese viburnum • Silver birch • Weigelia • liquidamber • Himalayan Birch • cherry.

The trees (and particularly the larger most established trees) are mostly deciduous. In summer, when these trees are in leaf, their density is such as to give the square the feeling of a small wood. The canopies of a number of the trees touch and cover much of the central footpath as well as the corners of the square. Viewed from most external angles it presents a bosky, billow of deciduous green (Figure 9.2). In winter, when views through to the surrounding buildings are less interrupted, it is possible to sense the original form of the square as shown in Figure 9.1.

The square is 'consumed' in all the common ways which can be expected of a small urban park in a wealthy commercial/residential inner-city area: by those

Figure 9.2 The square in late summer seen from the outside (Owain Jones)

passing by it in cars or buses, on bikes and on foot; by those walking, riding, or running through it; by those who look out over it from their home or place of work; and by all those who visit the square for various recreational purposes such as walking the dog, sunbathing, playing games, eating and reading during lunch breaks or after work, feeding the pigeons, or just sitting (figure 9.3). The trees are bound into many of these activities, for example providing a sensual amenity (views, sounds), shade, privacy, companionship, isolation from the city and habitat for urban wildlife. Some uses potentially conflict with each other, some will regularly be deemed as anti-social, and the square will also be implicated in a range of different complexities and othernesses associated with personal consumption of the space. Within all these different forms of consumption, the trees themselves will play roles which vary from the central to incidental, and from the conscious to the subconscious, interacting with people in all the ways we have already considered in earlier chapters. The trees have provided an ongoing material and symbolic presence in the square since they were first planted. Their growth has caused much controversy, but at the same time they have provided a thread running through the history of the square as it fell into dereliction and was eventually transferred to the ownership and upkeep of the civic authorities.

Figure 9.3 Using the square among the trees (Owain Jones)

Early History of Victoria Square

The square was built between 1840 and 1870, as the inner-city suburb of Clifton expanded through the speculative development of expensive residential houses. Two of the terraces which helped to form the square as a square, and the square gardens themselves, were built and owned by the Society of Merchant Venturers (SMV), a private organization which has been central to the economic history of Bristol and which still functions today. The deeds of the contract to form the first terrace and square gardens in front of it indicate that

> The said Master Wardens and communality shall and will with all . . . convenient speed lay out all that space of ground in the centre of Victoria Square . . . as and for pleasure grounds for the use of the owners and occupiers . . . and will enclose the same space . . . with a good and sufficient iron railing and shall and will preserve the same in good order and condition as a pleasure ground. (Title Deeds in the archives of the SMV)

The building of the square was part of the wider boom in the development of Clifton as a prestigious expansion of Bristol in the nineteenth century (Jones, 1992). According to Smith (1935) it was 'one of the most enlightened strokes of town planning which nineteenth century Bristol can display' suggesting 'a powerful atmosphere of graciousness and stability' (ibid.). However the building of the terraces that formed the square, and of the gardens themselves, proved to be far more problematic than these glowing assessments might indicate. McGrath (1975), for example, charts how the work undertaken by the SMV to set out the square gardens proved costly and problematic from the outset.

> The cost of laying out the land, making roads and providing iron railings round the central enclosure had been approximately £2,200 . . . The Society had, moreover, undertaken to lay out and maintain the ornamental plantation and gardens in the centre of the square, and maintenance was by no means cheap. In 1855 Messers Garraways signed a contract to look after the plantation for one year for £40. (339)

It is interesting to note that Garraways was also the plant nursery which was employed to plant Arnos Vale cemetery at roughly the same time (see Chapter 7). The mix of trees in the square, particularly the older trees, is characteristic of Garraways' planting regime (according to copies of their nineteenth-century catalogues which are still available). Nurseries such as these had considerable influence on the shaping of significant public and private spaces in developing Victorian cities through their favouring of certain planting regimes. Thus it was that the original gardens, although privately owned, assumed at this time certain 'civic' characteristics by the planting of trees which shared a common landscape architectural heritage, planning and visual 'feel' with other such planting elsewhere in the city. The trees in the square's gardens, then, not only co-constituted the particular place milieu of the square, but they also brought to the square something of the wider character of the cityscapes of nineteenth-century Bristol.

The overall development of the square's gardens, along with the building of the terraces, was slow and complex, due mainly to the prohibitive cost of the speculative building enterprise, as well as problems with builders and with the owners of the one terrace which was already in place. However, early engravings (Figure 9.4) show depictions of the square and gardens with shrubbery, flowerbeds and a large fountain. There is some question here whether this is a representational drawing of the square, or an artist's impression designed for 'marketing' purposes. However, the depiction does accurately portray the 14 houses of the 'Royal Promenade' terrace forming one side of the square, and is thought to present a likely picture of how the gardens would have looked. Indeed Jones (1992: 123) confirms the ornamental nature of the gardens by tracing the interactions between the SMV and other developers and neighbouring property owners, in which the SMV declare that they had 'laid out a square *of the most ornamental description*' (our emphasis).

A key characteristic of this speculative property development was the securing of the square gardens as a private, exclusive space for the use of residents only. Substantial ornamental railings completely enclosed the square to prevent public access, even to the extent that the footpath running through the middle was enclosed in a 'bird cage walk' with the two halves of the square being linked by a pedestrian tunnel underneath this path (now filled in). Access to the private gardens was via lockable gates set in each side of the square, to which only eligible users were given keys.

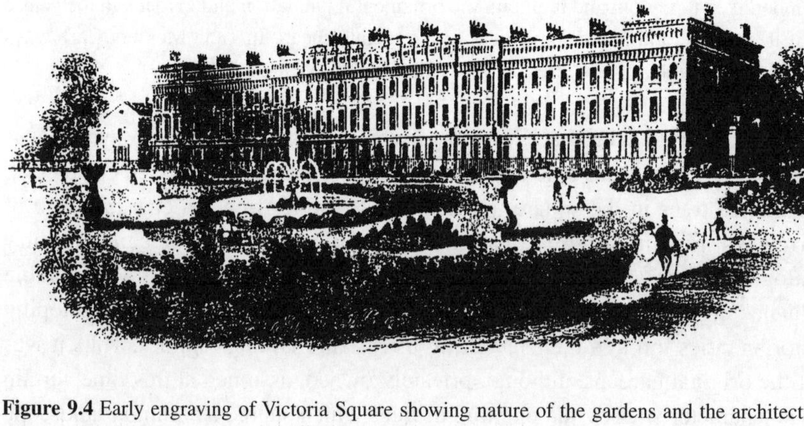

Figure 9.4 Early engraving of Victoria Square showing nature of the gardens and the architectural unity of the terraces

The Insistence of Trees

It is possible to chart the unfolding story of Victoria Square as a place, and of the developing presence of the trees in the square, through a substantial archive of letters, minutes, memoranda, and other documents kept in archive by the SMV. This narrative, in part, concerns the story of the gardens, which proved to be problematic in terms of upkeep, cost, and design, and of the trees in the garden which, as their size increased, began to play an increasingly dominant and often controversial role in the unfolding nature of the square. It is also the story of the struggle to keep this space private and of its eventual transfer to public ownership.

Once the gardens were established by the SMV, a garden committee was formed from the key-holding residents to provide liaison with the SMV. A gardener was employed to tend to the grounds of the square, and funds were raised by an annual subscription from the key-holders and by donations from the SMV who were committed in the terms of the initial contracts to contribute to the upkeep of the gardens. This binding commitment to the upkeep of the gardens was to 'give the Society considerable trouble' and as a consequence 'Victoria Square was the most ambitious and the most troublesome scheme that the Society became involved with' (McGrath, 1975: 336). The legal nature of the agreement brought the SMV into persistent conflict with key-holding and fee-paying residents of houses in the square. Even with the garden committee to act as intermediary between residents and the SMV, there were conflicts both over the management of the gardens (including here the decisions being taken by the committee) and over the unsatisfactory level of maintenance possible when 'limited' SMV funds allowed the employment of only one gardener. Thus the SMV archive is replete with letters of complaint about the square gardens. These letters address issues of upkeep, the developing presence of the trees, the actions or inactions of the garden committee, the struggle to keep the square an exclusive private space and finally its transfer to public ownership.

In 1874, almost twenty years after the square had been planted by Garraways, the SMV received a report that stated that the 'trees were overcrowded and that there were no keys to the gate, so that the public used the gardens "often, we fear, when dark . . . for immoral purposes"' (McGrath, 1975: 341). This is one of the earliest references to the trees being a problem in the square, suggesting that quite a high volume of trees had originally been planted and that they had by this time grown considerably. Even deciduous trees can seem to grow 'quickly' over a twenty-year period. Mitchell (1996), for example, tells of a common lime (one of the types of tree recorded in the square) which grew to a height of 50 ft in some forty years.

In the early twentieth century, after about half a century of growth, the letters about the gardens settled down into a repetitive pattern of exchanges about the size and position of the trees in the square, and about the ongoing struggle to keep the gardens in a good state and as a private amenity. In particular, the trees were seen by some residents as problematic in terms of blocking light to their houses, providing cover for 'unsociable activity', and disturbing the garden and architectural aesthetics of the square. These complaints often led to trees being thinned, topped or even felled. Such action, in turn, prompted letters from other angry residents who objected very strongly to the trees 'being mutilated' or harmed in any way.

A letter of 1920 tells of a resident's sadness that 'an exceedingly fine and handsome tree has been "destroyed"' and that 'for nearly 20 years I had enjoyed the privilege of sitting in the graceful shade and coolness of this tree'. This letter signals a series of voluminous exchanges between residents, the garden committee and the SMV throughout the 1920s. For example,

> Sir, May I draw attention to the extensive cutting of the trees which has been going on in Victoria Square Gardens for the past three or four weeks. Many of the best trees have already been cut down and others so badly mutilated that they may never resume their graceful forms . . . Mr Robinson, one of the tenants of No 23, says he is 'privately responsible'. He says the gardens are a wilderness, but we fail to see how disfiguring the trees can improve this, it would be much more to the purpose if he concentrated his attention on the undergrowth and the weeding of the paths.

Other letters from the same period give voice to a range of concerns relating to the trees in the square:

> There is a very big and ancient tree in front of this house . . . the result is we never get sun in our bedroom or any section of the house from year's end to year's end. Could you allow this tree to be removed, or at least allow it to be seriously lopped. (1925)

In response to this particular threat:

> I am in sore mental distress about the contemplated removal of the finest tree, apparently quite sound, in the Victoria Square Garden . . . this will damage the unique and rural charm of this beautiful garden. (1925)

Eventually some trees were cut back in 1925. Three years later a similar sequence occurs:

> I have hoped to run up against you and to have spoken about the trees (lime and copper beech) opposite us here and in particular as to the huge lime tree which I have been watching spread its branches for something like 38 years until in summer and autumn, while the leaves are out [,] it has become practically a 'nuisance' to us, especially on

dull days like those last summer, when it absolutely interferes with the light into the rooms even up to my study above the drawing room and the maids find the same thing in the kitchen. Personally I should like to see this tree, which is no longer a garden, but a forest tree, thoroughly lopped of some of its main limbs. (9 March 1928)

Action was taken on the receipt of these new complaints, and a number of trees felled and thinned. In response a petition of 26 residents opposed to tree-cutting was presented to the SMV. One protestor wrote:

Three trees have been cut down, the last of which was one of the finest lime trees in Bristol. [T]he committee are not to be trusted . . . we are afraid the copper beeches will be next . . . The birds in the garden were delightful . . . but repeated interference with the trees has driven them away. The trees were a great protection from the winds in winter and from the dust and petrol fumes in summer and also gave a sense of privacy in the garden, now there is practically nowhere one can sit in comfort without being overlooked. (5 April 1929)

After the Second World War, when the nature of the square and gardens had altered substantially (see below) a similar 'battle of the trees' occurs. In 1953 Mr Claremont, who ran a dental practice at no. 28 Victoria Square, wrote a series of letters about the square to the SMV. First he states that he is pleased that the square was not to be handed over to the Bristol Corporation, and that 'the privacy already enjoyed by the residents is to be maintained'. However, his main concern related once again to the impact of the growth of particular trees:

since [we took] this house in 1948, two trees [in front of the house] have got larger and the combined foliage in the summer months is obstructing the light from our dental surgeries. It would be a great help if 1) the trees could be thinned or 2) the tree behind the chestnut cut down. Could you take an opportunity of viewing the trees before the meeting of the standing committee? . . . There always seems to be considerable division of opinion over the Trees in the square, and I am quite sure that if we start thinning out, let alone cutting down we shall be inundated with protests!

After some delay and further exchanges of letters, in 1954 The SMV wrote to Mr Claremont saying that the lopping of the tree would not satisfy his demands and that felling was the only option. The society would, however, not meet the cost of this, but would allow Mr Claremont to have the tree removed at his own expense. The chestnut tree opposite his property was felled in 1955. However, this action again provoked a flurry of letters from the residents of the neighbouring properties, objecting to the tree management in the square.

May we know by whose orders a lovely tree in its prime has been cut down in the gardens of Victoria Square? [I]t has created a considerable amount of indignation

> amongst quite a number of residents and has made a nasty gap in what was a delightfully leafy and shady part of the garden. (25 May 1955)

> Some of us here still feel very sad about this piece of vandalism, after all the tree was much too far away to affect anyone's light at all let alone seriously. It was a superb tree in its prime and as such was an amenity of the square in which we all delighted and was part of our common possession. (15 June 1955)

Meanwhile the trees were presenting other problems, dangers and developing interactions with the urban milieu into which they were projecting themselves. In 1954 the SMV received a message from Redland Police Station that the limb of a tree had fallen across the path running through the Gardens and that the Bristol Corporation had been called out to remove it. Subsequently the SMV were charged £12.7.00 by the City Engineer for the clearing of a large limb of a beech tree which was 'dangerous and completely blocking the central walk through the open space'. The SMV contested this charge, but on discussion with the gardener came to accept it. At least three council staff had worked 'well into the night' to clear the fallen limb. The first cuts had to be made from ladders and the limb carried about 'a quarter of the foliage of this very large tree'.

In 1958 The Bristol Omnibus Company wrote to the SMV with further complaints about the growth of trees in the square: 'the overhanging trees in this park are sweeping the roofs of our vehicles causing a certain amount of damage, and I now request your permission to have these trees lopped to obviate the trouble'. The SMV granted permission for this to be done, but the incident marked a new phase in how trees in the square were interacting with the changing city environment. Private motor cars where also coming more and more onto the scene, and the parking of cars around the square sparked off a fresh round of letters of complaint. Such letters initially highlighted how the cars themselves were perceived as a nuisance by some local residents, destroying the peaceful and tranquil nature of the square. Soon, however, concern switched to the potential danger of the trees to the cars. The risk of branches falling onto the vehicles, and the attendant nuisance of leaf litter, bird faeces and sticky residues (from trees such as sycamores) to the paintwork of the parked cars, became matters of considerable complaint and contestation.

These flurries of exchanges over the trees in the square mark in one sense their ongoing persistence of growth, the timescales over which their agency is performed and their significance and, for some, the problematic materiality which comes with their eventual size. It also marks their slow (in human terms) but eventual material and symbolic colonization of this space and the human resistance this faced.

The Decline of the Gardens

While it was the impacts of the growth of the trees in the square gardens that tended to dominate the concerned approval or disapproval of residents, the upkeep of the gardens themselves was also proving to be problematic. The archive of letters show that through the early and middle parts of the twentieth century there were increasing problems in keeping the gardens in good order and securely private. The correspondence reveals exchanges about unreliable gardeners, 'unofficial' use of the square, and a gradual decline in upkeep. The archival evidence tells a story of decline and the struggle to uphold the imagination of the landscape of the garden – the expected level of privacy and order anticipated from the original designs and agreements – and the practical materiality of the space – in terms of how it looked, how it was experienced, how it was 'kept'. For example, the minute book of the SMV in 1916 notes that 'the Society paid £50 to the Garden Committee but that the gardens were not being satisfactorily kept up'. Moreover the removal of the railings during the Second World War caused considerable problems to the SMV and objections from residents. Even at this time of community coming together, the loss of privacy for the gardens was resented by local residents. Accordingly, in an effort to restore the private regime of access to the gardens, a metal post and wire fence barrier was erected in the 1950s around the perimeter of the gardens and along the edges of the pathway running through them. This much less grand defence also suffered from lack of upkeep, and by the end of the decade the state of the gardens was warranting drastic thinking by the SMV.

In 1961 The Surveyor of the Society, after negotiation with Forest and Orchard Nurseries, proposed to the SMV that 'it would be worth spending £130 opening up and grubbing and pruning the shrubberies (not the specimen trees)'. Here the idea that the trees should remain and the surrounding gardens be diminished begins to emerge. In the same report, other future options for the square were discussed, including the radical proposals to remove the now dilapidated fencing, and to make the gardens semi-open, although with clearly signed notices denoting it as a private park. The surveyor also suggested that it might be worth 'trying to organise a Committee of Residents' to take a renewed interest in the gardens but added that 'the square is now of such a mixed character that I myself am doubtful whether any success would be achieved'. This comment indicates the shifting social composition of residents around the square. By now many of the houses were divided into flats and the area did not retain the same exclusive residential status as it had previously enjoyed. The continuing poor condition of the garden is reflected in letters of 1962 which suggest 'the square garden is still in a deplorable state' and that 'the present gardener has allowed the work to get so far in arrears that it seems unlikely he will ever really get the garden in order'. A further letter written in 1964 paints a picture of final dereliction:

> The garden continues to deteriorate at an accelerating rate: the fence is broken for most of its length and some of it is missing, trees are broken, shrubs are overgrown, in need of expert attention and covered with bindweed in season, paths are disintegrating, the trees may be dangerous and need lopping . . . and the puny efforts of one nice old man on some Saturday mornings are quite ineffectual in stemming the tide of advancing chaos. As owners of property facing the square we feel that the condition of the gardens is becoming a disgrace.

In 1965, when the SMV received complaints from the Chief Public Health Officer about the state of the square they began to think seriously about how to change their relationship to it and to resolve what had for them become a public embarrassment, attracting comment in the local media.

From Private Space to Public Amenity

Originally the square was conceived as a privileged private space and part of a package of ownership and amenity which came with the prestigious nature of the town houses being built by the SMV. The space of the square was subjected to very strict regulatory control; as we have told, access to the square was restricted by the railings and locked gates and exclusively accessed by the distribution of keys to the owners of the new houses around the square. Initial access was restricted to owners of houses built by SMV, and thus even residents of houses in Landsdown Place (which forms the north-east side of the square and was not an SMV development) were excluded. The minutes of the Society show that an application for a key to the garden by a resident of Landsdown Place was refused in 1855. This extreme exclusivity was relaxed in the following decades. By 1875 the minutes record that applications for keys to the gardens from residents of Landsdown Place were being accepted in return for an annual fee.

Securing the gardens as a private space was an ongoing achievement which was not always smoothly accomplished. In 1874 the minutes report that 'there were no keys to the locks of the gates which were left open. The public were making a thoroughfare through the garden, and many persons having no rights habitually resorted there'. Consequently new locks were put on the gates and new keys distributed to eligible residents. These efforts to maintain the gardens as a private space persisted almost up to the time when ownership and management of the square was passed from the SMV to the City Council. But as before, there were considerable fluctuations in the success of these security measures. And these really took a significant blow when the imposing perimeter railings were removed during the Second World War (as were so many others throughout Britain, ostensibly to release much needed raw material to help the war effort). After the war it was deemed too expensive to replace the railings in their previous form, but the SMV were under pressure to maintain the private nature of the space. As a result, a chain link fence supported on metal posts was erected around the square. However, as we have told, the new fence was neither the aesthetic equivalent of the original nor as long-lasting. Its broken and battered state added to the more general air of malaise of the square and compromised it as a private space in practical and symbolic terms. The original railings had been part of the integral design of the square, as too was the notion of private space. Now this notion was being sustained by material articulations which failed in every other way to reflect the ethos of the square as a architectural entity.

Despite the 'unofficial' use of the square, and the persistent challenge to its private status, the SMV felt obliged to try to protect its security and privacy. Letters tell of frequent hostile engagements between the gardener and 'trespassers'. In 1964 The Society received a letter requesting that the children of Christchurch Primary Sunday School (located nearby) be allowed to use the gardens, if the weather was fine, after a party at nearby St Andrew's Hall. The Treasurer of the Society replied, politely refusing permission.

As the gardens in the square declined, the SMV discussed the possibility of the City Council taking charge of it under the Towns Garden Protection Act of 1863. This Act provided for just such a circumstance, but such a transfer of responsibility was deemed unlikely, due to the costs involved and because of the continuing legal liability borne by the SMV to contribute towards the upkeep of the gardens themselves. The precise problem for the SMV was that the form of the original legal management agreements, was such that, were the gardens not to be maintained properly by the City Council under any transfer of responsibility, the Society would then still be liable financially for their upkeep. Nevertheless, the SMV became determined to rid themselves of what had become both a considerable financial burden and a source of unwelcome public controversy. One potential option was to develop the centre of the square for residential building. This possibility was considered in February 1967, but a special committee of the SMV reported that 'the architectural value of the square was being increasingly appreciated' and thus that development was out of the question. There is also mention in the archives of developing some parking spaces on the square to relieve the ever growing pressure of traffic and parking. This too was rejected. It would not have been difficult (in architectural terms) to build on the centre of the square, and clearly such a plot in such a position would have had considerable value for the SMV. However, the square by now was an established open space, and an amenity, in a scenic sense at least, even if there still was no general public access. In particular, the presence of the trees, which now dominated both the current spatiality and the original architectural logic of the square, had secured it as an urban green space. The agency of the trees, when related to a wider context of awareness of environmental issues, campaigns for tree planting and an appreciation of the need for nature in urban space, had successfully negotiated an enduring presence for the square in some form which connected nature and amenity.

Trees and Nature in the City

Keil and Graham, (1998: 119) show how that 'in the post-Fordist city, nature has become a major discursive element in the production of urban space', and that within this process trees play a key role. We have discussed in Chapter 2 how trees can act as therapeutic presences and are considered as a panacea for urban ills. This is a message that has considerable discursive impact. In Nicholson-Lord's (2000) review of Community Forests and Urban Forests, for example, it was concluded that

> Trees provide a robust and cheap-to-maintain landscape – cheaper than parks and mown grass – that can absorb noise and crowds and yet provide a sense of intimacy. There is evidence for their therapeutic role . . . add to that their capacity to soak up carbon dioxide that generates global warming, provide shade from harmful solar radiation and combat traffic pollution linked to the rise of asthma . . . people are beginning to see that trees in cities don't just look nice. They're functional too . . . net contributor[s] to the quality of life in cities.

Alongside this appreciation of urban trees, however, there are significant concerns about the ability of trees to survive in urban environments. While trees bring manifest benefits to the urban, the urban presents manifest dangers to trees. Brown (1998) suggests that 'urban trees live an average of only 32 years compared with 150 for rural ones' and that 50 per cent of newly planted trees in urban areas die in their first year:

> In urban areas the traffic pollution, salt from clearing the roads in winter, and soil compaction under all the miles and miles of paving-slabs which deprive the roots of oxygen, all combines to stress the trees and kill them.

Problems of cabling have also impacted on urban trees, as the development of street-by-street networks for infrastructural services, and even house-to-house networks in more recent Cable TV networks, has involved sizeable programmes of mechanical digging which have inevitably disturbed the root systems of many urban trees. Britain's favourite trees – oak, ash, and horse chestnut – are particularly prone to these kinds of stress and Brown calls for a shift to planting trees likely to withstand the conditions more readily (such as river birch, alder, and pear). In addition, trees have also suffered from the decline of many urban parks. Regardless of a growing popular concern for the greening of urban environments, the financial restrictions experienced by local authorities have resulted in a broad squeeze on expenditure on parks and gardens, leading in some cases to lower levels of tree maintenance and a more general decline in the 'atmosphere' of some urban parks. Such changes were highlighted in 1999 in a report on 'Town and Country Parks' by the Parliamentary Committee on Environment, Transport and Regional Affairs, which stated that

> past models of municipal benevolence, embodied in high quality parks with excellent standards of horticultural display and bustling armies of gardeners and park keepers, have been eroded by the intensely competitive demands on leisure services budget. Though they may be remembered as places of childhood delight, many parks have now deteriorated and become unsightly, even dangerous places. (Brown, 1999)

The possibility of transferring Victoria Square into local authority management as a public asset, therefore, needs to be understood in this wider cultural climate of urban parkland. In many ways, the square was regarded as a considerable asset as, even with its somewhat restricted maintenance regime, it was in better condition than many other areas of urban parkland, particularly once all but the trees had been cleared prior to transfer. In addition, the nature of the square, with houses all around it and a busy straight footpath running though it means that it is not as vulnerable to vandalism and antisocial behaviour as are larger more isolated parks. As a consequence, the population of established, mainly thriving trees in the square presented considerable public amenity in a manageable environment. Moreover, the value of the trees – both aesthetically and ethically – to many local residents led to demands that they be protected in any future management scheme for the square.

Transfer of the Square to the City Council

In the mid-1960s the SMV resolved to develop plans in which the square could be restored to a state of management which would be both acceptable to the City Council in a deal to transfer responsibility, and suitable for a low-cost, low-maintenance management regime for the future:

> The preliminary work would involve the removal of all shrubs and bushed and vegetable growth, filling in the tunnel and its approaches, the removal of the remaining statuary and the fence around the north eastern half of the square, and finally the levelling off and re-seeding of the whole area with grass. (Memorandum, Victoria Square Gardens, Archives of the SMV)

In July 1967, the Society agreed to spend £2,000 to implement a 'clean-up' of the gardens and after that to let it at a nominal rent to the City Council who would maintain it as a public open space. All paths, flowerbeds, and any other remnants of the original gardens were removed, as was other problematic infrastructure, such as the tunnel under the central path. The square was put down to grass to make lawns for public use, thus establishing an easy-to-maintain format which would represent a minimal addition to the overall workload involved in maintaining the city's portfolio of parks.

Thus the format of the square as it is today was established. The trees became the sole survivors from the earlier configuration, 'moving' from private garden space to public park space and shaking off the exclusivity of the previous 100 years. As on the other sites, but in different ways and in different relational arrangements, they have projected themselves into new cultural contexts and the new regimes of management now implemented by the City Council.

As in Arnos Vale (see Chapter 7) these changes represent a reversal of the process described by Zukin in which public civic spaces fall into disrepair and are privatized. At Arnos Vale and in Victoria Square, private space has fallen into disrepair and has (or is soon to be, at Arnos Vale) taken into public management. In both cases, *trees have played a central role in this process*, but in Victoria Square the nature of the role, and the characteristics of the relational matrix in which the agency of trees was enacted, have been markedly different to those at Arnos Vale.

The agency of the trees in the square has been a significant co-constituent of the making and remaking of the square as a place, and of the character and aesthetics of resultant place milieu. This agency has been most evident in the characteristics and impacts of longevity and ongoing growth. The trees have been the focal influence of the changing nature of the square over the last 150 years. The efforts of the trees to colonize the open spaces of the square have been suppressed by management, so there is now a form of equilibrium between the 'push' of the trees and the check of management – an equilibrium which long ceased to exist at Arnos Vale. However even within this equilibrium, opportunities for relational change have occurred. For example, the spectacular Tree of Heaven on the south corner of the square now has a smaller companion alongside it. This younger tree, grown from a sucker of the parent tree, became established in the cover of some shrubby undergrowth, and has now reached a size which means it has gained recognition as a new tree presence, and is being allowed to grow.

The City Council is now responsible for the upkeep of the park, inheriting the legacy of the trees from the previous management regime. The Council Tree Officer told us that tree maintenance in the square had been on an 'ad hoc basis', responding to any urgent need for dealing with dead trees, unsafe branches and so forth. The officer hoped that future management would be on a more systematic basis in which regular maintenance (perhaps every four years) would be conducted, but the current policy seems very much to be to 'let the trees look after themselves'. The Council are now attempting to establish a system whereby each tree in their care will have a identification code and an individual history of maintenance which would be entered onto a central data base and accessible on hand-held computers used in field surveying. In this way, individual trees can now begin to have a coherent history and relationship with those who care for them. The ongoing relational agency of management in the square will therefore involve a policy of 'maintaining trees in their natural form as much as possible'. Somewhat ironically, this maintaining in natural form will mean in practice that trees will be maintained and managed from their earliest years, for example by removing weak branches, so that they grow in such a way as to be easily managed in later years – a process which suggests a managed rather than a 'natural' form. In effect, as the future of the tree population evolves under the management of the Council, the presence of trees should be of a more regulated 'steady state' nature than it has been up until now. In future, the policy for planting in the square and equivalent spaces in the city is to introduce a range of 'interesting and exotic species' while new planting of native species will be in the more 'natural' ecological environments of larger expanses of parkland and downland. It is possible, therefore, that as and when existing trees in the square need to be replaced in the future, the introduction of different exotic species may disturb the current steady-state, which is given a specific character by the current tree population.

The Square as a Place of Trees

Some of the trees in the square have (again) become very large and imposing presences in the place, particularly the beech in the centre of the square and the Tree of Heaven standing on the south corner. These trees now dominate the architectural logic of the square. Such is their size, and the expanse of their foliage, that it is now impossible to look across the square to the Royal Promenade on its North West perimeter, or to the South West terrace. Indeed, it is now very difficult to see the square as an architectural unity at all, which was the whole *raison d'être* of the design. Views into, out of, and across the square vary significantly according to the viewpoint in relation to the bigger trees. Interviews with residents suggest that they are in the main happy with the current state of the square, and that many have strong emotional attachments to, or aesthetic appreciation of the trees. Some residents do, however, continue to worry about views and domestic light levels being restricted by the trees, and about safety issues in terms of falling branches or of the potential for the trees themselves to fall down. But in contrast to that in the past, the likelihood of extensive thinning or felling of the trees is now radically diminished.

The square is now effectively characterized as 'a place of trees'. Valued older trees are supported and adapted in efforts to extend their life. A mulberry tree in the east corner has partly fallen over and is now supported on props. The massive beech in the centre of the square has its main limbs wired together in an effort to prevent them splitting from the main trunk. Such large limbs on trees right next to a busy path present a considerable degree of risk to the public, but such is the presence of the tree that every effort is made to negotiate this without felling or drastic lopping. Residents still remember and speak of a lovely old beech tree in the square, which lost a major limb in the 1950s and subsequently had to be felled. Such memories inspire popular support for efforts to 'prop up' veteran trees in the square. The council's aim is now to maintain the tree presence in the square in approximately its present form. Accordingly they have occasionally planted new trees to replace those which have fallen or died. This is not a straightforward process, however, as is illustrated by the case of a Wellingtonia which was recently planted in a central position in order to replace the beech. The Wellingtonia subsequently died, fuelling local rumours that it had been poisoned by some residents who resented the choice of tree and its position. Others residents, however, had watered it in the hope of keeping it alive.

The trees are now central to the identity of the square. Local residents, pedestrians and users of the park perceive it and experience it in various ways as a place of trees. Tree-gazing walks are held there (Figure 9.5) and the local civic pressure group takes a keen interest in the square, and in particular in any potential threat to the presence of the trees. Thus the square is not only valued by residents living on its immediate perimeter. Rather, it has become an integral component of the imagined and experienced geographies of the parish of Clifton, a key spatial set piece in one of the most desirable residential suburbs of the city.

For many residents the trees play a central role in their relationship with this place. One resident who has a first floor flat looking onto the square told us:

> In the spring they are lovely because obviously you have got all the fresh colours. In the autumn they are lovely because they are a blaze of colour. I rather like them in winter too, when you can actually see the structure of trees, especially against the sky. I mean the trees and sunset, and on the rare occasions when it snows . . . I go and look at them in the middle of the night as well. So there you are. Yes, I should say they have fairly pre-occupied me really, a major part of my life.

Another resident said,

> Oh yes I couldn't live without trees. I once said I would never live in the city, but it is because of the trees that I am living here within . . . one of the busiest cities in the country.

Figure 9.5 Tree gazing in Victoria Square conducted by Tony Titchen (Owain Jones)

Yet another commented on the many sensual 'treats' of living with such neighbours:

> It is very exciting up here in a storm, the movement of the trees, quite breathtaking, you feel sometimes as if they can't withstand it, they are bound to go over, but they come back and go over the other side, oh its very exciting.

Just as the orchard we considered in Chapter 6 was embedded in a wider notion of regional landscape, the square is embedded in notions of Clifton and even of Bristol as a place. It is an important part of Clifton in terms of architecture and of history, and as one of its green spaces. The Clifton and Hotwells Improvement Society (CHIS) is a very active and vocal organization monitoring local environmental issues and trying to take a lead in the conservation and enhancement of Clifton and its neighbouring parish of Hotwells. One of the Society's key areas of activity is to monitor trees in the locality. As in the square, other streets, small parks and even private gardens have a substantial range of significant trees. The Society monitors the condition of these trees and assesses any threat to them, attempting to ensure that replacement planting will ensure future generation of trees. The presence of this community of mature trees, of which those in the square are a significant element, is a key factor in the production of Clifton as a highly desirable, fashionable area of the city from both a residential and commercial perspective. As the Chair of CHIS summed up: 'Well, you imagine Clifton without trees, as beautiful as the buildings are! . . . but [with] a certain amount of trees, it's like a picture isn't it?'

Individual Trees

Although the square presents itself to many of its users and onlookers with the feel of a small wood, the actual number of trees located there is relatively small. As a consequence both in the square and in other parts of the locality, trees are in such numbers and in such forms that they can be seen, and related to, as individuals. These characteristics set the square apart from the tree-places discussed in Chapters 6–8, where the significant presence of trees has been in collective form. The capacity to relate to trees as individuals opens out some interesting implications for how trees, and tree-places, are constructed and reconstructed in relational agency. In particular, the valuing of individual trees in place constitutes that place as one of personal involvement, where specific practices of care, concern and ethical prompting are all manifest. Some aspects of these practices are manifest in support for and approval of management procedures, such as the propping up of the old mulberry tree with wooden stakes, and the wire reinforcement of the major branches of the beech tree which grows alongside the diagonal walkway. Residents and users of the square express their approval, and even sometimes delight, that steps are being taken to 'care for' these veteran trees. However, in addition to this institutional care for individual trees, local residents will sometimes take spontaneous action if they consider that a tree is under threat. We were told, for example, that in the drought of 1976 'people in the square . . . were carrying buckets of water from our houses and feeding water into this huge tree'. Here there are clear suggestions that strong emotional attachments are formed between local people and particular trees. Rather than seeing the square as some kind of mini-woodland which provides a landscape to look at, a space to walk through or rest in, or a habitat for wildlife, there is evidence here of a much more personalized relationship between people and the living nature of the tree. One resident, for example, (as quoted at the start of the chapter), narrated the following story to us:

> We had a lovely ash tree on the corner that was blown down in those gales, in the hurricanes, and that was terrible for those of us who lived here, and the person next door actually sat up watching it, watching it. I mean she actually saw it fall, and she actually sat and watched while they came, because the people had to come of course and cut it up and remove it, because it had crushed a car, and she sat there and cried and cried while they cut it up. [Interviewer: 'because?'] Well it had gone, it was dead, it was like watching a deathbed.

Such attachment transcends a nature–society relation based on visuality and material concern, reflecting instead an embodied emotional interconnection which opens up rather different avenues for understanding the interrelations between people and tree-places. Opportunities for ongoing interaction between people and particular trees, as in the square, seems to lead people to sense the palpable, living, individual identity of a tree (Harrison, 1991; Heinrich, 1997; Kaza, 1993; Perlman, 1994) resulting in a recognition of the tree's creativity and agency, and a sense in which these attributes 'demand' some form of ethical recognition.

In environmental philosophy, there have been some attempts to focus directly on 'individuals' as meaningful ethical beings (see Agar, 1995 and Jones, 2000), even if the notion of 'the individual' has come under critical scrutiny within the increasingly accepted wisdom of relational agency (Whatmore, 1997). However, this individuality still feels very problematic when particular trees are encountered in the flesh. In broad terms, society is just not used to prioritizing individual trees from this perspective. It is usually the collective presence of trees in the square, or in an orchard, or for that matter in Britain or globally, which seems important. The collective more abstract presence of trees, rather than the individual beings who make up that presence, is valorized. When individual trees are given priority it is usually because they are rare or spectacular, or that they offer aesthetic or amenity value. Such prioritization is anthropocentric, although sometimes reflecting the 'weak' anthropocentrism identified by Dobson (1995). Only rarely are trees treated as ethical 'others' in nature–society exchanges, particularly in any form of institutional exchange. However, the trees in the square – like 'Luna', the ancient redwood tree that Julia Hill lived in for a year to stop it from being felled in logging operations in California (Franklin, 1999) – do begin to emerge as ethical entities because they 'stand out' or have emerged as individuals in some way. This appreciation of trees as ethical entities is, however, only partially developed. Recognition of individual trees in the square as living (and sometimes dying) entities seems to have been driven by emotional attachment, which thus far seems unrefined by the rationality of wider ethical discourses. As a consequence individual trees remain as shadowy figures in ethical terms.

Beyond the Materiality of Place

The emerging story of Victoria Square, and the role which the trees have played in that story, opens out some interesting questions about the role of non-human agency in the making of places and in the representation of landscapes. As with the other tree-places we have researched (see Chapters 6 to 8) the historical development and present state of the square can be made sense of only if the agency of the trees is taken into account. Their presence, survival and growth have transformed the nature of the square and formed it as it is today, in a different relational network than previously. The trees now dominate the place and even make and perform it as a place; a place to visit, to walk through, to pass, to live and work by, that changes seasonally, daily and hourly, and over longer dimensions of tree growth and decay.

There are at least two major ways in which the non-human agency of trees has been implicated in the place-making of the square. First, we want to recognize that places are made in terms of the narratives which are constructed about them. As Curry (1999: 101) puts it:

> If as is common we imagine a place necessarily to be something like a location, we are immediately led to a particular way of thinking about it: places can be mapped, their locations specified in numerical terms, their borders found. This very metaphor, of course, undercuts our ability to see particular places as having to be maintained. Indeed, it would make more sense to compare a place to a conversation. For like places, conversations can be large and small, brief and long-lived. There can be multiple people involved, and the actors can change. Some people are good at keeping a conversation going and some are not.

Although Curry does not refer specifically here to agency or actors beyond the human realm, his analogy of place as conversation is helpful in our interpretation of tree-places such as the square. Rather than viewing Victoria Square in terms of mapped materiality, in which the living beings that are trees merely reflect zones of planting, we can more fruitfully recognize the square as an emerging conversation, in which the central narrative is wrapped around the living presence of the trees. Although the structure of ownership, the practices of management and the cultures of urban environmentalism have all been changing, and have contributed to the ongoing nature of the place-conversation, it is the trees which have been the focus of the place narrative. They, too, have contributed significantly to the conversation, both by their everyday presence and in terms of the threat to the stability of the conversation when they become vulnerable or at risk. It is the trees, in Curry's terms, which have been key agents in "keeping the conversation going".

Secondly, we want to recognize that places are made in terms of the active maintenance of specific practices – places, as Curry puts it are contexts 'within which human activities are carried out, and within which they make sense' (100). So, Wittgenstein's (1968) insight, that human practices are the basic elements of everyday life, needs to be placed (see Thrift, 1996b). The recognition of how we do things needs to be extended to an appreciation of how we do things here. The practices which have constituted the place of Victoria Square are many and various, including the changing regulation of access and use, the change from 'gardening' practices to 'park' practices, and the everyday practices of familiar encounter with a space which is somehow 'other' to the houses, pavements and roads which surround it. Throughout its history, however, the ritual practices and associated place-symbols of the square have been formed around the trees which, as we have seen, have in some cases become the subject of significant emotional and even ethical attachment. Without the trees, the square would not be how we do things here.

As with more expansive forms of landscape, tree-places such as the square are made both in material terms (planning, construction, planting and so on) and in imaginative terms. They become represented through place-myths and by the accretion of history, and they create an arena in which social relations are performed in never-ending production. Mitchell (2000) recognizes landscape as a 'vortex' in which all manner of contents swirl. Far from being merely a site across which the negotiations and outcomes of such contests are written, 'the landscape serves all at once as mediator, integrator and actor in these struggles' (139).

Tree-places such as the square can be viewed merely as some kind of commodity – a material entity to be struggled over in the social relations of production. However, it seems far more profitable to regard such tree-places as landscapes whose material form actively incorporates both the struggles which have occurred over it and, indeed, the very nature of these struggles. The square, and the trees which characterize it as well as constitute a significant part of its materiality, has been active in structuring practices and providing a place to live. It is this mix of textuality and materiality which make it potent as a place. Whereas the materiality of the place includes trees alongside bricks, mortar and concrete, the presence of nature in the form of the trees adds up to much more than materiality. The agency of the trees has been a fundamental co-constituent in the bricolage of place, as materialities have become reordered and recontextualized in order to communicate evolving place-meanings. It is the living active history, presence and becoming of trees which has exerted characteristic practice-forming agency in the square. It is the characterizing agency of trees which has integrated the square as a place, and provided a key moment of mediation between contesting and competing claims over the current and future management of the place.

–10–

Conclusions

> And this our life . . . finds tongues in trees, books in the running brooks, sermons in stones, and good in everything.
>
> (Shakespeare, *As You Like It*, Act 2 Scene 1, lines 15–18)

> The green trees, when I saw them first through one of the gates, transported and ravished me; their sweetness and unusual beauty made my heart to leap, and almost mad with ecstasy, they were such strange and wonderful things.
>
> (Thomas Traherne (1637–74), cited by Carey, 1999: 76)

> Val Plumwood argues in *Feminism and the Mastery of Nature*, that the environmental crisis has its roots in western culture's *dualizing* of humans and nature, creating 'a deep line of fracture between reason and nature', running through many societies and thinkers, *and systematically denying and obscuring the human dependence upon and immersion in nature*. The results are vast blind spots in our visions of ourselves and the world, through which modern forms of domination have been able to move, and indeed seem perfectly natural.
>
> (Weston, 1999b: 178, second emphasis ours)

In this concluding chapter we want to revisit the theoretical themes explored in Chapters 2 to 5 in the light of our research into the four different tree-places (Chapters 6 to 9). So far as culture, place and agency are concerned, we argue that the grounded studies of particular tree-places have already added to and developed the ideas discussed in the first half of the book. In each case, the detailed discussion of place-specific practices and processes has both illustrated and negotiated with the more abstract ideas with which we started out. In the case of ethics, however, we have refrained from further detailed discussion until this last chapter, partly at least because we wanted to review the four tree-places together in the context of ethical relations. However, there is another reason for 'leaving ethics till last': as warnings of environmental problems become increasingly compelling and alarming, we feel that this important issue lies at the heart of how humans relate to nature, in place. Our focus on ethics leads us to a final discussion of how time in general, and the notion of ecological time more specifically, represents a key factor in understanding non-human agency as performed by trees in an appropriate ethical framework.

Arbori-culture

The cultures of trees are both rich and dynamic. Trees are imagined according to a plethora of cultural constructs, circulating on different scales sometimes in hegemonic fashion, but often contested at more local levels. Arbori-cultures will be found folded and entwined within any particular place of trees. In our studies we have immediately encountered, for example, the orchardness of West Bradley, and the cemeteryness of Arnos Vale, as well as prevailing nationalistic interpretations of coniferous trees (which were then reversed locally) at Camerton. Alongside these macro-concepts, we have wanted to develop the idea that nature is vastly differentiated and that sub-categories of nature, such as trees, are themselves vastly variegated. This of course is not a surprising conclusion, but it is reached in the context of the paucity of attention given to nature in social theory and cultural geography, beyond gestures to it at *a very abstract generalized level*. If we are to break down the now infamous nature–culture divide, and our studies weave across it as we trace out the relational configurations and practices in the grounded world, then we have to insist that our approach will be as sensitive to otherness, difference, individuality in the realm of the non-human as it has become in the realm of the human. The sites we have considered are small, yet they are meaningful; meaningful in practical ways to the people bound up with them, and meaningful in conceptual ways too. The heritage represented by the trees planted on Camerton's spoil heaps became a fundamental facet of individual and community identity in the village. The natural oasis of Victoria Square offered sufficient access to the sights, sounds, smells and becomings of nature to allow some otherwise reluctant city residents to find an appropriate dwelling environment in an inner-city suburb. Trees play important, creative, even disruptive roles in the places we have narrated, and they are folded into very particular sets of relationships which are unique. In this way, the planned and ordered culture of a Victorian cemetery became a site of wild-life, and the enclosed tree-bounded private gardens of Victoria Square became a tree-centred public open space. Thus is the fabric of arbori-culture in place; thus is the fabric of human–non-human relational practices which operates here, there and everywhere.

Agency

The calls for the recognition of non-human agency in the performance of the world appear to us to be compelling. There remains, however, a considerable tension between the notion of relational agency – when that of any individual (be it human or otherwise) is subsumed by and incorporated into some creative network – and the notion that beings and things of various kinds do perform some kind of particular individual agency. Networks represent a most valuable frame of analysis, as illustrated by the rising levels of allegiance to Actor Network Theory in its various forms. The metaphor of networking also permits an exploration of the notion that power constitutes the result of relational agency within networks. However, networks may also be viewed as an achievement of what is networked, working together in some way. Networks exist precisely because different actants bring different qualities or creativities to the effort. In our view, then, alongside an appreciation of relational agency, there is still a need to understand the *creative contribution* of people, beings and things, and to tease out more precisely how this creativity is related to the qualities of any wider network. We are also convinced that by focusing analysis solely on networks, a range of between-spaces will be omitted from view. We believe that these between-spaces can often be relevant in terms of understanding particular places, and we also consider it extremely likely that between-spaces will not be devoid of agency, a factor which again suggests that individual creative contributions may be an appropriate starting point for the understanding of creative agency.

Natural actants, such as trees and the agencies they deploy, do seem to have been neglected substantially in the move away from very narrow views of human agency. This neglect seems puzzling because non-human actants were involved in networks and relational achievements before humans were around to be agents. We want to argue that neglect of non-human actants will lead precisely to an inability to see the world as full of creative meaningful others, and an unwillingness to grasp the *ethical implications which follow from recognizing creative otherness*. Trees do bring a creative agency into all manner of relational achievements which humans enrol, such as fruit production, timber production and landscape production. But they appear to work to other agendas and operate in other networks outside of or in conflict with human enrolled networks, and this distinction also merits attention and concern. We know that trees are not agents in the same ways that humans are, but to acknowledge this is not to deny that they are agents at all. Consider the transforming agency of the growth and spread of trees at Arnos Vale, turning networks of order into relative chaos. Consider how human monitoring of the trees and their agency was itself enrolled into processes of resisting landowner power. Or again, look at the agency performed by supposedly culturally alien conifer trees in the reformulation of wasteland into the locally cherished 'Little Switzerland' of Camerton, and the agency of the trees in Victoria Square whose longevity of presence and becoming has placed them as central place-signifiers in an elite city location. These different forms of agency need to be recognized, particularly in 'natural' objects such as trees which clearly have a life of their own, and can be unruly players in the development of the fabric of places. And, finally, the agency that emerges from embodied (relational) practice between (different) actors in material and symbolic places needs to be accounted for more fully.

Place

A nagging doubt has worried us throughout this work – that the sites we consider are not *places* at all, and that in fact the word *site* suits them better. In the end though, our doubt has been assuaged by the grounded studies we have undertaken. All the sites we have researched were considered to be places in many ways by different (local) people. The four sites were all places to visit in one way or another, or places of work, or places of ownership, or places of management. They were spatially bounded locations which were 'drawn' together by practices and narratives ranging from funding to management plans to bitter controversy. They were also bounded by fences or walls. Thus they have in one important sense a fixed spatial identity which chimes with conventional ideas of place. However, we have also emphasized that meanings, practices and materials constantly flow in and out of them, and that they are configured as places, and even parts of other places, in very different ways and on different scales. Places therefore need to be understood as dynamic flexing entities, which somehow retain some thread(s) of peculiar narrative which sustain them as places. 'A place may be a constant undergoing change . . . [and maybe is] a differential equation: flow upon flow; variation upon variation; differential upon differential' (Doel, 2000: 125), but there remain threads – presences, imaginings *which make the word 'place' still necessary*. As we have demonstrated, in places such as West Bradley and Victoria Square it is the trees which have contributed centrally to the sustaining place-narrative which offers these very threads, presences and imaginings on the local scale.

There is now a growing concern to link ideas of place and time. We have already discussed some of these concerns in Chapter 4, but others require further mention at this point (see in particular May and Thrift, 2001). For example, there has been considerable recent emphasis on how different places have different 'paces' (Shaw, 2001), and on how these paces are constructed, contested and differentiated in terms of power and lifestyle. We concur with this basic premise, but would add that places have multiple paces, and that different paces will be subject to complex gearing in the ongoing performance of that place. In this view, we are in closer agreement with Crang (2001) who claims that 'a place is not necessarily of singular time but a particular constellation of temporalities, coming together in a concrete place' (190; see also Parkes and Thrift, 1980).

All manner of beings, entities and materials contribute to these kinds of process, and our argument is that trees, with their prominent material presence, their vivid cultural baggages, their longevity, and the dynamics of their seasons and life cycles are key performers of place. The presence of trees in a place introduces a distinct time quality to that place. The apple trees of West Bradley convey a traditional facet of the Somerset countryside, even though many of the individual trees have been planted only recently. The mature, even veteran, trees of Victoria Square present almost timeless qualities to an inner-city suburb largely built some 150 years ago. The conifers of Camerton carry with them a strong sense of the heritage of the industrial site on which they were planted. Moving beyond the studies presented in this book, it is interesting to note how large developments and buildings, from the Crystal Palace to the new House of Commons offices, have used mature trees as central features of their key spaces. Crang (2001: 190) asserts that the city is a 'polychronic ensemble'. Although much of the talk of cities is about speed, fragmentation and flows, we would argue that city trees are key players in the polychronic ensemble, adding their distinct temporal tones to the gathering. This vital contribution by city trees is reflected in Silverton's (2001) description of London from the air,

> [it] seems less like a city than a scattering of buildings over gentle, wooded hills. Everywhere you look, there are trees. Big clumps of them. Great marching avenues of them. Long rows of them. Nor is this apparent greenness an illusion. London's tree population is currently 5.9 million, about three for every four humans.

In an increasingly urban and speeded-up world (Gleick, 1999) this time-presence of trees has been seized upon by many organizations and individuals who, in order to make the urban a saner place, call upon trees to become players and partners in the urban future.

Dwelling

As we have conducted this research, and in the writing of this book, we have become increasingly convinced that the concept of *dwelling* represents a fruitful way of dealing with the richness and dynamism of places. However, we also argue that dwelling, as currently proposed, requires some reformulation in order to meet the needs of the kind of grounded studies we have undertaken (see also Cloke and Jones 2001). First, we suggest that dwelling should not be used to denote any kind of necessary goodness or rightness in a particular situation, but rather that it should be invoked as a frame for understanding the richness or density of things actively together in the world. Secondly, any notion of dwelling being linked to some kind of conventional view of 'authenticity' seriously hampers its use as a concept. However, as the work of Common Ground shows, richness and place are linked, and the uniqueness contained within place, or as Common Ground put it 'local distinctiveness', *may* be deemed authentic in a certain immanent way, and *may* be something to value in the face of threat to that richness. Thirdly, dwelling needs to fully shake off its association with 'viewing' (framed) landscapes from without and, instead, to adopt a multi-sensed imagination-sensitive approach to the flexible movings and becomings which are immersed in the dwelt world of place. Dwelling is, or should be, about becoming. Game (2001), in her wonderful discussion of belonging, deploys many of the features of Heideggerian dwelling. She argues that to belong, to be at home, has distinct non-linear temporal qualities and this can be lived in the body, *in place,* and in the company of other humans and non-humans (for Game, with the sea and with horses). She also discusses verticality, 'poles, pillars, spires, steeples, temples, domes and bell towers' (236) which work to connect self, body, home, space, earth, sky, God, cosmos. Trees are beings which people can become 'at home with' (e.g. Kaza, 1993 and Heinrich, 1997), we suggest, and as well have stature which resonates with this symbolism of vertical extension. Game (2001: 239) in the end 'dares' to talk of paradise – 'Don't we say, "this is paradise" when we feel we belong – in connection with *places*, people, all sorts of experiences?' It is significant that in her discussion of the paradisal she turns to *place* not *space* or *networks* as the home of human beings. This paradise is, Game suggests, in part through connection with the cosmos, the world, or God, or childhood. We would add that it has often been claimed that woods and trees make such connections. As Emerson writes, 'in the woods, too, man casts off his years, as the snake his slough, and at what period soever in life, is always a child. In this wood we return to reason and faith' (Cited by Heinrich, 1997: 215).

Ethics

Connelly and Smith (1999) usefully note that 'it is not possible to "read off" ethical and political principles from concepts such as diversity, symbiosis and complexity' (40). However, they do suggest that ethical reasoning and ecological insights have a role to play by providing a 'critical standpoint from which to assess [current] political arrangements and decision-making processes' (ibid.). This we suggest goes some way toward highlighting the problems and the potential we have explored in our consideration of ethics. Our central question is *why* should ethics only apply to the human realm as they often seem to do. The usual answer to the question is that we are the only beings (as far as we know) who exercise moral judgement, and somehow we are separate from and above nature. But is this answer adequate, or even justifiable? We certainly have some serious doubts. To begin with, there seems to be a void at the very centre of this kind of answer: an assumed anthropocentrism which is responsible for vast swathes of environmental destruction in our world. If we are somehow above nature, then we are not making a very good job of our dominant position. If we are responsible for the stewardship of nature, then thus far we have failed to be good stewards as opposed to rampant resource-gatherers. In view of these realizations, there seems to be an urgent need for alternative ethical frames. Our basic alternative proposal is that ethical patterns need somehow to trace the relational patterns which perform the world. Thus we are interested in those views of ethics espoused by environmental philosophy, and in particular in the notion of relational ethics (Whatmore, 1997).

However, we also recognize that in all the complexity, ambiguity and aggravation that composes the world, very generalized ethical positions can serve only as a background against which other ethical patterns which match all the encounters of the world need to be measured. As Jacquie Burgess (2000) notes,

> Radical changes in policy evaluation include challenges to predominately instrumental and rational evaluation of policies which ignore or suppress the ethical/value dimension of these policies, one reason why the articulation of values is vital. (284)

Or as O'Brien and Guernier insist,

> Values are important in the debate about the environment not because some value or other in itself can or should be described as 'right' or 'wrong', but because value systems refer to the underlying principles about the 'proper conduct' of life in general and about ways of interpreting specific events in terms of more extensive commitments to particular social arrangements and political orders. They indicate the cultural plurality – and often ambiguity – within which notions of 'rightness' and 'wrongness' are formulated, contested and changed. (p. xiv, cited by Burgess 2000, 284)

We still face 'the unending struggle to live rightly in the world', to repeat Cronon's (1996) lovely phrase. So ethics needs to deal with situations, the actants involved and the places that arise out of them.

Proctor (1996) gives a convincing account of the ethical dimensions of the debates about the battle to save the Pacific Northwest old-growth forests (North America), considering the frames of intrinsic value and instrumental value, and ecocentrism and biocentrism in relation to the forests and the trees. He comes to two main conclusions. First, he suggests that an ethics of place is needed – 'an ethics rooted in, but not limited to, place' (294). Our conclusion is similar, in that we have called for ethics to pay attention to the dynamic interactions of particular encounters in particular places, although we argue that a background of more general ethical consideration needs to underpin this or connect it to the wider world. We also differ with Proctor in terms of scale. Compared with the size of our tree-places, the area he considers – which he says is 'small', – is in fact vast. Yet in our sites there are very particular formations of encounters which could not be generalized beyond their boundaries in any way. Clearly the forests of the

Pacific Northwest will share common features and themes (ecological, legislative or cultural) and thereby warrant a kind of *regional ethics*, but from the evidence of our research we would assume that there would be *micro-scales* of encounters within that. This, then, reinforces the argument we make about place. If Proctor and others (including us) call for an ethics of place, it must be on the understanding that place is understood as a multi-dimensional concept. Any location, any encounter, will be in a multiple of places which range from the very local to the very global.

Secondly, Proctor (1996) rightly suggests that environmentalists fighting for the forests 'should leave most of their ecological ammunition at home and instead encourage people to address more fundamental issues' so as 'to find and promote answers to moral questions that loom large in contemporary debates over nature' (297). To talk of intrinsic rights and bioethics in principle without facing up to the need to deal with *particular* nature in *particular* places and *particular* relations is to stop just where the going gets tough and meaningful. Do trees have intrinsic rights? How can this work in all the different ways that humans and trees interact? Applying this kind of thinking to the places we have researched leads us to the following conclusions and questions. First, the *creative* role of trees at the global, national and local levels, in biosphere production, habitat production, food and produce production, landscape production and place production, means that they need to be taken seriously. We have told how Common Ground have argued that felling trees should be a last resort, and that nurturing and increasing their presence should be a priority. However this maxim can only act as a background, albeit an important one. Once we begin to look at the relationalities, the multiple presences, in the places we consider, questions come crowding in.

Consider West Bradley orchard. As we have recounted, trees are routinely grubbed out and replaced in the ongoing management of the orchard. To argue against this on ethical grounds would seem implausible. For better or for worse, humans are bound to be in relationships of use with other beings, and we have to find effective, ethical formations of use. If a tree is rooted out and replaced with another to take up the burden of production (and place-making), that does not seem too shocking. If it is acceptable to replace one tree with another, then this would imply that it *is the presence of trees,* rather than the actual specific individual trees, which are of ethical resonance. But what about replacing one type of tree with another? This often happens, as older traditional types are replaced with new commercially bred varieties. Such replacement, it could be argued, represents an attack on biodiversity and the cultural and ecological richness that Common Ground is so concerned about. This may be a more serious question, and it points to an ethical imperative to preserve diversity itself, accepting that the death of a variety or species of plant (or animal) is more concerning than the death of any given individual. But then again, is it reasonable to ask the private owner who is seeking to run a commercially viable orchard to assume sole responsibility for these issues? If we are concerned with diversity should we help to preserve it by funding orchard owners?

In Victoria Square individual trees are recognized, loved, protected and given some form of 'rights' as living beings. Similarly, at Arnos Vale some trees are greatly valued and given recognition, while others are considered to be the equivalent of vermin. At Camerton, conifers were planted, and although often despised culturally as alien intruders into the English landscape, these trees became cherished, if not for their own intrinsic value then for the heritage and conservation signifiers which clung to them. Three reflections of the ethical consideration of trees emerge from our studies. First, trees that stand out as individuals, either because they are literally placed on their own and/or because they are distinctive in type, size, shape or age, seem to become particularly visible ethically (Jones, 2000). The treatment of these trees suggests that the liberal ethics of the individual human, and even the individual animal, can in some circumstances be stretched to the individual tree. By contrast trees – when seen collectively as a wood, or forest or orchard – suddenly become more invisible individually and the ethical focus falls, if at all, on the collective, such as on 'old-growth forest'. Thus it would be deemed wrong to clear the cemetery or the orchard of trees, but not so to cull individual trees which help to constitute those collectives. Secondly, trees which have been in place over time, and thus have grown to a certain size and venerability, achieve consequential status – particularly the so-called veteran trees. To pinch out a young horse-chestnut sapling in the cemetery is one thing, but to cut down the majestic mother tree is another. This distinction reflects the palpability of presence of being enjoyed by large trees.

Thirdly, 'working trees' (such as the apple trees in the orchard) are often viewed as mere extensions of human activity and are accordingly stripped of 'rights', whereas other trees – particularly when they have grown (perhaps from wild) to a certain status, and have transgressed human intention – seem to attract an independent status which is of much more significance. But should these trees be allowed to grow and seed freely? Such freedom to spread would unsettle the balance of Victoria Square, as it has done at Arnos Vale cemetery, where other habitats, the graves and graveside access have been compromised by the growing trees.

In the end, ethics should not just be about the contribution others make to the community nor about the assumption that if the contribution is meaningful then they are incorporated into the ethical fold. These issues are important, but beyond them lies a more Levinasian view of ethics which values the other as other, beyond any kind of reciprocal relationship (Jones, 2000). We showed in Chapter 5 how some tree protests have brought individual trees into ethical focus, and how some environmental philosophy tries to extend ethical consideration to non-human beings. In the end, trees need to be valued as ethically living beings just as humans are living beings. This is not to say they need the same type and degree of ethical consideration. Their being and living is very different to ours; for example, the life of some trees can be prolonged almost indefinitely by coppicing. We therefore need an ethical consideration of trees which is based in *their good and their vitality* (Attfield, 1981). Surely the key community, in all of the lifeless matter that seems to swirl around the universe and forms our solar system and our planet, is that of living things; they are meaningful beings in the key respect of being alive and we must respect and honour that in the many ways we use them. The story of the sequoia we told earlier points to an ethics based on the dignity of use.

Tree Timescapes

Finally we want to return to the issue of time, for our research has opened up questions about ecological time, and within that arbori-cultural time, which are the time dynamics of nature and the time dynamic of trees. These issues about the timescapes of nature in general and of trees in particular are significant in and of themselves, but also in relation to how trees gear with other temporal forms, notably those associated with social time. If, as Bail (1999) suggests, 'it is trees which compose a landscape', then they do so in their own time – a time at odds with notions of the speeded-up, instantaneous temporal nature of modernity. The timescape of trees reflects both the processes of ongoing growth and decay and the seasonal cycles of trees, and the shifting cultural and economic relational networks that trees inhabit. In a series of recent theoretical initiatives, time has been identified as a core theme in the understanding of nature (Macnaghten and Urry, 1998; Grange, 1997), environmental change (Driver and Chapman, 1996), environmental hazards and sustainability (Adam, 1998) and nature conservation (Adams, 1996). Within these initiatives there is an emerging debate over modern constructions of time, its abstracted condition and the increasing dominance of 'clock time' and 'instantaneous time' (Macnaghten and Urry, 1998), the twentieth century as the century of speed (Conrad, 1998), and 'the 24-hour society' (Krietzman, 1999). These modern manifestations of time are often seen to mark the 'triumph' of culture over nature and the obliteration of nature times (Adam, 1998). 'As Lefebvre suggests, with modernity lived time experienced in and through nature gradually disappears. It is no longer visible and is replaced by measuring instruments, clocks, which are separate from both natural and social space' (Macnaghten and Urry, 1998: 141).

In their important contribution to these debates, Macnaghten and Urry (1998) introduce the notion of glacial time (the very long-term cycles of nature such as ice ages or plate tectonics) which they equate to Macy's (1993) notion of ecological time. Here we suggest that Macnaghten and Urry hurry past an important distinction which is central to the approach we have adopted. Ecological time (and other forms of nature times, such as diurnal and tidal sequences) needs to be differentiated and analysed as separate from glacial time, and brought to the fore as a form of time in the complex construction of particular 'dwellings'. Donaldson (1996) discusses 'pre-capitalist', 'natural time' which comes in '"circadian" time (drawn from the solar and ecosystems), which gives rhythm to our "everyday-time"' (Scheibl, 1997: 350). He contrasts this with 'the *linearity, quantity* and *duration* of human life-time' (Scheibl, ibid.). Equally, in their introduction to 'the geographies of temporality', May and Thrift (2001: 3) acknowledge the importance of different 'nature times' – 'the diurnal, the rhythms of the seasons, the rhythms of the body to the turning of the tides'. Beyond this introduction, however, nature has only a fitful and/or background presence in the collection as a whole, while the social, the cultural, the political and the technological are foregrounded. A programme of research is required in order to address the various forms of nature times and how they *still* impact on social times: in such a programme the assumption of a simple historical model where modern time has replaced natural time will need to be challenged.

Consideration of the roles of trees in the construction of places highlights the importance and complexity of nature times. As Marshall (1992: 362) suggests, 'the process of nature is not . . . merely cyclic but a kind of "creative advance"'. The supposed dominance of modern clock time is in fact contested, or perhaps deflected or at least rendered complex, by all sorts of nature times. A survey of articles in the journal *Time and Society* shows that research into, and writing about, the complexities of time have mostly remained within the social realm, considering issues such as work, gender, leisure, money and management, with only limited reference to the times of nature. One exception is Hofmeister (1997) who claims that 'To create a time-sensitive approach to the interdependence of the ecological and socio-cultural systems, we must recognise the physical basis of the economy in time'. Macy (1993: 206) argues that we must 'reinhabit time' in the face of the 'temporal trap' of modern life and this is achieved by recognizing 'time in organic, ecological and even geological terms'.

Trees are the fulcrum all kinds of time-based constructions of social formations, and are bound up in the processes of place, production and consumption. The ecological timescales of tree growth and lifespan interact with the social to form a number of social/cultural/economic hybrid timescapes. Trees are planted for the *future* (as in the National and Community Forests), for the marking of symbolic moments of the *present* such as the various millennium planting initiatives (for example, by the Oaks Millennium Trust), and to establish a *permanence* through time (the Woodland Trust memorial planting scheme, and the National Memorial Arboretum). Trees are also protected for the veneration of the *past*, as in the

Veteran Trees Campaign, and are used in the restoration of historical landscapes through planting and clearing. All of these treescapes are in part manifestations of time (Thomas, 1998). Time can serve to reconfigure mature landscapes as quite different from how they originated. As a somewhat obvious example, the great landscape gardeners such as Repton and Capability Brown did not see their mainly tree-based creations in the forms that we see them now. Time can also be 'artificially' introduced, as seen in examples of instantaneous landscapes which are achieved through expensive, high-tech processes of transplanting well-developed trees from specialist nurseries to new developments. This is in effect a process of buying ecological or even arboricultural time (Figure 10.1). Jacobs (2000) and Hoskins (2001) both offer temporal narratives of places and landscapes in which trees play central roles. For Hoskins the time symbolism of Sydney's Centennial Park is in part articulated through the shifting tree types planted under differing regimes. For Jacobs the analysis of the landscape design work of Lassus demonstrates how 'playing with time' is a key device in creating a landscape narrative and sense of place. Trees, as in the designs of Lassus depicted by Jacobs, are key means of doing just this, through both their materialism and their symbolism.

Figure 10.1 Buying ecological (arboricultural) time (Owain Jones)

All these are examples of the ecological timescales of tree growth, interacting in complex ways with human social constructions of time. Tree time also, of course, interacts with economic cycles. Tree-related economic production and consumption are inevitably embedded within these tree timescales such that, for instance, 'in forestry 40 years is not even a rotation' (Trewin, 1998). Issues of the seasonal cycles of trees are also important. All of the tree-places we have researched went though significant seasonal changes, and these are important, even definitive, for those who interact with them. In the orchard, the temporality of work falls in with the seasonal cycles of the trees. Arnos Vale was seen by one regular visitor as 'bigger' in the summer and 'smaller' in the winter, because the 'leaf cover in summer blocks views, deadens sound penetration, and encloses you'. At Victoria Square the sound of the trees at night in a winter storm was an evocative place-making experience for some residents overlooking the square, and the trees in summer and winter bring markedly different qualities to their engagement with this place.

Our research points clearly to the fact that despite the undoubted transformation of time that has occurred within modern society, all manner of nature times can still be found in what Adam (1998) calls the 'timescapes of modernity'. Trees present a compelling example of this. We suggest that a much better understanding is needed in terms of how particular nature times differ from each other, interact with social time, are spatially embedded and arc implicated in notions of landscape and place. Addressing deeply embedded and taken-for-granted assumptions about time, nature and the environment is, according to Adam (1994, 1998) and Macnaghten and Urry (1998), critical in developing a more nuanced understanding of society and nature-society relations. As yet, issues of time, nature and environment have received little research attention apart from the pioneering efforts of those mentioned above.

One potential way forward is to use new techniques of visualization to depict nature times. Time-lapse photography, for example, has been used extensively in the popular media to illustrate the extremely active life of trees and plants, presenting a view usually closed off to us due to the fundamentally different timescales which trees and humans occupy. Future research could beneficially deploy time-lapse or long-exposure photography to convey a better, more visualized understanding of how the timescapes of nature, and in our case trees, interconnect with other timescapes (Brosse, 1998). It is our view that a better appreciation of the timescapes of nature will open up new understandings of some of the issues of agency, place and ethics which we have addressed in this book. Such technology may help us to advance yet further our argument about the importance of taking seriously the active creative life of trees.

> Silence ensues, broken only by the sound of an axe striking a tree in the orchard far away. (last line of *The Cherry Orchard*, Chekov, 1959: 398).

Bibliography

ACCES (1985) *Camerton Old Colliery: management scheme for wooded batch and pithead area*, ACCES: Bristol.

Ackroyd, P. (2000) *London: The Biography*, London: Chatto & Windus.

Adam, B. (1994) *Time and Social Theory*, Cambridge: Polity Press.

—— (1998) *Timescapes of Modernity: the Environment and Invisible Hazards*, London: Routledge.

Adam, B., Held, M., Geibler, K., Kummerer, K. and Schneider, M. (1997) 'Time for the Environment: the Tutzing Project "Time Ecology"', *Time and Society*, 6, 1, 73–84.

Adams, P.C., Hoelscher, S. and Till, K.E. (eds) (2001) *Textures of Place: Exploring Humanist Geographies*, Minneapolis: University of Minnesota Press.

Adams, W. (1996) *Future Nature*, London: Earthscan.

Agar, N. (1995) 'Valuing species and valuing individuals', *Environmental Ethics*, 17, 4, 397–415.

Agnew, J.A. (1989) 'The devaluation of place in social science', in J.A. Agnew and J.S. Duncan (eds) *The Power of Place*, London: Unwin Hyman.

Agnew, J.A. and Duncan, J.S. (eds) (1989) *The Power of Place*, London: Unwin Hyman Ltd.

Agyeman, J. (1993) 'Alien Species', *Museum Journal*, December.

Anderson, K. (1995) 'Culture and nature at the Adelaide Zoo: at the frontiers of "human" geography', *Transactions of the Institute of British Geographers*, NS 20, 275–94.

—— (1997) 'A walk on the wild side: a critical geography of domestication', *Progress in Human Geography*, 21, 4, 463–85.

Arnot, C. (1999) 'Where There's Muck' . . ., *Guardian*, Society Section, 28 April.

Atran, S. (1990) *Cognitive Foundations of Natural History*, Cambridge: Cambridge University Press.

Attfield, R. (1981) 'The good of trees', *Journal of Value Inquiry*, 15, 35–54.

—— (1991) *The Ethics of Environmental Concern*, Oxford: Blackwell.

Bachelard, G. (1988) *Air and Dreams: an Essay on the Imagination of Movement*, Dallas: Dallas Institute Publications.

Bail, M. (1999) *Eucalyptus*, London: Panther.

Baker, R. St.B. (1944) *I Planted Trees*, London: Lutterworth Press.

Baker, S., Kousis, M., Richarson, D. and Young, S. (eds) (1997) *The Politics of Sustainable Development: Theory, Policy and Practice within the European Union*, London: Routledge.

Bakhtin, M.M. (1981) *The Dialogical Imagination*, Austin: University of Texas Press.

Barker, C. (2000) *Cultural Studies: Theory and Practice*, London: Sage.

Barnett, A. and Scruton, R. (eds) (1998) *Town and Country*, London: Jonathan Cape.

Barrow, C.J. (1999) *Environmental Management: Principles and Practice*, London: Routledge.

Bates, B. (1997) 'Sacred Trees', *Resurgence*, 181 (www. gn.apc.org/resurgece/ articles/bates.htm)

Bauman, Z. (1993) *Postmodern Ethics*, Oxford: Blackwell.

Bender, B. (1998) *Stonehenge: Making Space*, Oxford: Berg.

Berg, P. and Dasmann, R. (1978) 'Reinhabiting California' in P. Berg (ed.) *Reinhabiting a Separate Country: a Bioregional Anthology of Northern California*, San Francisco: Planet Drum Foundation.

Berry, W. (1990) *What are People For?* San Francisco: North Point Press.

Birnbacher, D. (1987) 'Ethical principles versus guiding principles in environmental ethics', *Philosophica*, 30, 59–75.

Blakemore, J. (1984) 'Wind Series', photographs in R. Mabey (ed.) *Second Nature*, London: Jonathan Cape.

Bloch, M. (1998) 'Why trees, too, are good to think with: towards an anthropology of the meaning of life', in L. Rival, (ed.) *The Social Life of Trees: Anthropological Perspectives on Tree Symbolism*, London: Berg.

Borden, I. (1998) 'Body architecture: skateboarding and the creation of superarchitectural space', in J. Hill, (ed.) *Occupying Architecture: Between the Architect and the User*, London: Routledge.

Bosanquet, A. (2000) 'Trunk Calls', *Guardian*, 8 July.

Boyer, M. (1996) *Tree-Talk: Memories, Myths and Ttimeless Customs*, London: Thames and Hudson.

Braun, B. and Castree, N. (eds) (1998) *Remaking Reality: Nature at the Millennium*, London: Routledge.

Broad, K. (1998) *Caring for Small Woods*, London: Earthscan.

Brosse, J. (1998) Postface: 'The life of trees', in L. Rival (ed.), *The Social Life of Trees: Anthropological Perspectives on Tree Symbolism*, Oxford: Berg.

Brown, P. (1997) 'Greening of the Black Country', *Guardian*, Society Section, 3 September.

—— (1998) 'Dying young: Britain's trees wilting under urban stress', *Guardian*, 3 April.

—— (1999) 'The havens that have gone to hell', *Guardian*, 6 November.

Browning, F. (1998) *Apples: The Story of the Fruit of Temptation*: London: Allen Lane Penguin.

Bryson, B. (1998) *A Walk in the Woods*, London: Black Swan Books.

Buber, M. (1937) *I and Thou*, Edinburgh: T & T Clark.

Buchanan, A. and Cossons, N. (1969) *Industrial Archaeology of The Bristol Region*, Newton Abbot: David & Charles

Buell, L. (1995) *The Environmental Imagination, Thoreau, Nature Writing and the Formation of American Culture*, Cambridge, Mass.: Harvard University Press.

Bunce, M. (1994) *The Countryside Ideal: Anglo-American Images of Landscape*, London: Routledge.

Burgess, J. (1993) 'Not out of the woods yet', *Landscape Research Extra*, no. 12, Spring.

—— (2000) 'Situating knowledges, sharing values and reaching collective decisions: the cultural turn in environmental decision making', in I. Cook, D. Crouch, S. Naylor and J.R. Ryan (eds) *Cultural Turns/Geographical Turns: Perspectives on Cultural Geography*, Harlow: Prentice Hall.

Callicott, J.B. (1994) *Earth's Insights: a Survey of Ecological Ethics from the Mediterranean Basin to the Australian Outback*, Berkeley: University of California Press.

Callon, M. (1986) 'Some elements of a sociology of translation; domestication of the scallops and the fishermen of St Brieux Bay', in J. Law (ed.) *Power, Action and Belief: A New Sociology of Knowledge?* London: Routledge & Kegan Paul.

—— (1991) 'Techno-economic networks and irreversibility', in J. Law (ed.) *A Sociology of Monsters?* London: Routledge.

Callon, M. and Law, J. (1995) 'Agency and the Hybrid Collectif', *The South Atlantic Quarterly*, 94, 2, 481–507.

Cam Valley Wildlife Group (1998) Letter to Bath and North-East Somerset County Council Planning Committee, in reference to applications 98/03185/OUT and 98/03234/REM.

Camerton Heritage Committee (1993) *Camerton Heritage Project*, Camerton Heritage Committee: Camerton (nr Bath, UK).

Carey, J. (ed.) (1999) *The Faber Book of Utopias*, London: Faber & Faber.

Casey, E.S. (1993) *Getting Back into Place: Towards a Renewed Understanding of the Place-World*, Bloomington: Indiana University Press.

—— (1998) *The Fate of Place: a Philosophical History*, University of California Press, London.

—— (2001) 'Body, Self, and Landscape: a Geographical Inquiry into the Place-World', in P.C. Adams, S. Hoelscher and K.E. Till (eds) *Textures of Place: Exploring Humanist Geographies*, Minneapolis: University of Minnesota Press.

Castree, N. (2000) 'Nature' in R.J. Johnston, D. Gregory, G. Pratt and M. Watts (eds) *The Dictionary of Human Geography*, 4th edn, Oxford: Blackwell.

Chekhov, A. (1959) *Plays*, Harmondsworth: Penguin.

Cheney, J. (1989) 'Postmodern environmental ethics: ethics as bioregional narrative', *Environmental Ethics*, 11, 2, 117–34.

—— (1994) 'Ecofeminism and the reconstruction of environmental ethics', in K.J. Warren (ed.) *Ecological Feminism*, London: Routledge.

—— (1999) 'The Journey home', in A. Weston (ed.) *An Invitation to Environmental Philosophy*, Oxford: Oxford University Press.

Clark, S.R.L. (1977) *The Moral Status of Animals*, Oxford: Clarendon Press.

Clarke, J. (1976) 'Style', in S. Hall and T. Jefferson (eds) *Resistance Through Rituals: Youth Subcultures in Post-war Britain*, London: Hutchinson.

Clifford, S. (1996) 'Place, people and Parish Maps', in S. Clifford and A. King (eds) *From Place to PLACE: Maps and Parish Maps*, London: Common Ground.

Clifford, S. and King, A. (eds) (1993) *Local Distinctiveness, Place, Particularity and Identity*, London: Common Ground.

—— (eds) (1996) *From Place to PLACE: Maps and Parish Maps*, London: Common Ground.

Cloke, P. and Jones. O. (2000) 'From Wasteland to Woodland to "Little Switzerland": Environmental Management in Place, Culture and Time', in X. Font and J. Tribe (eds) *Forest Tourism and Recreation*, Oxford: CABI Publishing.

—— (2001) 'Dwelling, place, and landscape: an orchard in Somerset', *Environment and Planning A*, 2nd, 33, 649–66.

Cloke, P., Milbourne, P. and Thomas, C. (1996a) 'The English National Forest: local reactions to plans for renegotiated nature-society relations in the countryside', *Transaction, Institute of British Geographers*, 21, 552–71.

—— (1996b) 'From Wasteland to Wonderland: opencast mining, regeneration and the new National Forest', *Geoforum*, 27, 2, 159–74.

Cloke, P., Milbourne, P. and Widdowfield, R. (2000) 'Partnerships and policy networks in rural local governance: homelessness in Taunton', *Public Administration*, vol. 78, 111–34.

Common Ground (1989a) *Orchards: A Guide to Local Conservation*, London: Common Ground.

—— (1989b) *Pulp!* Summer, London: Common Ground.

—— (1991) *Tree Dressing Day*, Information Booklet, London: Common Ground.

—— (1994) *The Apple Broadcast*, London: Common Ground.

Condry, W. (1974) *Woodlands*, London: Williams Collins and Sons.

Conley, V.A. (1997) *Ecopolitics: The Environment in Poststructuralist Thought*, London: Routledge.

Connelly, J. and Smith, G. (1999) *Politics and the Environment: From Theory to Practice*, London: Routledge.

Conrad, P. (1998) 'The World Changes Gear', *Observer*, Review, 30 August.

Cosgrove, D. (1984) *Social Formation and Symbolic Landscape*, London: Croom Helm.

Coward, R. (2000) 'Harvesting the Forbidden Fruit', *Guardian*, 25 October.

CPRE (1996) *Trees and Woods: A Campaigner's Guide*, London: CPRE.

Crang, M. (1998) *Cultural Geography*, London: Routledge.

—— (2001) 'Rhythms of the city: temporalised space and motion', in J. May and N. Thrift (eds) *Timespace: Geographies of Temporality*, London: Routledge.

Crang, M. and Thrift, N. (eds) (2000) *Thinking Space*, London: Routledge.

Creswell, T. (1996) *In Place/Out of Place: Geography, Ideology and Transgression*, Minneapolis: University of Minnesota Press.

Cronon, W. (ed.) (1996) *Uncommon Ground: Rethinking the Human Place in Nature*, New York: Norton.

Crouch, D. (1996) 'Making sense of our place: A critical review of Parish Maps', in S. Clifford and A. King (eds) *From Place to PLACE: maps and Parish Maps*, London: Common Ground.

—— (2001) 'Spatialities and the feeling of doing', *Social and Cultural Geography*, 2, 1, 61–75.

Crouch, D. and Matless, D. (1996) 'Refiguring geography: the Parish Maps of Common Ground', *Transactions of the Institute of British Geographers*, NS 21, 236–55.

Curry, D. (2000) 'Defending Middle-Earth', in L. Coupe (ed.) *The Green Study Reader: From Romanticism to Ecocriticism*, London: Routledge.

Curry, M. (1999) '"Hereness" and the normativity of place', in J. Proctor and D. Smith (eds) *Geography and Ethics: Journeys in a Moral Terrain*, New York: Routledge.

Curry, M.R. (2000) 'Wittgenstein and the fabric of everyday Life', in M. Crang and N. Thrift (eds) *Thinking Space*, London: Routledge.

Daniels, S. (1988) 'The political iconography of woodland in later Georgian England', in D. Cosgrove and S. Daniels (eds), *The Iconography of Landscape*, Cambridge: Cambridge University Press.

—— (1992) 'Place and the geographical imagination', *Geography*, 7, 4, 310–22.

—— (1999) 'Trees and woods in British art', in A. Miles, *Silva: The Tree in Britain*, London: Ebury Press.

Davis, D. (1988) 'The evocative symbolism of trees', in D. Cosgrove and S. Daniels (eds), *The Iconography of Landscape*, Cambridge: Cambridge University Press.

Dawkins, R. (1996) *River Out of Eden*, London: Phoenix Books.

de Certeau, M. (1984) *The Practice of Everyday Life*, Berkeley: University of California Press.

Deleuze, G. and Guattari, F. (1987) *A Thousand Plateaus. Capitalism and Schizophrenia*, London: The Athlone Press.

Demeritt, D. (1994) 'The nature of metaphors in geography and environmental history', *Progress in Human Geography*, 18, 163–85.

Denes, M. (2000) 'Scary Fairy Tales, review of "In a Dark Wood" by A. Craig', (Fourth Estate) *Telegraph,* Arts and Books, 22 July.

Dobson, A. (1995) *Green Political Thought*, 2nd edn, London: Routledge.

Doel, M. (1999) *Poststructuralist Geographies, The Diabolical Art of Spatial Science*, Edinburgh: Edinburgh University Press.

—— (2000) 'Un-glunking geography: Spatial Science after Dr Seuss and Gilles Deleuze', in M. Crang and N. Thrift (eds) *Thinking Space*, London: Routledge.

Donaldson, M. (1996) *Taking our Time: Remaking the Temporal Order*, Nedlands: University of Western Australia Press.

Down, C.G. and Warrington, A.J. (1971) *The History of the Somerset Coalfield*, Newton Abbott: Davis & Charles Ltd.

Doyle, T. and McEachern, D. (1998) *Environment and Politics*, London: Routledge.

Driver, T. and Chapman, G. (eds) (1996) *Time-scales and Environmental Change*, London: Routledge.

Duncan, J.S. (1990) *The City as Text: The Politics of Landscape Interpretation in the Kandyan Kingdom*, Cambridge: Cambridge University Press.

Dunk, J. and Rugg, J. (1994) *The Management of Old Cemetery Land: Now and the Future*, Crayford: Shaw and Sons Ltd.

Edlin, H.L. (1948) *Forestry and Woodland Life*, London: Batsford.

—— (1970) *Trees, Woods and Man*, 3rd edn, London: Collins.

Ehrenfeld, D. (1992) 'Places', in P. Sauer (ed.) *Finding Home: Writing on Nature and Culture from Orion Magazine*, Boston: Beacon Press.

Eisenberg, E. (1998) *The Ecology of Eden: Humans, Nature and Human Nature*, London: Picador.

Ellen, R. (1993) 'Rhetoric, practice and incentive in the face of the changing times. A case study in Nuaulu attitudes to conservation and deforestation', in K. Milton (ed.) *Environmentalism: The View from Anthropology*, London: Routledge.

Emel, J. and Wolch, J. (1998) 'Witnessing the Animal Moment', in J. Wolch and J. Emel (eds) *Animal Geographies: Place, Politics and Identity in the Nature-Culture Borderlands*, London: Verso.

Entrikin, J.N. (1991) *The Betweenness of Place*, Baltimore: Johns Hopkins University Press.

Evans, M. (1996) 'Languages of racism in contemporary Europe', in B. Jenkins and S. Sofos (eds) *Nation and Identity in Contemporary Europe*, London: Routledge.

Evans, P. (1992) 'A policy for forestry and woodland', in P. Conford, (ed.) *A Future for the Land: Organic Practice from a Global Perspective*, Bideford: Green Books.

—— (1998) 'Barking Mad', *Guardian*, Society Section, 7 October.
—— (1999) 'Long Live Trees', *Guardian*, Society Section, 29 December.
—— (2000) 'Myths and Memories', *Guardian*, Society Section, 29 November.
Fairbrother, N. (1970) *New Lives, New Landscapes*, Harmondsworth: Penguin.
Fitzsimmons, M. (1989a) 'The matter of nature', *Antipode*, 21, 106–20.
—— (1989b) 'Reconstructing Nature', *Environment and Planning D, Society and Space*, 7, 1–3.
Fitzsimmons, M. and Goodman, D. (1998) 'Incorporating nature: environmental narratives and the reproduction of food', in B. Braun and N. Castree (eds) *Remaking Reality. Nature at the Millennium*, London: Routledge.
Forestry Commission (1985) *Broadleaved Woodland Grant Schem*e (revised November 1985), The Forestry Commission: Edinburgh.
—— (1996) *Press Release 461*, 8 November. (www.forestry.gov.uk)
Frankena, W. (1979) 'Ethics and Environment', in K. Goodpaster and K. Saure (eds) *Ethics and the Problems of the 21st Century*, Notre Dame: Notre Dame University Press, 3–20.
Franklin, S. (1999) *The Time of Trees*, Milan: Leonardo Arts.
Frazer, J. (1993) *The Golden Bough: a Study in Myth and Religion*, Ware: Wordsworth.
Game, A. (1991) *Undoing the Social: Towards a Deconstructive Sociology*, Buckingham: Open University Press.
—— (2001) 'Belonging: experience in sacred time and space', in J. May and N. Thrift (eds) *Timespace: Geographies of Temporality*, London: Routledge.
Gates, P. (2000) *Trees in Trouble. A New Campaign to save the World's Rarest Species*, supplement to BBC Wildlife Magazine, October, Bristol: BBC Wildlife Magazine.
Gil, J. (1998) *Metamorphoses of The Body*, Minneapolis: University of Minnesota Press.
Gleick, J. (1999) *Faster: The Acceleration of Just About Everything*, London: Little Brown.
Goin, P. (1996) *Humanature*, Austin: University of Texas Press.
Goodwin, B.C. (1994) *How the Leopard Changed its Spots*, London: Weidenfeld & Nicolson.
Goodwin, M. (1998) 'The governance of rural areas: some emerging research issues and agendas', *Journal of Rural Studies*, 14, 1, 5–12.
Goodwin, M. and Painter, J. (1996) 'Local governance, Fordism and the changing geographies of regulation', *Transactions of the Institute of British Geographers*, 21, 635–49.
Gordon, S. (1997) 'How many kinds of things are there in the world? The ontological status of societies', in J.D. Greenwood (ed.) *The Mark of the Social: Discovery or Invention?* Lanham: Rowman and Littlefield.

Grange, J. (1985) 'Place, body and situation', in D. Seamon, and D. Mugerauer (1985) *Dwelling, Place and Environment: Towards an Understanding of Person and World*, Dordrecht: Matinus Nijhoff.

—— (1997) *Nature: An Environmental Cosmology*, Albany: State University of New York Press.

Graves, R. (1961) *The White Goddess*, London: Faber & Faber.

Greer, G. (2000) 'Time to wage a proper war against the rabbits', *Telegraph*, Weekend, 14 October.

Gregory, D. (1989) 'The crisis of modernity? Human geography and critical social theory', in R. Peet and N. Thrift (eds), *New Models in Geography*, Vol. II, London: Unwin Hyman.

—— (1994) *Geographical Imaginations*, Oxford: Blackwell.

Grove-White, R. (1997) 'Environmental sustainability, time and uncertainty', *Time and Society*, 6, 1, 99–106.

Guattari, F. (2000) *The Three Ecologies*, London: The Athlone Press.

Guignon, C.C. (ed.) (1993a) *The Cambridge Companion to Heidegger*, Cambridge: Cambridge University Press.

—— (1993b) 'Authenticity, moral values, and psychotherapy', in C. Guignon (ed.) *The Cambridge Companion to Heidegger*, Cambridge, Cambridge University Press.

Hadfield, M. (1967) *Landscape with Trees*, London: Country Life Ltd.

Hall, S. (1996) 'For Allon White: metaphors of transformation', in D. Morley and D.-K. Chen (eds) *Stuart Hall*, London: Routledge.

Haraway, D. (1991) *Simians, Cyborgs, and Women: the Reinvention of Nature*, New York: Chapman & Hall.

—— (1992) 'The Promise of monsters: a regenerative politics for inappropriate/d others', in L. Grossberg, C. Nelson, and P. Treichler (eds) *Cultural Studies*, New York: Routledge.

—— (1994) 'A game of cat's cradle: science studies, feminist theory, cultural studies', *Configurations* 1, 59–71.

Hardy, T. (1978) *Under The Greenwood Tree*, Harmondsworth: Penguin.

Harmer, R. and Kerr, G. (1995) 'Creating woodland: to plant trees or not?', in R. Ferris-Kaan (ed.) *The Ecology of Woodland Creation*, Chichester: John Wiley & Sons.

Harris, M.S. (1998) 'Being homesick, writing home', in P. Panting (ed.) *Fresh Tracks, Writing the Western Landscape*, Victoria: Polestar Books, 253–64.

Harrison, C.M. and Burgess, J. (1994) 'Social Constructions of Nature: a case study of conflicts over the development of Rainham Marshes', *Transactions of the Institute of British Geographers*, NS, 19, 291–310.

Harrison, F. (1991) *The Living Landscape*, London: Mandarin Paperbacks.

Harrison, R.P. (1992) *Forests: The Shadow of Civilisation*, Chicago: University of Chicago Press.

Harvey, D. (1996) *Justice, Nature, and the Geography of Difference*, Oxford: Blackwell.

—— (1999) *Spaces of Hope*, Berkeley: University of California Press.

Hayden, D. (1995) T*he Power of Place: Urban Landscapes as Public History*, Cambridge, Mass.: MIT Press.

Hebdige, D. (1979) *Subculture: the Meaning of Style*, London: Routledge.

Hecht, S. and Cockburn, A. (1989) *The Fate of the Forest*, London: Verso.

Heinrich, B. (1997) *The Trees in My Forest*, New York: HarperCollins.

Hofmeister, S. (1997) 'The Tutzing Time Ecology Project. Nature's temporalities: consequences for environmental politics', *Time and Society*, 6, 2/3, 309–22.

Hornsby, J. (1997) 'Agency and causal explanation', in A.R. Mele (ed.) *The Philosophy of Action*, Oxford: Oxford University Press.

Hoskins, I. (2001) 'Marking Time: History and Identity in Sydney's Centennial Park', *Studies in the History of Gardens and Designed Landscapes*, 21, 1, 41–53.

Hubbell, S. (1993) *Broadsides from the Other Others: a Book of Bugs*, Boston: Mariner Books.

Hutton, M. (1999) 'The Psychology of tree relations': paper presented at the 'For the Love of Nature?' Conference, Centre for Human Ecology, Findhorn, Scotland.

Ingold, T. (ed.) (1988) *What is an Animal?* London: Unwin Hyman.

—— (1993) 'The temporality of landscape', *World Archaeology*, 25, 152–74.

—— (1995) 'Building, dwelling, living: how people and animals make themselves at home in the world', in M. Strathern (ed.) *Shifting Contexts: Transformations in Anthropological Knowledge*, London: Routledge.

—— (1997) 'Life beyond the edge of nature? or, the mirage of society', in J. Greenwood (ed.) *The Mark of the Social*, London: Rowman and Littlefield.

—— (2000) *The Perception of the Environment: Essays in Livelihood, Dwelling and Skill*, London: Routledge.

Jackson, P. (1989) *Maps of Meaning: an Introduction to Cultural Geography*, London: Unwin Hyman.

Jacobs, P. (2000) 'Playing with Time', *Studies in the History of Gardens and Designed Landscapes*, 20, 4, 325–39.

James, N.D.G. (1990) *The Arboriculturalist's Companion*, Oxford: Blackwell.

Johnston, R. (1996) 'A place in geography', in E.M. Rawling and R.A. Daugherty (eds) *Geography into the Twenty-First Century*, Chichester: John Wiley & Sons.

Jones, D. (1992) *A History of Clifton*, Chichester: Phillimore and Co.

Jones, O. (2000) '(Un)ethical geographies of human–non-human relations: encounters, collectives and spaces', in C. Philo and C. Wilbert (eds) *Animal Spaces, Beastly Spaces: New Geographies of Human-animal Relations*, London: Routledge.

Jordan, A. and O'Riordan, T. (1999) 'Environmental problems and management', in P. Cloke, P. Crang, and M. Goodwin (eds) *Introducing Human Geographies*, London: Arnold.

Karacs, I. (2000) 'The swastika in the woods', *The Independent*, Review, 6 December.

Kaza, S. (1993) *The Attentive Heart: Conversations with Trees*, Boston: Shambhala.

Keil, R. and Graham, J. (1998) 'Reasserting nature: constructing urban environments after Fordism', in B. Braun and N. Castree (eds) *Remaking Reality: Nature at the Millennium*, London: Routledge.

King, A. and Clifford, S. (1993) 'The Apple, the Orchard, the Cultural Landscape', in S. Clifford and A. King (eds) *Local Distinctiveness, Place, Particularity and Identity*, London: Common Ground.

Koziell, S.P. (2000) 'A tale of two apples', *Resurgence*, 198, 44–5.

Krebs, A. (1999) *Ethics of Nature*, New York: de Gruyter.

Krietzman, L. (1999) *The 24 Hour Society*, London: Profile.

Kropotkin, P. (1992) *Ethics: Origin and Development*, Dorchester: Prism Press.

Laidlaw, W.B.R. (1960) *Guide to British Hardwoods*, London: Leonard Hill Books.

Latour, B. (1993) *We have Never Been Modern*, Hemel Hempstead: Harvester/Wheatsheaf.

—— (1994) 'Pragmatogonies: a mythical account of how humans and nonhumans swap properties', *American Behavioral Scientist*, 37, 6, 791–808.

—— (1997) 'Trains of Thought: Piaget, Formalism, and the Fifth Dimension', *Common Knowledge*, 6, 3, 170–91.

Law, J. (1994) *Organizing Modernity*, Oxford: Basil Blackwell.

Law, J. and Hassard, J. (eds) (1999) *Actor Network Theory and After*, Oxford: Blackwell.

Lee, N. and Stenner, P. (1999) 'Who pays? Can we pay them back?', in J. Law and J. Hassard (eds) (1999) *Actor Network Theory and After*, Oxford: Blackwell.

Legg, P. and Binding, H. (1998) *Somerset Cider: The Complete History*, Tiverton: Somerset Books.

Leslie, A. (1981) *The Gilt and the Gingerbread*, London: Hutchinson.

Lewington, A. and Parker, E. (1999) *Ancient Trees*, London: Collins & Brown

Ley, D. (1995) 'The case of the missing sequoias', *Ecumene*, 2, 2, 185–210.

Light, A. and Katz, E. (1996) 'Introduction: environmental pragmatism and environmental ethics as contested terrain', in A. Light and E. Katz (eds) *Environmental Pragmatism*, London: Routledge.

Lippard, L.R. (1997) *The Lure of the Local: Sense of Place in a Multicentered Society*, New York: New Press.

Little, B. (1969) *Portrait of Somerset*, London: Robert Hale.

Louden, J. (1843) *On the Laying Out, Planting and Management of Cemeteries, and on the Improvement of Churchyards*, London: Longman, Brown, Green and Longmans.

Lovelock, J. (1988) *The Ages of Gaia: A Biography of Our Living Earth*, Oxford: Oxford University Press.

Lowenthal, D. (1978) 'Finding valued landscapes', *Progress in Human Geography*, 2: 373–418.

—— (1979) 'Age and Artefact', in D.W. Meinig (ed.) *The Interpretation of Ordinary Landscapes*, New York: Oxford University Press.

—— (1985) *The Past is a Foreign Country*, Cambridge: Cambridge University Press.

Luke, T. (1999) 'Eco-managerialism: environmental studies as a power/knowledge formation', in F. Fischer and M. Hajer (eds) *Living with Nature: Environmental Politics as Cultural Discourse*, Oxford: Oxford University Press.

Lutley, W. (1992) *Making Space: Protecting and Creating Open Space for Local Communities*, London: Open Spaces Society.

Lynn, W.S. (1998a) 'Animals, Ethics and Geography', in J. Wolch and J. Emel (eds) *Animal Geographies: Place, Politics and Identity in the Nature-Culture Borderlands*, London: Verso.

—— (1998b) 'Contested moralities: animals and moral value in the Dear/Symanski debate', *Ethics, Place and Environment*, 1, 2: 223–44.

Mabey, R. (1980) *The Common Ground: a Place for Nature in Britain's Future?* London: Hutchinson.

—— (1990) 'Foreword' to N. Sinden, *In A Nutshell. A Manifesto for Trees and a Guide to Growing and Protecting Them*, 2nd edn, London: Common Ground.

—— (1993) 'Nature and Change: The Two Faces of Naturalisation', in S. Clifford and A. King (eds) *Local Distinctiveness: Place, Particularity and Identity*, London: Common Ground.

—— (1996) *Flora Britannica*, London: Chatto & Windus.

—— (1997) *The Oxford Book of Nature Writing*, Oxford: Oxford University Press.

Macmillen, N. (1990) *Coal from Camerton*, Bath: Avon Industrial Buildings Trust.

Macnaghten P. and Urry, J. (1998) *Contested Natures*, London: Sage Publications.

Macy, J. (1993) *World as Lover; World as Self*, London: Rider.

Mahner, M. and Bunge, M. (1997) *Foundations of Biophilosophy*, Berlin: Springer.

Malpas, J. (1998) 'Finding Place: spatiality, locality and subjectivity', in A. Light and J.M. Smith, (eds) *Philosophies of Place, Philosophy and Geography III*, Lanham: Rowman & Littlefield.

Marshall, P. (1992) *Nature's Web: Rethinking our Place on Earth*, London: Cassell.

Massey, D. (1991) 'A Global Sense of Place?', *Marxism Today*, June, 24–9.

Massey, D. and Jess, P. (eds) (1995) *A Place in the World?*, Oxford: Oxford University Press.

Massingham, H. J. (1988a) 'Apples', in E. Abelson (ed.) *A Mirror of England: an Anthology of the Writings of H.J. Massingham (1888–1952)*, Bideford: Green Books.

—— (1988b) 'The Curse of the Conifer', in E. Abelson (ed.) *A Mirror of England: an Anthology of the Writings of H.J. Massingham (1888–1952)*, Bideford: Green Books.

Matless, D. (1991) 'Nature, the modern and the mystic, tales from early twentieth century geography', *Transactions of British Geographers*, NS 16, 272–86.

Mauzé, M. (1998) 'Northwest coast trees: from metaphors in culture to symbols for culture', in L. Rival, (ed.), *The Social Life of Trees*, Oxford: Berg.

May, J. and Thrift, N. (eds) (2001) *Timespace: Geographies of Temporality*, London: Routledge.

McEwen, I. (1998) 'Move Over Darwin . . .' (review of 'Consilience' by E.O. Wilson) *Observer, Review*, 20 September.

McGrath, P. (1975) *The Merchant Venturers of Bristol*, Bristol: The Society of Merchant Venturers of the City of Bristol.

McManus, P. (1999) 'Histories of forestry: ideas, networks, silences', *Environment and History*, 5, 185–208.

McPhail, R. and Ward, D.E. (1988) *Morality and Agency*, Lanham: University of America Press.

Meinig, W.D. (1979) 'Symbolic Landscapes. Some Idealizations of American Communities', in D.W. Meinig (ed.) *The Interpretation of Ordinary Landscapes* New York: Oxford University Press.

Mele, R.A. (ed.) (1997) *The Philosophy of Action*, Oxford: Oxford University Press.

Mele, R.A. and Moser, P.K. (1997) 'Intentional Action', in R.A. Mele (ed.) *The Philosophy of Action*, Oxford: Oxford University Press.

Merchant, C. (1992) *Radical Ecology: The Search for a Liveable World*, London: Routledge.

Merrick, (1996) *Battle for the Trees*, Leeds: Godhaven Inc.

Midgley, M. (1983) *Animals and Why they Matter*, Athens, GA: University of Georgia Press.

—— (1996) *Utopias, Dolphins and Computers: Problems of Philosophical Plumbing*, Routledge: London.

Miles, A. (1999) *Silva: The Tree in Britain*, London: Ebury.

Mitchell, A. (1996) *Alan Mitchell's Trees of Britain*, London: HarperCollins.

Mitchell, D. (2000) *Cultural Geography: a Critical Introduction*, Oxford: Blackwell.

Moffat, A.J. and Buckley, G.P. (1995) 'Soils and restoration ecology', in R. Ferris-Kaan (ed.) *The Ecology of Woodland Creation*, Chichester: John Wiley & Sons.

Monk, J. (1992) 'Gender in the landscape: expressions of power and meaning', in K. Anderson and F. Gale (eds) *Inventing Places*, Melbourne: Longman.

Morris, M.G. and Perring, F.H. (eds) (1974) *The British Oak: Its History and Natural History*, Faringdon: E.W. Classey Ltd (For the Botanical Society of the British Isles).

Morton, A. (1991) *The Trees of Shropshire*, Shrewsbury: Airlife.

Muir, R. (1999) *Approaches to Landscape*, Basingstoke: Macmillan.

Murdoch, J. (1995) 'Actor-networks and the evolution of economic forms: combining description and explanation in theories of regulation, flexible specialisation, and networks', *Environment and Planning A*, 27, 731–58.

—— (1997) 'Inhuman/nonhuman/human: actor-network theory and the potential for a non-dualistic and symmetrical perspective on nature and society', *Environment and Planning D, Society and Space*, 15, 731–56.

—— (1998) 'The Spaces of Actor-Network Theory', *Geoforum*, 29, 4, 357–74.

Murdoch, J. and Abram, S. (1998) 'Defining the limits of community governance', *Journal of Rural Studies*, 14, 1, 41–50.

Naess, A. (1973) 'The shallow and the deep, long range-ecology movement', *Inquiry*, 16, 95–100

—— (1989) *Ecology, Community and Lifestyle*, Cambridge: Cambridge University Press.

—— (1997) 'Sustainable development and the deep ecology movement', in S. Baker, M. Kousis, D. Richardson, and S. Young (eds) *The Politics of Sustainable Development: Theory, Policy and Practice within the European Union*, London: Routledge.

Nash, C. (1993) ''Embodying the Nation': the West of Ireland Landscape and National Identity', in M. Cronon and R. O'Connor (eds) *Tourism and Ireland: A Critical Analysis*, Cork: Cork University Press.

NCB (1970) *Review of Research on Properties of Spoil Tip Materials*, Wimpey Laboratories Ltd, Hayes, Middlesex.

Nesmith, C. and Radcliffe, S. (1993) '(Re)mapping Mother Earth: a geographical perspective on environmental feminisms', *Environment and Planning D, Society and Space*, 11, 379–94.

Niall Phillips Architects (1999) *Arnos Vale Cemetery Regeneration Study: Stage 1 and 2 Report*. Bristol: Niall Phillips Architects.

Nicholson-Lord, D. (2000) 'Trees of Life', *Guardian,* Society Section, 19 July.

O'Riordan, T. (1989) 'The challenge for environmentalism', in R. Peet and N. Thrift (eds) *New Models in Geography, Vol I*, Boston: Unwin Hyman.

Owen, L. (undated) *History of Arnos Vale*, unpublished.

Packenham, T. (1997) *Meetings with Remarkable Trees*, London, Phoenix Illustrated.

Parker, K.A. (1996) 'Pragmatism and environmental thought', in A. Light and E. Katz (eds) *Environmental Pragmatism*, London: Routledge.

Parkes, D.N. and Thrift, N. (1980) *Times, Spaces and Places: Chronogeographic Perspective*, Chichester: John Wiley & Sons.

Peck, J. and Tickell, A. (1994) 'Too many partnerships . . . the future for regeneration partnerships', *Local Economy*, 9, 3, 251–65.

Pepper, D. (1986) *The Roots of Modern Environmentalism*, London: Routledge.

—— (1996) *Modern Environmentalism: An Introduction*, London: Routledge.

Perlman, M. (1994) *The Power of Trees: The Reforesting of the Soul*, Woodstock: Spring Publications.

Peterson, A.L. (2001) *Being Human: Ethics, Environment, and Our Place in the World*, Berkeley: University of California Press.

Phelan, P. (1993) *Unmarked: The Politics of Performance*, London: Routledge.

Philo, C. (1995) 'Animals, geography, and the city: notes on inclusions and exclusions', *Environment and Planning D: Society and Space*, 13, 655–81.

—— (1998) 'Animals, geography, and the city: notes on inclusions and exclusions', in J. Wolch and J. Emel (eds) *Animal Geographies: Place, Politics and Identity in the Nature-Culture Borderlands*, London: Verso.

—— (2000) 'More words more worlds: reflections on the "cultural turn" and human geography', in I. Cook, D. Crouch, S. Naylor and J.R. Ryan (eds) *Cultural Turns/Geographical Turns: Perspectives on Cultural Geography*, Harlow: Prentice Hall.

Philo, C. and Wilbert, C. (2000) *Animal Spaces, Beastly Spaces: New Geographies of Human–Animal Relations*, London: Routledge.

Plumwood, V. (1993) *Feminism and the Mastery of Nature*, London: Routledge.

—— (1999) 'Paths beyond human-centeredness: lessons from liberation struggles', in A. Weston (ed.) *An Invitation to Environmental Philosophy*, Oxford: Oxford University Press.

Preddy, S. (1999) Written response to email questionnaire sent by Owain Jones.

Proctor, J.D. (1996) 'Whose Nature? The Contested Moral Terrain of Ancient forests', in W. Cronon (ed.) *Uncommon Ground: Rethinking the Human Place in Nature*, New York: Norton.

—— (1998) 'Ethics in geography: giving moral form to the geographical imagination', *Area*, 30, 1, 8–18.

Rachel, J. (1994) 'Acting and Passing: Actants and Passants, Action and Passion', *American Behavioral Scientist*, 37, 6, 809–23.

Rackham, O. (1996) *Trees and Woodland in the British Landscape*, London: Phoenix.

—— (1997) *The History of the Countryside*, London: Phoenix.

Radford. T. (2001) 'Warning over disappearing forests', *Guardian*, 21 August.

Redclift, M. (1993) 'Sustainable development: needs, values, rights', *Environmental Ethics* 2, 1, 3–20.

Regan, T. (1998) 'The case for animal rights', in S.M. Cahn and P. Markie (eds) *Ethics: History, Theory, and Contemporary Issues*, New York: Oxford University Press

Relph, E. (1989) 'Responsive methods, geographical imagination and the study of landscape', in A. Kobayashi and S. Mackenzie (eds) *Remaking Human Geography*, London: Unwin Hyman.

Rhodes, R.A.W. (1996) 'The new governance: governing without government', *Political Studies*, 44, 652–57.

—— (1997) *Understanding Governance: Policy Networks, Governance, Reflexivity and Accountability*, Buckingham: Open University Press.

Ridley, H.N. (1930) *The Dispersal of Plants Throughout the World*, Ashford: L. Reeve and Co.

Rival, L. (ed.) (1998a) *The Social Life of Trees: Anthropological Perspectives on Tree Symbolism*, London: Berg.

—— (1998b) 'Trees, from symbols of life and regeneration to political artefacts', in L. Rival, (ed.) *The Social Life of Trees: Anthropological Perspectives on Tree Symbolism*, London: Berg.

Rolston III, H. (1999) 'Ethics on the Home Planet', in A. Weston (ed.) *An Invitation to Environmental Philosophy*, Oxford: Oxford University Press.

Routley, R. and Routley, V. (1980) 'Human chauvinism and environmental ethics' in D. Mannison (ed.) *Environmental Philosophy*, Canberra: Australian National University Press.

Samuel, R. (1995) *Theatres of Memory*, London: Verso.

Schama, S. (1995) *Landscape and Memory*, London: HarperCollins.

—— (2000) *A History of Britain*, London: BBC Worldwide Ltd.

Scheibl, R. (1997) Review of Donaldson (1996) *Time and Society*, 6, 2/3, 349–50.

Schilling, C. (1993) *The Body and Social Theory*, London: Sage.

Schroeder, R.A. (1995) 'Contradictions along the commodity road to environmental stabilisation: foresting Gambian gardens', *Antipode*, 27, 4, 325–42.

Seamon, D. and Mugerauer, D. (1985) *Dwelling, Place and Environment: Towards an Understanding of Person and World*, Dordrecht: Matinus Nijhoff.

Seymour, J. (1983) *The Woodlander*, London: Sidgwick & Jackson.

Shackley, S. and Wynne, B. (1995a) 'Global climate change: the mutual construction of an emergent science-policy domain', *Science and Public Policy*, 22, 218–30.

—— (1995b) 'Integrating knowledges for climate change: pyramids, nets and uncertainties', *Global Environmental Change*, 5, 113–26.

Shaw, J. (2001) '"Winning territory" changing place to change pace', in J. May and N. Thrift (eds) (2001) *Timespace: Geographies of Temporality*, London: Routledge.

Shields, R. (1991) *Places on the Margin: Alternative Cultures of Modernity*, London: Routledge.

Shiva, V. (1989) *Staying Alive: Women, Ecology and Development*, London: Zed.

Shoard, M. (1980) *The Theft of the Countryside*, London: Temple Smith.

Sibley, D. (1995) *Geographies of Exclusion*, London: Routledge.

—— (1999) 'Creating geographies of difference', in D. Massey, J. Allen, and P. Sarre (eds) *Human Geography Today*, Cambridge: Polity Press.

Silverton, P. (2001) 'Green and Pleasant Land', *The Observer Magazine*, 18 March.

Sinden, D. (1989) 'Orchards and places', in Common Ground, *Orchards: A Guide to Local Conservation*, London: Common Ground.

—— (1990) *In a Nutshell: A Manifesto for Trees and a Guide to Growing and Protecting Them*, London: Common Ground.

Singer, P. (1993) *Practical Ethics*, 2nd edn, Cambridge: Cambridge University Press.

Skinner, J. (1971) *Journal of a Somerset Rector, 1803–34*, Oxford: Oxford University Press.

Slater, C. (1996) 'Amazonia as edenic narrative', in W. Cronon (ed.) *Uncommon Ground: Rethinking the Human Place in Nature*, New York: Norton.

Smith, A. (1935) 'The days of elegance when a butler was a necessity', *Bristol Evening Post*, 13 December.

Smith, D.M. (1998) 'Geography and moral philosophy: some common ground', *Ethics, Place and Environment*, 1, 1, 7–34.

Smith, M.J. (1998) *Ecologism: Towards Ecological Citizenship*, Buckingham: Open University Press.

—— (ed.) (1999) *Thinking Through the Environment*, London: Routledge.

Smith, J.A., Light, A. and Roberts, D. (1998) 'Introduction: philosophies and geographies of place', in A. Light and J.M. Smith (eds) *Philosophy and Geography III: Philosophies of Place*, Lanham: Rowman and Littlefield.

Sprin, A.W. (1998) *The Language of Landscape*, New Haven: Yale University Press.

Stoker, G. (1996) 'Governance as theory: five propositions', Mimeo, Department of Government, University of Strathclyde.

—— (ed.) (1997) *Partners in Urban Governance: European and American Experience*, London: Macmillan.

Stone, C. (1972) 'Should Trees have Standing? Towards legal rights for natural objects', *Southern Californian Law Review*, 45, 2, 450–73.

Stone, P. (1994) *Orchards in Somerset – The County Council's Approach*, Taunton: Somerset County Council.

Sutherland, P. and Nicholson, A. (1986) *Wetland: Life in the Somerset Levels*, London: Michael Joseph.

Tall, D. (1993) *From Where We Stand: Recovering a Sense of Place*, Baltimore: Johns Hopkins University Press.

Tansley, A.G. (1968) *Britain's Green Mantle: Past, Present and Future*, London: George Allen & Unwin.

Thomas, G.S. (1998) *Trees in the Landscape*, London: John Murray Ltd.

Thoreau, D.H. (1972) *In the Maine Woods*, (ed. J.J. Moldenhauer), Princeton: Princeton University Press.

Thrift, N. (1996a) *Spatial Formations*, London: Sage.

—— (1996b) '"Hereness" and the normativity of place', in J. Proctor and D. Smith (eds) *Geography and Ethics: Journeys in a Moral Terrain*, New York: Routledge.

—— (1999) 'Steps to an ecology of place', in D. Massey, J. Allen and P. Sarre (eds) *Human Geography Today*, Cambridge: Polity Press.

—— (2000) 'Afterwords', *Environment and Planning D, Society and Space*, 18, 2, 213–56

Torgerson, D. (1999) 'Images of place in green politics: the cultural mirror of indigenous traditions', in F. Fischer and M. Hajer (eds) *Living with Nature: Environmental Politics as Cultural Discourse*, Oxford: Oxford University Press.

Toulson, S. (1989) 'Landmark Trees', in *Pulp!,* Summer Edition, London: Common Ground.

Trewin, C. (1998) 'The New Men of the Trees', *The Field*, April.

Tsouvalis, J. (2000) 'Socialized nature: England's royal and plantation forests', in I. Cook, D. Crouch, S. Naylor and J.R. Ryan (eds) *Cultural Turns/Geographical Turns: Perspectives on Cultural Geography*, Harlow: Prentice Hall.

Tsouvalis-Gerber, J. (1998) 'Making the invisible visible: ancient woodlands, British forestry policy and the social construction of reality', in C. Watkins (ed.) *European Woods and Forests: Studies in Cultural History*, Wallingford: CAB International.

Urry, J. (1988) 'Cultural change and contemporary holiday-making', *Theory, Culture and Society*, 5, 35–55.

—— (1990) *The Tourist Gaze*, London: Sage.

Valentine, G. (1989) 'The Geography of Women's Fear', *AREA*, 21, 4, 385–90.

Vitale, A.T. (1997) *Leaves in Myth, Magic and Medicine*, New York: Stewart, Tabori and Chang.

Von Maltzahn, K.E. (1994) *Nature as Landscape: Dwelling and Understanding*, Montreal: McGill-Queen's University Press.

Vycinas, V. (1969) *Earth and Gods: An Introduction to the Philosophy of Martin Heidegger*, Dordrecht: Martinus Nijhoff.

Warren, K.J. (ed.) (1994) *Ecological Feminism*, London: Routledge.

Watkins, C. (ed.) (1998a) *European Woods and Forests: Studies in Cultural History*, Wallingford: CAB International.

—— (1998b) 'A solemn and gloomy umbrage': changing interpretations of the ancient oaks of Sherwood Forest', in C. Watkins (ed.) (1998a) *European Woods and Forests: Studies in Cultural History*, Wallingford: CAB International.

Webb, P. (1997) Tall Trees, *The Countryman*, High Summer (August/September).

Weston, A. (1996) 'Before environmental ethics', in A. Light and E. Katz (eds) *Environmental Pragmatism*, London: Routledge.
—— (1999a), 'Is it too late?', in A. Weston (ed.) *An Invitation to Environmental Philosophy*, New York: Oxford University Press.
—— (1999b) 'Epilogue: going on', in A. Weston (ed.) *An Invitation to Environmental Philosophy*, New York: Oxford University Press.
Whatmore, S. (1997) 'Dissecting the autonomous self: hybrid cartographies for a relational ethics', *Environment and Planning D: Society and Space*, 15, 37–53.
—— (1999) 'Hybrid geographies: rethinking the "human" in human geography', in D. Massey, J. Allen and P. Sarre (eds) *Human Geography Today*, Cambridge: Polity Press.
—— (2000) 'Heterogeneous geographies: reimagining the spaces of N/nature', in I. Cook, D. Crouch, S. Naylor and J.R. Ryan (eds) *Cultural Turns/Geographical Turns: Perspectives on Cultural Geography*, Harlow: Prentice Hall.
Whatmore, S. and Boucher, S. (1992) 'Bargaining with nature: the discourse and practice of "environmental planning gain"', *Transactions of the Institute of British Geographers*, NS, 18, 166–78.
Whatmore, S. and Thorne, L. (1998) 'Wild(er)ness: reconfiguring the geographies of wildlife', *Transactions of the Institute of British Geographers*, NS, 2, 435–54.
—— (2000) 'Elephants on the move: spatial formations of wildlife exchange', *Environment and Planning D: Society and Space*, 18, 185–203.
Whitt, L.A. and Slack, J.D. (1994) 'Communities, environments and cultural studies', *Cultural Studies*, 8, 1, 5–31.
Wilkinson, G. (1979) *Epitaph for the Elm*, London: Arrow Books.
Williams, M. (1990) 'Clearing the Forests', in M.P. Conzen (ed.) *The Making of the American Landscape*, London: HarperCollins.
Williams, Raymond (1985) *The Country and the City*, London: Hogarth Press.
Williams, Rosalind (1992) *Notes on the Underground: an Essay on Technology, Society, and the Imagination*, Cambridge, Mass.: MIT Press.
Williams, R.R. (ed.) (Undated) *Cider and Juice Apples, Growing and Processing* Bristol: Bristol University Printing Unit.
Williams, W.J. (1976) *Coal Mining in Bishop Sutton North Somerset, c.1799–1929* (no other details provided).
Wilson, A. (1992) *The Culture of Nature*, Oxford: Blackwell.
Winterson, J. (2000) 'Soul purpose', *Guardian*, Society Section, 29 March.
Wittgenstein, L. (1968) *Philosophical Investigations*, 3rd edn, trans. G Anscombe, Basingstoke: Macmillan.
Wolch, J. and Emel, J. (1995) 'Bringing the animals back in', *Environment and Planning D: Society and Space*, 13: 632–6.
—— (eds) (1998) *Animal Geographies: Place, Politics and Identity in the Nature-Culture Borderlands*, London: Verso.

Woolgar, S. (1991) 'Configuring the user: the case of usability trials', in J. Law (ed.) *A Sociology of Monsters?* London: Routledge.

Wright, P. (1992) 'The disenchanted forest', *Guardian*, Weekend, 7 November.

Young, I. (1990) *Justice and the Politics of Difference*, Princeton: Princeton University Press.

—— (1992) 'Communication and the other: beyond deliberate democracy', in S Benhabib (ed.), *Democracy and Difference*, Princeton: Princeton University Press.

Zelter, A. (1998) 'Grassroots campaigning for the world's forests', in L. Rival (ed.) *The Social Life of Trees: Anthropological Perspectives on Tree Symbolism*, London: Berg.

Zimmerman, M.E. (1993) 'Heidegger, Buddhism and Deep Ecology, in C. Guignon (ed.) *The Cambridge Companion to Heidegger*, Cambridge: Cambridge University Press.

Zukin, S. (1996) *The Cultures of Cities*, Oxford: Blackwell.

Index

Index